Praise for *Holding Her Head High*

"*Holding her Head High* is a wonderful book that I wish I had as a resource during my years as a single mom. It is filled with stories through the ages about the strength and tenacity of women who not only raise children but also contribute to the world in so many different ways. Janine Turner captures what it's like to be a single mother and offers lessons for us all."

DORO BUSH KOCH
Author, *My Father, My President*

"For every mother who thinks they are merely ordinary, Janine Turner has skillfully illustrated that their destiny and that of their children is divinely purposed. Through the stories of remarkable women Janine challenges mothers to look deep within themselves to find the woman God created them to be. I hope you will be inspired to use your influence and God-given authority to help your children fulfill their destiny."

VICTORIA OSTEEN
Co-pastor, Lakewood Church

"As a 15-year-old mother I will never forget the day I looked into my newborn son's eyes. I was overwhelmed with a feeling that no matter what happened I could never let him down. I knew it was an awesome responsibility and that there were exceptional odds against us, but somehow I knew we were going to be alright. Ironically, I only had that feeling one other time in my life—24 years later—on November 21, 2006, when Mayor Adrian Fenty appointed me to be the first female Chief of Police in the Nations Capitol, Washington, D.C. When I read Janine Turner's book I realized that I am not the first single mother to make history, just one of many. *Holding Her Head High* signifies hope for single mothers. The strengths exhibited by these women will be an inspiration to anyone."

CATHY L. LANIER
Chief of Police, Metropolitan Police Department, Washington, D.C.

"*Holding Her Head High* is a fascinating read about single mothers across the ages finding ways to not only survive but thrive despite their trying circumstances. Janine Turner's wonderful book can inspire today's single mothers to help their children overcome life's challenges."

ROXANNE SPILLETT
President, Boys & Girls Clubs of America

"Janine Turner has written an important account of arguably the most important people in the world—mothers. *Holding Her Head High* chronicles twelve women who raised their children by themselves and at the same time blazed paths in history. Their achievements inspire. Their stories impress. Their values inform. Every mother should read this beautiful book."

KAY GRANGER
U.S. Congresswoman, 12th District of Texas

"This unique book tells in a very special way the little-known stories of a dozen remarkable women such as Alexander Hamilton's mother—women of strong character and strong faith."

MYRNA BLYTH
Former Editor-in-Chief, *Ladies' Home Journal*

"Janine articulates some amazing stories of the mothers in her book. Clearly, her resilient spirit and passion give us hope to serve as the force behind this type of role model for other single mothers."

LINDA ARMSTRONG KELLY
Author, *No Mountain High Enough: Raising Lance, Raising Me*

"*Holding Her Head High* is a powerful series of mini-biographies of some of the world's most courageous and influential women. This well-researched book gives glimpses into the overwhelming struggles and amazing victories of single mothers throughout history. These are stories of astounding bravery, daunting difficulties, and soaring hope. Janine has done a brilliant job. Two thumbs up!"

JANE ABRAHAM
President, Abraham Strategies, LLC
Board Member, The Nurturing Network

"Turner has presented all women, and all men who love women, with a singular gift: history's lessons of heroic single motherhood. Those lessons are an earnest invitation to every woman facing life's cruel obstacles to persevere, to love, to think independently, and to laugh. Never preachy, Turner brings together a party of women anyone would love to join. Each found love, her genius, and her life work through love of her family and her calling."

MARJORIE DANNENFELSER
President, Susan B. Anthony List

"May God speak from these powerful pages of history into the truth of your life right now. Our loving God can lift your head high. He can make your life beautiful and give your children even more than you could dream for them. Read these inspiring words and put your hope in His faithfulness."

ANGELA THOMAS
Best-selling Author, *My Single Mom Life*

"In 2002, when Janine Turner walked away from Hollywood to move to Texas and raise her daughter, she was one of the most popular actors on the big or small screen. Unlike so many celebrities in today's culture, she found a way to balance a career with what is most important to her—being a devoted mother to Juliette. In *Holding Her Head High*, Janine introduces us to twelve women who step out of the pages of history to mentor the single mothers of today. These eloquently profiled women will inspire mothers everywhere."

CATHY GILLESPIE
Women's Vote Strategist

"As minister to single mothers and fathers I see the incredible struggles daily. *Holding Her Head High* gives single parents a refreshing breath of hope. The dynamic stories of these astounding women demonstrate how single mothers—and all of us—can overcome adversity, achieve success, and change the world for our children through unswerving faith in God. Thank you, Janine, for empowering each of us to become all that God intends for us."

PAM WILLINGHAM
Single-Parent Family Minister,
Richland Hills Church of Christ, Fort Worth, TX

"The single mothers in *Hold Your Head High* illustrate the inherent determination that all mothers have to make a better life for their children, and prove again and again that knowledge and mutual respect can overcome stigma and poverty."

KATHLEEN COONEY CLARKE
Assistant Executive Director,
Development & External Affairs, Inwood House

"I love this book because it dispels a horrible myth: As a single-parent mother, the best I have to hope for is survival for my mediocre emotionally damaged children. Janine's excellent research proves what we now know to be true. Women who are willing to work hard and dare to dream can provide everything their children need to not only succeed, but change their world for the better. She truly provides hope in hard times to the women who need it most."

GARY RICHMOND
Pastor to Single Parents, First Evangelical Free Church, Fullerton, CA
Author, *Successful Single Parenting*

"Learning to rely on oneself and one's inner strength are important challenges facing single mothers. Thank you to Janine Turner for highlighting single mothers throughout history who took on the challenges of their situations, cared for themselves and their children, and made such a remarkable difference."

ANNE NEUBERGER
President, Sister to Sister

holding her head high

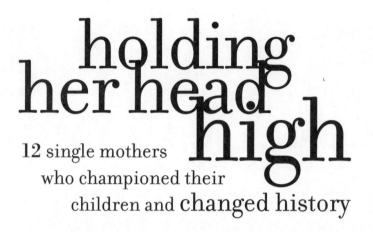

holding
her head
high

12 single mothers
who championed their
children and changed history

Janine Turner

THOMAS NELSON
Since 1798

NASHVILLE   DALLAS   MEXICO CITY   RIO DE JANEIRO   BEIJING

Published in Nashville, Tennessee by Thomas Nelson. Thomas Nelson is a registered trademark of Thomas Nelson, Inc. Published in association with David Hale Smith Literary Agency.

Thomas Nelson, Inc., titles may be purchased in bulk for educational, business, fundraising, or sales promotional use. For information, please email SpecialMarkets@ThomasNelson.com.

All Scripture quotations, unless otherwise indicated, are taken from The New King James Version (NKJV®), 1979, 1980, 1982, Thomas Nelson, Inc., Publishers.

Other Scripture references are from the following sources: The Holy Bible, New International Version (NIV). ©1973, 1978, 1984, International Bible Society. Used by permission of Zondervan Bible Publishers. The King James Version (KJV).

Managing Editor: Adria Haley
Interior Design: Mandi Cofer

Library of Congress Cataloging-in-Publication Data

Turner, Janine.
    Holding her head high : 12 single mothers who championed their children and changed history / Janine Turner.
      p. cm.
    Includes bibliographical references.
    ISBN 978-0-7852-2324-5 (hardcover)
    1. Single mothers—History. 2. Women—History. 3. Children of single parents.
I. Title.
HQ759.915.T87 2008
306.874'32091821—dc22

2008000647

Printed in the United States of America
08 09 10 11 12 13 QWM 9 8 7 6 5 4 3 2

For all single mothers past and present
and for Juliette

contents

ACKNOWLEDGMENTS

I consider any piece of work, whether artistic or business, a team effort. An analogy I often use is of a painting. It all starts with a blank canvas and every member of the team contributes with a concept, color, and shape. These contributions create the painting, and one aspect intertwines with the other. As a first-time author, standing back to appraise the completion of my first book, I realize that I have many contributors to acknowledge.

Of course, I must thank God, for without Him all has no meaning. I thank Him for planting the desire in my heart to write this book about single mothers and for the fortitude to bring it to fruition! I thank Him for my most precious blessing, Juliette, whose sweet, adventurous spirit continually breathed inspiration into my words.

I thank Jonathan Merkh for seizing upon an idea I had referenced and visualizing the concept for this book: single mothers throughout history. I thank him for giving me the opportunity to actually *write* the book! By believing in me as an author, he unlocked a deeply rooted desire. I thank Michael Broussard for introducing me to Jonathan Merkh and for David Hale Smith, my literary agent, who diligently and skillfully guided me through the mysterious process of publishing.

I thank Thomas Nelson Publishers for giving me the canvas and for being an entity that truly wants to make a difference in the world. I thank Joey Paul, a prince, for his earnest enthusiasm and devotion. I thank Debbie Wickwire for being the cohesive force that combined all of the elements with vision, grace, and a heart of gold.

I thank Mary Hollingsworth, a glorious child of God and a most talented, loving editor, who graciously exhibited the patience of Job. She gently walked me through the editing, shaping process, as I routinely perceived everything as both a nuance and a necessity!

I am eternally grateful to Rhonda Hogan for her infinite knowledge regarding the most formidable task of permissions. I thank Lady Lisa Nichols, who assisted me through the hallowed halls of history, Isabel Seeman at the Hockaday Library—a magnificent resource, the Southlake Library, and Cathy Gillespie for her continued inspiration and guidance.

And last but not least, I thank the glorious twelve women in this book. They were the colors of this painting. I was merely the brush. I grew to love them with a respect and awe that only great character can generate.

How Did a Baptist Girl from Texas End Up as a Single Mom?

Before you were conceived I wanted you;
Before you were born I loved you;
Before you were here an hour I would die for you;
This is the miracle of life.

—MAUREEN HAWKINS

Wow! If you could see the way I look right now . . . like an author who's been intimately immersed in the writing of her book. My hair, which is currently red and short, is spiking up everywhere, and my glasses are blurry from so many smudge marks. My house has been obliterated by research. Books are stacked in hallways and pathways, and paperwork is piled in every nook and cranny. This has all occurred, of course, as I have nurtured my daughter: driven her two hours to and from school every day, accompanied her to extracurricular activities, been lunch-bunch mom and third-grade musical chairman, fixed her meals, helped with homework . . . well, you get the picture.

This book has been my professional baby for about as many months as it takes to gestate a real one. I dare say pregnancy and childbirth were a cakewalk compared to this. The publishing process has been arduous and painstaking, but it has also been immensely fascinating and rewarding. I am eternally grateful that God has given me this wonderful opportunity because, ironically, by telling these women's stories, I have been transformed. I even garnered the courage from these women to pick up and move from Texas to New York City with my daughter!

I have always experienced a gravitational pull toward biographies. I remember as a third grader, my daughter's age, sitting on the floor of my elementary school library and reading biographies—Betsy Ross, Pocahontas, Martha Washington. History was alluring to me. As an adult I have continued to be drawn to biographies, because they offer unique and invaluable insights into the way other people viewed life and met their challenges. I have relished these moments as a researcher and writer, because the work has provided the vehicle to share my own experiences, strength, and hope. As an actress, I'm called to be the mouthpiece for the screenwriter's words. This time the words are my own.

My Journey

I am a single mother, and every day I thank God for my beautiful, sweet gift, my little girl, Juliette. After God, of course, my devotion is unreservedly to her. I've often reflected, *How did a Baptist girl from Texas end up as a single mother?* My pregnancy, however, was the most miraculous event of my life. I would read to her in the womb, play Mozart, and pray with her. I even felt the joy when she kicked, literally, to the music of a Broadway show.

As my pregnancy progressed, however, it became increasingly evident that my journey as a mother was to be a singular event. One day I predicted that my daughter's father would not be there when our baby was born. He responded by holding me tightly and saying that, yes, he would be there. I knew in my heart he would not. Call it women's intuition, but I knew. This is not how I envisioned the drama of my life, the joy of bringing a child into the world, but life presented itself to me in this way. Yet I have thanked God every day that I'm a mother, even if a single mother, because God has blessed me with sweet Juliette. And I have never, for one moment, doubted that God designed Juliette to be born, no matter the circumstances. God wanted Juliette to be here. God sees eternity in perspective.

How did I do it? How *do* I do it? My faith. My faith has been my foundation. From pregnancy to present day, with immense joys, I have also walked through judgment and fear. I've been knocked down, had to reach for the hand of God, dusted myself off, and gotten back up again. During these times, I've had only Him to rely on for guidance and for coping with the complex and varied challenges of motherhood—spiritually, emotionally, financially, physically. If my life had been picture perfect then I might not have reached out to God the way that I have ardently and consistently done. Consequently, I have enjoyed a rich friendship with God, and so has my daughter. God has taught me to hold my head high. I'm on my knees in praise every morning and every night. God is great.

My Mission

There's one thing I believe fervently, and that is that 90 percent of single mothers never intended to be single mothers. Most young girls, as they daydream about the day when they will have children, rarely say, "When I grow up I want to have a child and raise the child without the father." Or, "When I grow up I want to get a divorce and raise my children all by myself." It rarely happens.

I wrote this book to inspire these women. I wrote it so that single mothers of today would not feel alone, troubled, burdened, shamed, or depressed. When the concept of this book—single mothers of history—first came to me, I was concerned that I wouldn't be able to find enough single mothers in history or enough information to render a worthwhile book. Boy, was I wrong! I was stunned by the number of single mothers through the wide span of the centuries. We may think single motherhood is a modern phenomenon, but it's not.

The definitions of single motherhood are quite complex. Throughout the annals of history a woman could have been a single mother as a concubine, a widow, a divorcée, due to constraints of society or war, or by sheer choice. Today these definitions still apply. A woman may be a single mother who lives with the father, or she may not live with the father. Single mothers may experience manageable relations or unmanageable relations with the father. Single mothers may be entirely on their own with *no* presence of the father. The age range is also wide, then and now. Single mothers range from teenagers to the forties to grandmothers raising children as single mothers.

The U.S. Census Bureau data published in 2004 reports that approximately 43 percent of women raising children are single mothers; this number is likely higher today. 51 percent of women in America are not married.[1] The wisdom that the women of this book impart to us is that we are not alone. Women have been doing it for centuries and through tragic circumstances in social environments that, for the most part, pale to any we could encounter today.

As I spent many months with the women in this book, I feel as if God opened windows for me to peer inside their lives. Rays of light and inspiration emanated from the pages. It's as if these women came alive and sat beside me as I told their stories; sometimes I think they did. I wept with them, laughed with them, echoed their sentiments, and rallied them to victory. I would marvel at how timely their issues were, how they mirrored mine. These women rose from the ashes like a phoenix and became glorious stewards of their wounds. They were remarkable, brilliant, and brave.

As I researched and documented them, a trend emerged. These women were not just single mothers who championed their children. They were women who changed history. They didn't set out to change history. They did it by merely trying to survive with dignity, faith, and compassion. In the process they left their indelible marks on history. I found their choices in life to be uplifting, inspiring, and amazingly modern, no matter the era. These women not only had a message about motherhood, they had a message about life. They propelled the issues of their particular battles into progressive movements. They took their children with them on this passage of passion, and they were transformed as well. These women didn't just raise their children; they raised their nations. As a result, I became genuinely enthusiastic about my destiny in life as a mother and a woman—if they can do it, I can too!

I researched a great many women, but I chose twelve who model great virtues: determination, dignity, love, hope, spirit, morals, grace, forgiveness, character, stewardship, and justice. Primarily, though, the ones I chose were women of great faith, because faith is everything in my view. Faith in God is the primary purpose in our lives—to serve and honor Him. And I believe faith is an absolute, unquestionable necessity for children. It gives their lives meaning and purpose. It shapes their characters and perspectives as future humanitarians, citizens, and children of God. Thus, all of these single mothers radiate faith and signify hope.

These courageous women span seventeen centuries. They embraced the birth of Christianity, ruled countries, endured wars, birthed a country, withstood torments of slavery, pioneered west, and battled the inequities of men's and women's rights. They range from an Augusta of Rome, to a queen of France, a medieval feminist, a trailblazer, a visionary, a devout humanitarian, the first female printer, a revolutionary icon, a slave mother, pioneer mothers, and a single mother who was the first woman to be admitted to the bar of the United States Supreme Court and officially run for the office of president of the United States. (No, it was not Hillary Clinton.)

Their range is wide but the bond is close. They were mothers, single mothers, women—beautiful, spirited, intelligent, witty, sensuous, strong, and devout. These single mothers succeeded in life, in spite of life. They championed their children and changed history, because they walked into the winds of destiny holding their heads high.

Janine Turner

I can do all things through Christ who strengthens me.

—Philippians 4:13

*What breadth, what beauty and power of human nature
and development there must be in a woman
to get over all the palisades, all the fences,
within which she is held captive!*

—ALEXANDER HERZEN

CHAPTER ONE

The Roman Empire— Setting the Stage

27 BC–AD 476

After the death and resurrection of Jesus, the conversion of Constantine may have been the most implication-laden event in western history.

—James Carroll, *Constantine's Sword*

Rome. The Roman Empire. Vast. Vacillating. Murder and intrigue. Senators and emperors. War and warriors. Proudly civilized and grandly grotesque. Christians in chains and children's cries. A culture poised on the brink of change. Who will be their leader?

The Roman Empire was vast, from western Asia to Britain and Spain, from the Danube River in Central Europe to the edge of the Sahara Desert in North Africa. The eastern part of the empire survived until AD 476 and the Western Empire survived as the Byzantine Empire until AD 1453.

The early Roman population was pagan, tolerating the bane of human behavior, and could be easily justified as a religion steeped in evil, as exhibited in the games and circuses in places such as the Coliseum, which exhibited public displays of torture, violence, and death. Romans entertained themselves with triumphs, games, and great spectacles that concluded with slaughters of animals *and* humans. It was barbaric and cruel. Paganism also tolerated all sexual mores in their temples, ranging from sodomy to orgies, prostitution to bestiality and sadomasochism.

After the death and resurrection of Christ, Christians were subjected to horrific executions. The early church sustained an intense period of savage persecution, and Christians were brutally martyred by the Roman government up to twenty-five years before Constantine. And there was no collective, social consciousness that exhibited restraint or remorse. Infants' spirits were snuffed out as they were given as human sacrifices to the false gods. "Paganism prevailed in the land of the prophets." Darkness reigned.

The Father

By Roman law, the family was strictly patriarchal. The *paterfamilias,* the father, was the head of the Roman family. He owned the property acquired by his sons and had the right to sell his children into slavery or expose them. Women did have a few advantages compared to other centuries—they could divorce their husbands and control their own property. A woman was held under the legal control of the father until his death, even if she were married. After the death of her father, she was under the legal hand of her husband. If a woman was raped, she could not seek recourse, only her father or husband could press charges. A man could, by law, kill his wife if she was caught in an adulterous affair, but if a man committed adultery, he was not punished. Women had no status or political rights.

Marriage and childbearing were considered a woman's purpose in the Roman Empire. Marriages were arranged by the parents, and a young girl was usually married by the age of sixteen. The bride brought a dowry to the marriage, but unlike later centuries and societies, the dowry was not to be touched in case of unforeseen circumstances, such as divorce. Capturing a woman was a way of getting around a fixed marriage and was, perhaps, a way of getting the parents to accept a true love. However, this practice was later forbidden because it forbad the father the right to decide what was best for his daughter. Interestingly, divorce was very easily obtained during Roman times. A marriage was not considered holy, only a loose contract. Marriages were dissolved by mutual consent, the couple simply declaring their desire to divorce before seven witnesses.

The father also had control of a child's fate. Infanticide was an accepted act in the Roman culture. After birth a child was set at the feet of the father, who would lift the child into the air, deciding if the child should live or die. A wife could be disowned if she denied the father that decision. Infanticide was widely accepted, considered legal, and justified by philosophers such as Plato and Aristotle. Baby girls were more susceptible to the act of infanticide due to the considerable expense of wedding dowries. Roman law also forbad a man from taking in an abandoned child and saving it. Alarmingly, children were sometimes sealed in the foundations of bridges to strengthen the structures dating back to the walls of Jericho. Lloyd de Mause states, "To this day, when children play 'London Bridge is falling down' they are acting out a sacrifice to the river goddess when they catch a child at the end of the game." Disregard for children permeated all lands.

Light into Darkness

Then Christ. Light breathed into darkness. Christianity's mission was to spread "the light" through all ethnic cultures. Matthew 19:13–14 says,

> Then little children were brought to Jesus for him to place his hands on them and pray for them. But the disciples rebuked those who brought them. Jesus said, "Let the little children come to me, and do not hinder them, for the kingdom of heaven belongs to such as these." (NIV)

Children have value? Children belonged to the kingdom of heaven? This concept was revolutionary! Everyone, even the little children, was created in God's image. The Epistle of Barnabas prohibited infanticide, and following this law was considered essential to the "way of light." Infanticide was considered murder. Various Christian pamphlets taught, "You shall not commit infanticide." However, as long as Christianity was an underground religion hiding from persecution, efforts remained almost ineffectual.

CONSTANTINE

Entering the world stage next was Constantine, whose conversion to Christianity and breadth of change he brought to Christians, Christianity, and to the Christian church is, according to James Carroll, author of *Constantine's Sword*, "the second greatest story ever told." Carroll expresses that "after the death and resurrection of Jesus, the conversion of Constantine may have been the most implication-laden event in western history."

Constantine unified a suppressed church and a scattered band of disciples. As the leader of the world's biggest empire, his acceptance of Christ paved the way for the end of persecutions of Christians and propelled the illumination of Christ's light upon a dark, barbaric land. Disciples could now spread the word about how, with Christ's intervention, the human spirit can transcend the limitations of evil and partake in the supernatural. The Christian way of life was to offer alternative behaviors to murder and perverse sexuality. Christians had been in hiding. Jerusalem had lain as a wasteland but the scene was set to change. God had chosen Constantine through a divine vision to be a facilitator of unity for Christians and the Christian church.

Constantine, the son of Helena Augusta.

Then Christ. Light breathed into darkness . . . Jesus, by reaching out to little children, validated and honored the life of a child.

—JANINE TURNER

SAINT HELENA AUGUSTA

Devoted Single Mother

AD 248–330

SNAPSHOT	Eighty-year-old Helena, desiring to emulate Jesus, washes the Holy Virgin's feet
MOTHER MOMENT	Helena proudly sitting by her son as he resides over the Nicea Council as they compose the Nicene Creed
CHALLENGE	Abandoned by her lover
STEWARDSHIP	Fiercely devoted to her God, her son, and humanity
SCRIPTURE	A voice of one calling: In the desert prepare the way for the LORD, make straight in the wilderness a highway for our God. (Isaiah 40:3 NIV)

CHAPTER TWO

Listen for God's Higher Calling

Constantine and his mother, Helena, became the instruments through which Christ, the Christians, and the Christian church transitioned from a dispersed, persecuted brotherhood of disciples to the everlasting foundation of faith that it is today.[1]

—JAMES CARROLL

Third century Rome. Colonnades and Roman baths. Coliseums and perverse pagan pageantry. Heat on your shoulders. Sand on your feet. Hear the echoing of a child's laughter and the cries of a broken heart. Hear the fervent, frightened prayers of Christ's disciples whispering in the hallowed halls.

How do I write about a woman who lived seventeen hundred years ago and make it relevant to those of us who are single mothers today? What could we possibly have in common with a woman who walked around the Roman Empire in a toga and thong shoes before it became a ruins ? (Well, we do wear flip-flops.)

I'm amazed at the way history plays upon the affairs of the heart. Times change but passions never do; love, betrayal, joy, sadness, depression, revival, abandonment, loyalty, despair, and faith—all these emotions resonate, regardless of the timeline. The only aspect that changes is the playing field of history.

Helena was a woman like any other. In her youth she was a waitress in a hotel. She fell in love with a promising soldier destined for high places who was strong, powerful, rich, and handsome. She was loyal, smart, poor, and beautiful. What is extraordinary about Helena's story is that she was an ordinary girl, a stable girl, a pagan, who ultimately becomes a saint and co-ruler of the Roman Empire, an Augustus, "grandmother to the Caesars."[2] The son she bore, Constantine, becomes not just an emperor of the Roman Empire, but after an epiphany from God, he becomes the first *Christian* emperor of the Roman Empire.

I am intrigued, comforted, and inspired by God's continual manifestation of great feats from the humble. By Helena's example we may hopefully become aware that the seeds of opportunity to do great works lie within everyone, including a single mother like Helena. You can never be too humble, too meek, too poor, too destitute, or too sinful that God cannot raise you up and make you resolute, hopeful, a beacon for humanity and your children who can hold your head high. It is the seeking, acceptance, and willingness God desires—His only prerequisites. We may also become aware that a mother whose lover abandons her, a single mother, is capable of overcoming hardships and despair with amazing results. Watch what God can do!

Timeless Scenario: Boy meets girl. Boy and girl fall in love. Boy and girl have a son. When presented with fortuitous gain, boy abandons girl for younger, more socially acceptable girl. Boy dies. Girl reunites with son. Girl and son serve their God.

Sound familiar? Well, then, let's walk together on this timeless journey through the Roman Empire.

FACT OR MYTH?

Due to scarcity of records, Helena's life must be told with a delicate fusion of fact and myth; it was, after all, almost two thousand years ago. Details of Helena's life were recorded by Roman historians, philosophers, and by bishops documenting their church histories. Many historians debate every historical perspective, contradicting this and that, eventually resulting in their own versions of truth about Helena.

After assimilating all the information, I realized I have to acquiesce to my spiritual impulses regarding her life, and one definitive arises: Helena was a mother—a fiercely loyal, dedicated mother. Abandoned by her lover, her son sought her back into his life and validated her. She became one of the most important figures in the Roman Empire. A mother who worshiped Christ and who would walk to the ends of the earth, literally, to uphold both her God and her son. At approximately age eighty, she took a pilgrimage to Jerusalem, then an abandoned wasteland, to "pray at the places where Christ's feet had touched the ground"[3] and to find the relics of Jesus, including the True Cross.

From Innkeeper to Augusta

Helena was presumably born in Drepanum, Bithynia, which was in northwest Asia Minor (probably Turkey today), around AD 248. Constantine later renamed Drepanum as Helenopolis to honor his mother. Helena, rumored to be part Jewish, was not born into a prestigious family of wealth or power. According to St. Ambrose of Milan, she was a *stabularia*, defined as a woman from the stables. During the third century, stables were associated with inns, insinuating that she was an innkeeper or servant at an inn. Not considered a lofty occupation, there was a social stigma associated with being a female innkeeper. Though born of questionable descent, Helena was regarded as a woman of sound and solid character.

It was here that Helena met Constantius, a firmly built soldier with a rosy complexion, who was kind and keen. They fell in love in AD 270 when Helena was twenty-two years old. Whether they were married or not is debated by scholars. One version claims they were married; another says she was his concubine. Either way there was love between them and great plans by God for their son, Constantine.

Helena's story is an example of how God works through the majestic, and seemingly more often, the humble. Our earthly preconceived judgment of those we see as unworthy and their plights cannot compare to God's compassion or vision for such people. Only He sees the world with eternity in perspective.

Helena and Constantius probably made their home together in

Dalamaia, Constantius's home region. When Helena was twenty-four years old, Constantine was born in Naissus in AD 272 or 273. He matured mirroring his mother. He was tall and good looking, and his intellect was sharp and quick. And Helena instilled into her son a sense of values and moral fiber.

In AD 289, however, everything changed for Helena. Constantius—soon to be Caesar to Maximian—severed his relations with Helena to marry Theodora, a more acceptable woman laden with social status. So Helena was abandoned by Constantius because she was not wealthy or from a socially, politically reputable lineage. She could give him her love, but that was not enough. Her heartbreak was surely intensified by this humiliation. Then, adding insult to injury, Constantine was removed from Helena's custody as a type of political hostage.

Constantius had three children with his new wife, Theodora, which threatened Constantine's claim to power. Who would succeed Constantius—the son of a woman innkeeper or the son of a royal woman? Helena's pain and circumstances were universal: a woman is abandoned by the man she loves because he desires another woman.

History books of that time reveal facts, but not feelings. Yet Helena surely grieved. She lost the love of her life and her precious son. Emptiness and sorrow must have permeated her soul. She disappeared into obscurity, her name disappearing from the history books. She seemingly became obsolete.

This was a time in Helena's life when she could not possibly fathom the works God had in store for her. In the midst of her darkness, she could not meditate upon what is now prevalently displayed in history. She could not perceive God's plans. Furthest from her thinking was that one day she would be revered as a saint; she wasn't even a Christian. But Helena was obviously a woman of courage and fortitude. She didn't spiral down into self-pity. She waited for light to dispel darkness, for it always does.

In AD 305 when Diocletian was sixty years old, he abdicated the throne to his Caesar and demanded that Maximian act accordingly. Maximian did so with rancor, and Constantius was promoted to

Augusta of the eastern region. Upon receiving the title of Augustus, Constantius prepared to lead his legions into Britain. Constantine escaped Diocletian's control and rushed to join his father, arriving just as his ship was set to sail.

While in Britain, Constantius became ill and died in York. Constantine was at his deathbed, and he was instantly hailed by his father's troops as Augustus, emperor of the Western Roman Empire. Interestingly, it was Constantine, Constantius's son with Helena, the mother of his child from humble heritage and mundane social status, not Theodora's royal-blooded son, who was heralded as the new emperor. God had a plan. He looks after the humble and meek, the poor and destitute, the widow and fatherless.

One of the first things Constantine did upon becoming Augustus was to reunite with his mother and bring her to his side at his imperial court. He honored her with dignity, love, and respect, giving her a position of prominence and independence. He minted bronze coins bearing her effigy, honoring Helena as *Nobilissima femina.* In AD 324 Constantine bestowed upon his mother the enormously significant, honorable title of Augusta. She was forty-six years old. This time he acknowledged her as an Augusta by minting gold coins bearing her portrait, which were circulated throughout the land.

God's Plan Revealed

Upon becoming Augustus, not surprisingly, Constantine was thrown into many battles. Maximian, the former Augustus, decided to reclaim his title. Constantine won that battle and then had to fight Maximian's son, Maxentius, who had decided *he* wanted to be Augustus. Heeding the call of battle after battle, Constantine and his weary, ravaged troops were in Maxentius's territory preparing for the famous battle of Milvian Bridge.

Constantine was still a pagan. Yet, before the battle of Milvian Bridge, Constantine experienced a dramatic and transforming vision from Christ. He saw something shining in the sky, the cross of Jesus accompanied with the words *In Hoc Signo Vinces,* meaning "Conquer by This Sign." Eusebius, Constantine's historian, reports,

He said that about noon, when the day was already beginning to decline, he saw with his own eyes the trophy of a cross of light in the heavens, above the sun, and bearing the inscription, "Conquer by this."[4]

God had called upon Constantine because He knew Constantine's and Helena's hearts. As a result, their lives would never be the same again, because they heeded God's call. Constantine realized he had been chosen by the Christian God for a divine purpose; so he was heartened and inspired, yet his generals tried to dissuade him from taking his demoralized, exhausted troops into battle. However, Constantine now knew he would reign victorious, and he decided to enter the battle of Milvian Bridge. Knowing that his victory depended on putting his faith in Jesus, Constantine raised a cross on a spear and rallied his troops with his newfound faith, his sign from Christ.

Constantine was victorious in the battle of Milvian Bridge and, thus, humbled by the vision he had received from God, he became a Christian. Helena also became a Christian, and to quote James Carroll in *Constantine's Sword*, the "second greatest story ever told" ensued.

Eusebius, describing Helena's passion and devotion for Christ, wrote,

> She [his mother] became under his [Constantine's] influence such a devout servant of God, that one might have believed her to have been from her very childhood a disciple of the redeemer of mankind.[5]

James Carroll describes the impact on the Christian movement this way:

> Constantine and his mother, Helena, became the instruments through which Christ, the Christians, and the Christian church transitioned from a dispersed, persecuted brotherhood of disciples of the everlasting foundation of faith that it is today.[6]

Constantine, the son of a humble innkeeper and single mother was chosen by God to validate and protect Christ's disciples and the Christian movement. As emperor, Constantine dutifully and passionately endorsed and upheld Christianity, unifying the word and works of Christ.

Within a year of the Milvian Bridge vision, Constantine decided to aid Christians with his political influence and end persecution of the church. He issued the *Edict of Milan*, granting universal freedom of religion. The decree, sounding very much like aspects of the Constitution of the United States of America, stated,

> Since we saw that freedom of worship ought not to be denied . . . to each man's judgment and will the right should be given to care for the sacred things according to each man's free choice.[7]

In another letter he states both his faith and the freedom people would have, who have not yet been convinced of the truth, to take part in pagan cults. Constantine continued to appoint pagans to his government, yet he had no tolerance for the pagan traditions of morally deficient acts such as temple prostitution, inspection of entrails, and infanticide. Constantine knew the odds were against him in regard to forcing all pagans to become Christians. And though there were some acts of intolerance for the blatantly evil practices of paganism, Constantine's reign was not defined by violent acts of intolerance. His prayer was for the pagans to be enlightened and convert to Christianity, as he had done, peacefully and not by force. And he prayed to that end.

Many modern critics of Constantine theorize that he used Christianity solely to aid his own political ambitions and to augment his greed for power. These criticisms warrant rational responses such as: Who really knows Constantine's heart? Only he, Helena, and God. Also, if an emperor wanted to gain political ground, why would he do it with a new, unpopular, insignificant, unacknowledged religion? The masses were still pagans. Surely there were easier ways to solidify power. Constantine was a brilliant, respected strategist and leader. He didn't need to defend the underdog religion to rally his influence.

Logically, my assessment as a person, not a historian, is that Constantine was motivated by his passion, love, and respect for Christ. His life's mission was to honor Him, though at times he failed as all humans do. If this resulted in a breathtaking transformation, unity, and permeation of Christianity throughout the Roman Empire, it was by Christ's power and design.

HELENA'S MIRACLE

Helena's life was transformed as well. Mercifully, Helena, in her days of woe, didn't give up before the miracle. God lifted her out of the mire and gave her a willingness and passion to serve. As always Helena was still holding her head high. Out of the pain from her lover's lack of loyalty ensued a fierce and relentless loyalty to Christ, her son, and the people. She observed with awe and assisted with diligence as Constantine became the first Christian emperor. He legitimized Christianity across his empire, shedding light upon a newfound definition of humanity. Helena, year after year, was by his side as his confidant, his advisor.

Constantine had giant hurdles to jump to enlighten the Roman Empire about Christianity—this new and mysterious religion. In this effort and campaign he used Helena as his diplomatic representative to help facilitate his new missions of mercy. One of his first Christian acts was to manifest two measures regarding infanticide. He provided imperial money to parents overwhelmed with children and gave all the property rights of exposed infants to those who took them in and supported them. Other Christian acts followed, such as assistance to the poor and needy, a hallmark of Christian charity. Exiled Christians were allowed to come home, and he released Christians employed as slaves and reinstated their civil rights. There was also restoration for the stolen goods of Christians and the churches.

Helena brought to fruition these acts of benevolence across the empire. She became "one of the pillars upon which the security of the *republica* rested,"[8] and historian Eusebius stated that Constantine had put the imperial treasury in her hands and even insinuates that Helena was his co-ruler.[9]

Helena was generous with her time, money, and land. History reveals a connection between Helena and the southeast corner of Rome. Her humanitarian efforts included overseeing the building of many churches and basilicas. Helena and Constantine were inspired and, thus, responsible for presenting Christians with beautiful places of worship. Three of eight inscriptions discovered in the area are to her.

Constantine and Helena built a basilica honoring the martyrs of the Great Persecution during Diocletian's reign. The church of *SS Marcellinus e Pietro* was built in honor of Peter and Marcellinus in the *Via Labicana* and is one of the oldest basilicas in Rome. A mausoleum was built right next to it, and Helena dedicated an engraved golden scyphus (drinking vessel), representing her religious devotion to the newly built church on her land. Some scholars believe that Constantine may have built the basilica because Helena initiated and insisted upon it.

Helena also gave her residence in Trier, Germany, to Agricus, the bishop of Trier from AD 314–330, for use as the city's cathedral. She presented the bishop with several relics of Christ (found on her trip to Jerusalem), as well as the remains of the apostle Matthias. It has been reported that Helena was instrumental in the genesis of the Abbey of St. Maximin at Trier. Civic-minded, she repaired public areas such as the baths that had been destroyed, which were subsequently renamed Thermae Helenae. The aqueducts were also built under her supervision, as proven by inscriptions dedicated to her by Julius Maximiliannus.

CONSTANTINE'S ACCOMPLISHMENTS

Because Constantine was the son of a single mother, and because the ramifications of his reign are vastly relevant to Christians and Christian worship today, I am including some of Constantine's accomplishments.

Constantine was concerned about the lack of unity and differing interpretations between Christians—differences Christians sought to resolve through prayer and communion. Yet the priests could not define Christ and the Trinity or how Jesus was God. They couldn't even decide on a date for Easter. Constantine's perspective was that only a church with unity of vision and direction could represent Christianity effectively to the pagan masses. Constantine was looking for unity within his faith. Thus, tolerance of natural differences between Christian religions and religious interpretations were soon to become unacceptable. In a century when the church was waning, the brotherhood of disciples was wandering, and Christians were routinely martyred, Constantine, through Christ's guidance, provided Christians and the Christian church the much-needed sense of direction, protection, and unification that elicited strength, respect, and relevancy.

THE NICENE CREED

The Christian debate and theological opacity was soon to end with an act representing Constantine's desire for clarity that reverberates to this day in church services all over the world—the Nicene Creed. In AD 325 Constantine summoned all of the church's approximately two hundred and fifty bishops to Nicea to debate, discuss, and draw conclusions about these questions. His letter to them stated, "Wherefore I signify to you, my beloved brethren, that all of you promptly assemble at the said city, that is at Nicea." Constantine would not let them adjourn until a resolution of unity had been achieved. As always, Helena was by his side. The Nicene Creed provided the unity of Christian theological vision and doctrine he felt was vital for the survival and expansion of the church. Helena was proud of her son as he sat on his golden chair in Nicea leading this historically significant event, participating to the point that he was noted as one of the principal authors.

The Nicene Creed has been recited in various forms in churches through the centuries and remains a fixture in many services today as follows:

We believe in one God, the Father almighty, maker of all things, visible and invisible. And in one Lord Jesus Christ, the Son of God, begotten from the Father, only begotten, that is, from the substance of the Father, God from God, light from

HOLDING HER HEAD HIGH

light, true God from true God, begotten not made, of one substance with the Father, through whom all things came into being, things in heaven and on earth, who for the sake of men and for the purpose of our salvation came down and became incarnate, becoming man, suffered and rose again on the third day, ascended into the heavens, and will come to judge the living and the dead . . .

The creed was expanded upon, and today it is recited "and became man. For our sake he was crucified under Pontius Pilate; he suffered, died, and was buried. On the third day he rose again in fulfillment of the Scriptures." I note this expansion of the creed because I find it to be rather interesting. According to James Carroll, the original Nicene Creed did not mention the death of Jesus or the crucifixion. It's thought that the emphasis on Pontius Pilate, which is in direct contrast with the Gospels (Pontius Pilate in the Bible symbolically washed his hands clean of the death of Jesus), was added to accuse Pilate, who was a pagan, and thus the pagan religion. The new phrase "in fulfillment of the Scriptures" was later added to affirm that the Jewish "prophecy" had been fulfilled.

The original creed took many years to accomplish and more than a dozen councils. It was finally culminated in AD 381 during the Council of Constantinople. What is interesting is the shift of emphasis from the incarnation and resurrection represented in the first version of the creed to the death of Jesus and the heart of redemption in the revised versions. The cross of Jesus' death was evolving into *the* reverent symbol representing Christianity. The shift was due to the culmination of many events: Constantine's vision, the Council of Nicea, the Nicene Creed, and Helena's claimed discovery of the True Cross.

HELENA'S PILGRIMAGE

Helena was a reverent Christian and a devoted single mother at the side of her son all of her days. As an Augusta she bestowed her compassion and benevolent acts of kindness throughout the land. Remarkably, it was at the end of her life that Helena endured her most grueling mission and defined her profound purpose. When Helena was almost eighty years old she took her most famous excursion. When most women are ready for their rocking chairs, Helena decided to go on a pilgrimage to Jerusalem. She was the first woman, the first person, to go on such an adventure because pilgrimages had not existed before that time. Her pilgrimage was not based on penance, as they were later in the Middle Ages, but on discipleship.

Besides her benevolent acts of charity and reverent acts of worship, it was her vastly significant discoveries of Golgotha (the place where Christ was hung on the cross), Christ's Sepulcher (His tomb), the Place of the Nativity (His birthplace), and Christ's seamless robe that were to change the perception of Jerusalem forever. The forsaken wasteland was to become the center of Christianity. Christians had abandoned Jerusalem due to both the call of evangelism and the fear of persecution. The Jews had staged two revolts against the Roman Empire, resulting in the destruction of the temple by the Romans, just as Jesus had predicted. The Jews were expelled from Jerusalem and the coastal plains where Caesarea was located. They were confined to Galilee and the Golan Heights in the north. Jerusalem was still beautiful, filled with vegetation, but the glorious city on the hill had been taken over by pagans. They had built altars, temples, and statues of their gods over the archeological treasures of Christ.

Helena decided to go on this long and tedious journey for numerous reasons. As noted before, she wanted to "pray on the ground where Jesus's feet had walked."[10] She also wanted to pray for her son and her grandsons. Constantine wanted to unify the eastern part of the Roman Empire by spreading the gospel through generous acts of charity and peace. Helena sought to honor her son's convictions and mirror his benevolence by teaching Christianity and inspiring conversion. Constantine also wanted his mother to oversee the building of lavish and magnificent churches. These basilicas were to serve as statements of strength of the Christian church and to accommodate the influx of many new converts.

Thus, as an aged yet able woman, a devout and pious Christian, and a fiercely dedicated mother, Helena ventured into a long, arduous trip to Jerusalem, the holy city. She would serve as an example of Christian charity, peace, and love, and her discoveries would draw millions to the church. Her journey was recorded in the historical documents by Eusebius. He writes that Helena was pious, humble, abounding with good deeds, generous, and charitable; filled with kind acts of helping the poor and the helpless. She visited Constantine's soldiers and gave them generous bonuses; she initiated and executed the release of prisoners; she gave money to the poor and lavished money upon the churches she visited. And she didn't overlook any church on the way—even at the smallest towns she stopped and prayed at their altars. She gave money to all who approached her, clothed the poor, and prayed with the sick. She was steadfast in her belief that she was responsible for the less fortunate. Through Christ, she held her head high and helped others do the same.

HELENA'S DISCOVERIES

One of the most fascinating aspects of Helena's pilgrimage was her discoveries. According to both legend and scholars, Helena had a vision from God that she was to uncover the three crosses of the crucifixion and identify the True Cross upon which Jesus died. Is it a myth or is it real? There are many accounts of such discoveries, and churches across the world claim to house these sacred relics. It's documented in church histories and by scholars such as Ambrose (his is believed to be the oldest account), Socrates, Paulinas, Theodoret, Gelasuis of Caesarea, Sozomen, Rufinus, Paulinas of Nola, Sulpicius, and Severus, to name just a few!

One version is presented by Sozomen, who records it this way:

I. Helena journeys to Jerusalem to search for the True Cross.
1. Helena comes to Jerusalem to pray and visit the holy places.
2. She searches for the cross which is, like the tomb, hard to find.
3. Enemies of Christianity have covered the place with a heap of sand, have surrounded Golgotha and the tomb with a wall and have set up a temple and statue for Aphrodite.

4. The place comes to light, not under the directions of a Jew, but by means of a divine signs and dreams.
5. Constantine orders the sand to be removed: the tomb is revealed and on the other side of the same place three crosses and the titulus appear.
6. The True Cross cannot be identified because the titulus has become separated from it. Moreover, the crosses are jumbled together because the Roman soldiers, who had taken Jesus and the thieves down from their crosses, have thrown the crosses away.

II. The Identification of the True Cross
1. A noble woman, native of Jerusalem, lies dying.
2. Macarius and Helena are standing at her deathbed and Macarius prays for a sign from God.
3. After the touch of two of the crosses is of no avail, the third instantly cures the woman.
4. A dead person has also come back to life at the touch of the Cross.

III. Construction of the Church, the sending of the nails and part of the Cross to Constantine, the preservation of the Cross in Jerusalem
1. A large part of the Cross is preserved in Jerusalem in a silver casket.
2. Another part is sent by Helena to Constantine together with the nails: the latter are incorporated in the emperor's helmet and are included as part of the bridle of his horse.
3. Reference to Zechariah 14:20 and the prophesy of the Sibyl.
4. Constantine orders a church of great beauty to be built on the site of the discovery.
5. Helena builds churches in Bethlehem and on the Mount of Olives.

IV. Helena's other activities (and information about the empress)
1. Helena invites holy virgins to a banquet and serves them at the

table. She presents the churches in the cities of the East with suitable gifts, helps the poor and those who have lost their property, and releases others from captivity, exile, and mines.

2. She is given the title of Augusta and coins with her portrait are minted; the imperial treasury is put at her disposal.

3. Palestine is named after her. She dies at the age of 80, but she is not forgotten because towns in Bithynia and Palestine are named after her.[11]

So Helena evidently fulfilled her dream of discovering the True Cross of Jesus. It was reported that she persisted and found it beneath the rubble of a long forgotten piece of land adorned with a statue of Aphrodite built by pagans. It may have been disguised by a statue of Venus, which was built by the Roman pagan leader Hadrian during the second century. It was in the second century that the Romans had renamed Jerusalem as *Ailia Capitolina*. After Helena discovered and evacuated this spot, she then honored it with a beautiful basilica called the *Martyrium*, a glorious church. To this church Helena dedicated the True Cross in a silver casket.

It's interesting to note that Eusebius did not mention the discovery of the True Cross. It was told by St. Ambrose, bishop of Milan, in AD 395. Yet the discovery of the True Cross was also documented by many other theologians and scholars. Eusebius knew that the discovery of the Cross would most certainly change the focus of attention from Caesarea to Jerusalem, and time would prove his fear true. Eusebius also believed that the focus of Christianity should be on the resurrection and not on the crucifixion, the heart of redemption. Various churches to this day still debate this topic.

Helena's discovery, coupled with Constantine's vision of the burning cross at Melvian Bridge, provided further impetus for the cross to be the center of Christianity, and the idea spread rapidly. Helena sent pieces of the True Cross to her son Constantine to be put into his helmet and his horse's bridle. She had a silver shrine made to hold the fraction of the True Cross that was to remain in Jerusalem. Pieces of the True Cross were the most revered church relics in the Middle Ages and were spread throughout Europe and Byzantium. The antiquated superstition "knock on wood" originates from the fascination and reverence of the True Cross. Today a piece of the True Cross is contained in the bronze cross atop the obelisk in St. Peter's Square in Rome.

It is widely believed that Helena discovered many other things as well while on her pilgrimage in Jerusalem. Her discoveries ranged from the womb to the tomb of Christ. She discovered the Nativity Cave in Bethlehem where Christ was possibly born, and there she built the Church of Nativity over the site. She also may have discovered the tomb of Jesus, the Sepulcher. Helena supervised the building and decorating of the Church of the Holy Sepulcher to honor this sacred spot. It was destroyed by fire in AD 614 but was rebuilt. It remained until AD 1009 when Egyptian Calioh Al-Hakim destroyed the church and had Jesus' tomb hacked down to bedrock. The church was rebuilt yet again by the French Crusaders in the early twelfth century. Today the Church of the Holy Sepulcher is occupied by the Greek Church, the Roman Catholic Church, and the Coptic and Armenian clergy.

Helena also built a church on the Mount of Olives. Eusebius states that she built these churches and dedicated them to God, endowing them with many gifts. Another belief is that she discovered the seamless robe of Jesus (probably an undergarment). As stated in John 19:23–24, the seamless robe of Jesus was not torn because it had no seam:

> When the soldiers crucified Jesus, they took his clothes, dividing them into four shares, one for each of them, with the undergarment remaining. This garment was seamless, woven in one piece from top to bottom.
>
> "Let's not tear it," they said to one another. "Let's decide by lot who will get it." (NIV)

Helena had the robe sent to the church in Trier, Germany, and it is now housed in the Cathedral of Trier. It has been on display for pilgrimages many times during the sixteenth century, once during the seventeenth century, three times in the nineteenth century, and three times in the twentieth century. The last time it was on display was in 1996 when it was viewed by more than a million people.

The courage and tenacity Helena exhibited during her lifetime and on this first pilgrimage, yet her last journey, was monumental in scope and vast in its religious implications. Constantine certainly played a hand in the decisions, and it was done with his imperial funding, but it was Helena who made the journey and brought it to fruition. Helena once again exhibited that for her God and her son she would travel to the ends of the earth.

The annuls of history are fuzzy and incomplete, especially ones from more than seventeen hundred years ago. Did Helena really make all these discoveries? Only God knows. There is much written documentation that she did, and these articles of discovery are in churches to this day. There is no doubt about her ardent desire to worship Christ. There is no doubt about her devotion to Christ and to her son. There is no doubt about her loyalty and her insatiable thirst to help others. There is no doubt that she was a single mother who held her head high, intent on healing others with empathy, compassion, and dignity. During the process, she healed herself. Therein lies the gift of service. And there is no doubt that she was a light of God and an honest example of His grace.

Amazing as all of this was, Helena was simply a humble stable girl who loved a man, birthed his son, and ended up a single mother. It is, however, the way she lived her life and the choices she made that wrought her uniqueness and inspiration. She pursued her life, with all its heartbreak and challenges, with a resolute character and a willingness to walk with Christ. She instilled in her son a moral fiber and a sense of duty that would one day make him a vastly successful Augustus.

Constantine represented both masterful military victories and the humanizing of a barbaric world with a fierce loyalty to Christ. His leadership resulted in the cessation of senseless murders of adults and infants and inspired a new definition of compassion and social order. He became the first Christian emperor and, thus, one of the world's most important Christians.

According to Eusebius, Constantine, who ruled from AD 306–429, was responsible for the monumental triumph of Christianity over paganism. He ended the persecution of Christians. His insistence on a unified vision of Christianity resulted in the Nicene Creed, which confirmed Jesus as God and clarified the Holy Trinity.

> [Constantine] dedicated his life to finding a unity, a binding of himself and his Christian subjects in a common goal—the gift of living in a settled, tranquil world and by their piety and faithfulness earning salvation.[12]

Helena, the Saint

Helena was a fiercely devoted mother to her son, and Constantine was a fiercely devoted son to his mother. What a special woman Helena must have been. She spent her life standing by her son's side and doing whatever he asked of her. She died fittingly in the presence of her son in AD 330. She was buried in Rome in the mausoleum of the Church of *SS Marcellinus e Pietro.*

Helena is a prominent saint in the Greek Church, and many Eastern churches are dedicated to her. After her death the position of *progenetrix* of the dynasty was recognized. So the next time you put a cross around your neck or recite the Nicene Creed, you may reflect upon the goodness of God and the perseverance of Constantine and Helena, his mother—a single mother.

Though Helena's time was ancient, her message is modern: *Never be defeated by circumstances. Go to church and worship God.* If for some reason you feel judged as a single mother, then find another church, because Christianity is the essence of forgiveness and not about the ill-considered judgments of mere men. Only God is the Judge, and only God knows the inner sanctuary of your heart.

Life Lesson: Listen for God's Higher Calling

Helena listened and illustrated God's strength and transformational power through grace, humility, love, and devotion. As Helena exemplified, we need to be stewards of our wounds—transform our personal wounds into gifts that help others. You can be a conduit for healing, and the healing will be mutual. Then you will be full of joy and peace, living your destiny and being a positive example for your children. You'll be teaching them how to cope, how not to be defeated by pain. Children emulate what we do; so hold your head high, because from you they will learn how to transform despair into divine inspiration.

Listen for God's higher calling. He is there. He knows your name, your capabilities, your talents, your influence. He knows your heart.

Helena, the saint, the queen,
the friend to the nuns and priests,
the patroness of armies,
the benefactress of churches,
the devoted mother of the Emperor.

—CHRONICLER

chapter three

The Middle Ages—
Setting the Stage

AD 500–1399

*As late as the fifteenth century, if we are to believe the
great popular preachers of the day, the streams and cesspools
of Europe echoed with the cries of abandoned babies.*[1]

Medieval times. Castles and moats. Royal courts and peasant poverty. Church bells and frankincense. Prayers and communion. Wild galloping horses and streets of mud. Ravaging diseases and herbal medicines. Barons and knights and war . . . war . . . war. Who will ease their pain?

The Middle Ages, or medieval times, extended over a broad period of time. Some scholars refer to the era as a millennium, while others restrict it specifically from AD 500–1399. Regardless, it is considered a time when the social vista for women was bleak. Their rights, status, and futures deteriorated. Families considered the birth of daughters a burden, and they were more likely to be subjected to infanticide. Girls were perceived and treated as incapable of taking care of themselves, ironically because they were prohibited from doing so. The burden of a sizable dowry was the family's only hope for their daughter's fortuitous marriage. Unlike in Roman times, the dowry was no longer protected for the woman. Once she was married, it became the man's property, and he could do with it as he desired.

Some women lived into their eighties, but the average age of death was thirty-three. Because the age of mortality was so young, marriage was permissible for a girl at the age of twelve. Marriage was permissible for boys at the age of fourteen, though boys generally waited until they were older to marry. Girls were not considered able to bear children until the age of fifteen, thus the youngsters were allowed to play ball, read, and study together until they reached puberty. There is some indication that fifteen may have been a more realistic age for marriage.

Once they entered the dangerous world of producing babies, girls did so repeatedly and often. Their lives were continually jeopardized by the rapid rate of pregnancies. They were not likely to yield any influence over their often older husbands, yet they could enjoy an intimacy with their children as they became formidable figures in the direction of their lives.

Rarely is childbirth given a second thought in modern society; mostly it's taken for granted. And yet, to ponder that with every sexual opportunity and fulfillment, with every expression of love for her husband, the woman risked her life is foreign to us in modern times. She never knew if her consummation of sex would yield a pregnancy, and if it did, if she would withstand it or die. The number of women who died in childbirth was exceedingly high and continued to be until the twentieth century. In this respect, for a woman to express her love for her man throughout the centuries of time has truly been the ultimate sacrifice.

Young girls were frequently relieved of the dangers of pregnancies due to the deaths of their husbands. A substantial percentage of widows were teenagers, some as young as ten. The majority of these teenage widows had already borne children—the teenage and single mothers of medieval times. In Florence in 1427, more than half the adult population of women were widows. Many women took over the duties of their deceased husbands' affairs as regents and chose not to remarry but to devote themselves to the futures of their children. Thus, these women, who were supposedly incapable of taking care of themselves, repeatedly disproved this myth.

STRENGTH AND STAMINA

The medieval noblewoman's life was not one of idle times, romping around castle grounds. Stamina was her middle name. She was like a drill sergeant over a small army. She was responsible for the well-being of her employees, including everything from laying hands on them when they were sick to paying their bills and making sure they were well fed. The food sources were her domain, such as fishing, gaming, herb gardening, and caring for the spice houses. Manufacturing clothing was also her responsibility, from sheering the sheep to spinning, weaving, and tailoring. These chores were in addition to her duties as a mother, overseeing her children's education by hiring their chaplains, chambermaids, and tutors, and checking on their progress.

A noblewoman also provided their cultural life and entertainment as she single-handedly defended her domain against attacks. She had to allow time in her day to visit and endow the poor with money and listen to the needs and wants of her audience as she ate her noonday meal, repeated again during her evening meal. Her day included attending chapel in the early mornings and evenings. She did all this as she developed her cunning ability to laugh and be harmonious, discerning who within her household was her ally, and know who was desirous of her death!

Children of medieval times were at risk. Noblemen and -women were more inclined to love, honor, and care for their children than in earlier times, but infanticide continued as a common practice. Unlike the ritual of the *susceptio* by the *paterfamilias* in Rome when the child was accepted or rejected by the father, medieval women were motivated by the shame of being seduced or abandoned with an illegitimate child. Many were motivated by poverty. Infanticide was the act of the poor and the desperate. Church councils, documents, and laws of the time refer consistently to acts of infanticide.

In the legend of Pope Innocent III, he was inspired by a dream to order fishermen to cast their nets into the Tiber River. The fishermen threw their nets into the waters, and as the nets were heaved up onto the boat they revealed eighty-seven drowned babies. A second sweep revealed three hundred and forty more. The Pope was so shocked by this horror that he funded the hospital Santo Spirito for the purpose of aiding unwanted babies. Remembrances of this event still illuminate the walls of this hospital.

It was the example of Jesus' love for children that shed light on this tragic purging of babies. Christ is referred to as the "King of children." St. Benedict of Nursia insisted that the advice of children be sought in important matters, "for often the Lord reveals to the young what should be done."[2] Churches offered services for orphans and foundlings, but none made this service its specific mission until the fifteenth century. Orphanages bearing shelter for foundlings, illegitimate children, and orphans started to then dot the landscape of Europe. Some, appallingly, were for unwanted children of legitimate birth only.

Among the wide speculation and many free-floating facts debated by scholars of medieval children, there is random consensus as to when the definition and awareness of "childhood" came to fruition. Many believe it was in the latter part of the Middle Ages. As for the well-being of the wanted child and the medieval reevaluation of childhood, it wasn't until the twelfth century that education was even considered for these children. It wasn't until the fourteenth century that social thinking shifted toward the welfare of the child's health and survival. Writers began expressing sentiments that children should be treated with special care and considered a blessing. Until then children had been routinely beaten, and this was considered acceptable. Vincent of Beauvais, a thirteenth-century author, warned against the beating of children and explains, "Children's minds break down under excessive severity of correction; they despair, and worry, and finally they hate. And this is the most injurious; where every-thing is feared, nothing is attempted."[3]

Do not embitter your children,
or they will become discouraged.

—COLOSSIANS 3:21, NIV

QUEEN BLANCHE OF CASTILE

Passionate Single Mother

AD 1188–1252

SNAPSHOT	Tender twelve-year-old Blanche weeping sadly, dries her tears, deciding to accept her destiny
MOTHER MOMENT	Fervently riding her horse through the streets, summoning help for her son
CHALLENGE	Powerlessness over her destiny
STEWARDSHIP	Passionately fulfilling her destiny
SCRIPTURE	Be shepherds of God's flock that is under your care, serving as overseers— not because you must, but because you are willing, as God wants you to be; not greedy for money, but eager to serve; not lording it over those entrusted to you, but being examples to the flock. (1 Peter 5:2–3 NIV)

CHAPTER FOUR

Choose God's Greatness

Louis, who King of France was made
In everything truly obeyed
His mother's wishes, Blanche the Queen;
'Twixt him and her came none between,
Him did she love as never mother
Loved a son, or loved a brother.

—CHRONICLERS OF FRANCE

Twelfth-century France. Pungent perfumes and garlic garlands. Bells toll and swords collide. Long heavy gowns and monks' robes of austerity. Horses' sweat and damp, musky halls. Always an uprising. Always a coup. Never a peaceful moment.

It is almost nine hundred years ago, a millennium. Yet again, the love, passions, joys, sorrows, fear and bravery, sickness and death are synchronous in the scope of time. Pain is universal. Love is eternal. So let's go into the world of medieval France and parlay the worlds of ancestry. Let's watch the knights fly by in their saddles and the archer's arrow spear through the air. Let's learn how a weeping, frightened young girl, powerless over her destiny, finds the inner strength to overcome adversity, raising nine children as she rules the country of France.

A queen. How can we relate to a queen? Even if she were a widowed single mother, a queen's life is one of luxury, dripping in wealth, ensconced in splendid castles, followed by priests to assist her every benevolent moment, and ladies-in-waiting willing to aid her every whim. How is her life challenged?

As I researched, I realized I was wrong, most wrong. I became enlightened to the enormous weight a queen carries on her shoulders. I realized a queen never *chooses* to become a queen. She is *born* a queen. Her only choice, not even choosing her husband, lies within her heart: Does she choose to become a queen of merit or a queen of malice? Does she choose greatness or meekness, happiness or discontentment? Herein lies my choice of Queen Blanche of Castile for this book.

Blanche, thrust upon despairing turning points of life, chose to persevere with dignity, grace, efficiency, and tremendous effort. She chose to follow God's vision for her life as a ruler, a mother, a child of His. Heeding the call of the hurricane force of responsibilities and challenges, her greatness emerged. She, by sheer will and tenacity, coupled with her unshakable faith, *became* great. And though it was almost nine hundred years ago, the emotions and situations are both contemporary and eternal.

I am impressed at the scope of undertakings that awaited Blanche upon her husband's death. Fiercely devoted to her husband, she vowed to never marry again. Thus alone (because other than her Lord, who could she really trust?), she sought to take charge of her duties as a widow with nine children and pregnant with the tenth.

Many widowed queens ruled as regents for their sons but few with the aptitude, honor, and benevolence of Blanche. And she was not just a regent; she became the ruling queen, preserving the kingdom for her young son, Louis IX, who would later be named a saint. She was an ancient equivalent of a modern-day working single mother. She made wise choices based on a sense of humanity founded in her Christian faith.

Timeless Scenario: Girl is born into a rich, powerful family. Girl marries boy from a rich, powerful family. The girl and boy are powerless over their decisions and their lives. Girl and boy are suppressed by parents and society. Girl and boy fall madly in love. They have many children. Boy dies. Girl is devastated. Girl must now take over the family business. She is a single mother with nine children. Girl builds her successes as a single mother and a leader on the foundation of God. Girl is constrained by circumstances but chooses God's greatness.

BORN TO RULE

Very little historical documentation survives about Blanche of Castile and her son King Louis IX; the reasons why are unclear. It's ironic that more data does not exist because Blanche and Louis were both prolific and faithful rulers.

Blanche was born on March 4, 1188, in the castle of Palencia in Castile. She was the daughter of Alfonso VIII, king of Castile, and Eleanor of England, daughter of Henry II of England and his queen, Eleanor of Aquitaine. Blanche's parents were very much in love and inseparable. Eleanor of Aquitaine was infamous for her strength, defiance, and maternal fortitude.

It was Blanche's grandmother, Eleanor of Aquitaine, who whisked her from her homeland in Castile to the foreign castles of France. She had arranged for Blanche to marry the young prince of France, Louis VIII. Blanche had, of course, no say in the matter. It didn't matter if, at the tender age of twelve, she was devastated to be separated from her parents. She was a means to an end—a pawn in the game of royal chess. Her grandmother was disappointed in her son, King John of England, an irresponsible and despised ruler who since the age of seven had refused holy communion. Blanche was to be the pledge of peace between the two kings—her future husband's father, King Philip of France, and King John of England. Beautiful, passionate, brilliant Blanche was also the conduit for Eleanor of Aquitaine's daring dream—the union under one crown of France and England. Blanche's life was not her own. As she traveled with her grandmother to her new destination, she no doubt passed the hours listening to Eleanor's dissertations about the responsibilities of being a queen and emboldening her with her grand ambitions.

The lectures had little effect on the sensitive, tender Blanche, for she succumbed to constant sobbing after her marriage to young King

Louis VIII on May 23, 1200. Only after a visit with St. Hugh, at the beckoning of her most concerned thirteen-year-old husband, did Blanche dry her tears. What St. Hugh said to her is unknown, but he who made children smile, caused animals to sway, and was constantly followed by a swan, surely must have spoken of God. This strength would be her constant companion in years to come. Blanche must have been resilient, because once again she was faced with a choice in regard to how she meditated upon her fate. Lonely and dreadfully homesick, she must have longed for her mother and father. Through this delicate time, Blanche nurtured her own inner strength and resources, one of which was her faith in God. The self-assurances of divine purpose must have been her solace during her nights in a strange and foreign land.

After her marriage, Blanche played court games with Louis VIII, and together they studied grammar, music, geometry, astronomy, Latin, and the Bible. As an aspiring poet she wrote:

> Love, who too late has captured me,
> Has taught me by his mastery,
> O Queen of Heaven, sovereign Lady,
> That he who would your praises sing
> And hymn the joy that is lasting
> Must love and serve you above all things
> O Queen and maiden, fleur de lis.

This sweet time with her husband allowed them to enjoy one another's company and learn to respect each other. In time she grew to love him with all her heart. They were inseparable, bound by friendship and a mutual respect. Louis VIII was her everything. He was all she had. They didn't enter into a sexual relationship until about five years after the marriage. Then it proved to be a beautiful union. She became pregnant and lost her first child at the age of seventeen. Pregnant again at the age of twenty-one, she adoringly presided over the ceremonies as her husband was knighted. She soon thereafter bore their second child, a son. They named him Philip.

As the years passed, Louis gallivanted throughout the kingdom, engaging in battles, as Blanche was birthing babies. As she bounced babies on her hip, she engaged in the administrative duties and responsibilities of France. Blanche always worked beside her husband and was well acquainted with domestic and foreign affairs. Her duties included overseeing the castle and lands, and attending to the vast number of nobles, courtesans, and peasants who constantly swarmed the castle with incessant requests. She was determined to be an active participant in her children's education, adamant that Christianity was intrinsically woven into their studies.

In AD 1213, at the age of twenty-five, Blanche gave birth to twins, but they didn't live. Sorrow certainly permeated her heart as she endured the loss of her second and third babies. Resilient, though, more pregnancies were to follow. On April 25, 1214, she gave birth to another son, Louis, named after his father.

Shortly thereafter, when Blanche was twenty-six years old, she felt the stunning blow of losing both her parents. King Alfonso died on August 16, 1214. Her mother, Eleanor, overcome with grief, died two months later on October 31, 1214. Legend says she died of a broken heart. Alfonso and Eleanor were buried side by side, a novelty for the times. Blanche was touched by this endearing act of passionate love, and it was her influence that motivated her son to build the Royal Mausoleum at Saint Denis. After her parents' deaths, the only one left in Blanche's life was her husband, Louis VIII, whom she passionately adored and leaned upon as a confidant for security, compassion, and love.

The Magna Carta

Louis VIII spent many years in England fighting the dismal English king John Lackland. (He was named Lackland because, unlike his brothers, he had received no land rights on the continent at birth; therefore, he *lacked land*.) King John was an unpopular, irreverent ruler, and he was continually creating ill will against himself and his kingdom. When he unfairly taxed his barons, the results were historic. They revolted and would not reunite with King John of England, with significant repercussions.

The barons seized the window of opportunity that King John's ineptitude warranted. They insisted that he sign the famous Magna Carta on July 19, 1215. This Magna Carta, Latin for "great charter" or "great paper," required the king to renounce certain rights, respect certain legal procedures, and accept that the will of the king could be bound by law. It stated that a committee of twenty-five barons could meet at any time and overrule the king. The Magna Carta was the precursor for the Constitution of the United States and Bill of Rights.

King John, of course, didn't honor this agreement, and war ensued. The First Barons' War involved Louis VIII, who fought honorably and was given the name Louis the Lion for his bravery. In AD 1216 he claimed the English crown as Blanche's birthright in keeping with Eleanor of Aquitaine's dream. Louis was proclaimed king of England for a short while but was never actually crowned. He found that the country of England did not embrace him, resulting in a sticky situation. He reached out to his father, Philip, king of France, but Philip refused to help his son. Blanche, though, did not refuse. She was incensed. She would never abandon her husband, leaving her blood to the wolves. Blanche had Latin blood running through her veins, and she was a fierce protector of her family. To put it in contemporary terms, you didn't mess with Blanche of Castile. When a situation warranted, she responded like a mama bear with her cubs.

Showing her mettle, Blanche decided to take matters into her own hands to save her husband. Most likely pregnant with her son Robert, she rode on horseback throughout Louis's lands and urgently sought the barons' aid for her husband in England. She succeeded in putting together two fleets. One fleet was under the command of Eustace the Monk, and the other consisted of an army under the command of Robert of Courtenay. All of her efforts were in vain, however; she only succeeded in demonstrating blind devotion to her husband. This righteous passion resonated deeply within her character and when awakened would be fierce. Louis was a lion and Blanche was a lioness.

King and Queen of France

Next in the line of momentous events was the death of Blanche's father-in-law, King Philip. He died on July 14, 1223, at the age of fifty-eight. On his deathbed he spoke these parting words: "Fear God, glorify God's church, give justice to God's people, protect the poor and the humble against the encroachments of the overbearing. My son, you did never cause me grief."[1]

Louis was a man of integrity, which was mirrored in Blanche's integrity. They truly were an idealistic couple bound together with a religious, moral code of ethics and a genuine sense of mutual love and respect. One month later Blanche stood by the man she adored as she and Louis VIII were crowned king and queen of France. The ceremony took place at Rheims on August 6, 1223. They were both thirty-five years old. As Blanche stood beside her king, she was described as "well endowed in body, in carriage, in beauty rich with nature's noblest gifts."[2]

Preceding the coronation, during twenty-three years of marriage and eighteen years of consummated marriage, Blanche had conceived and birthed nine babies, with subsequent children to come. She birthed a daughter at the age of seventeen whom she lost. Her second child, Philip, had died at age nine in 1218. She had given birth to twins on January 26, 1213, who didn't live. By the age of thirty-five Blanche and Louis had bravely withstood the agony of the loss of four children. However, on this glorious day of coronation, as Blanche looked into the eyes of her fiercely loyal, royal lover, her confidant, her teacher, her friend, she was surrounded by the manifestations of that love—her five surviving children: Louis IX, Robert, Jean, Alphonse of Toulouse, and Philippe of Dagobert.

The love that Blanche and Louis shared was deep and rich and romantic. His moral fiber was beyond reproach. The court and nobles all knew of Louis's devotion to Blanche. His heart, body, and soul were for Blanche.

Lost Love

On October 29, 1226, after Louis's siege of Avignon, many of

Louis's key people fell ill and died. Louis himself was exhausted from the tedious battles in abnormally hot weather. He decided to begin his journey home. He was only able to make it as far as Montpensier, however. How he must have yearned to see his Blanche. Having no communication must have been agonizing, and the fear of dying without her by his side must have been tragic. Feeling the impending doom, he made his confidants swear to recognize his son Louis IX as his successor. Having before made his intentions clear that Blanche was to rule the country, he died on November 8, 1226. He never got to see his sweet Blanche or precious children again. Forever he was severed from his lover, his friend, the mother of his children, and his children.

> The King died on the Sunday next after the octave day of All Saints. Jesus Christ have his soul, for he lived a good Christian, always in great holiness and purity of body so long as life as he had. For none ever discovered him to have commerce with woman other than her whom he took in marriage.[3]

In contrast, Louis's father, King Philip, had not been a virtuous man regarding marriage. In fact, at one time the church refused its services throughout the land, such as holy communion and the ringing of church bells, because Philip had refused his bride the morning after the wedding. He had her imprisoned and he married another woman.

Louis, however, chose a different path for his life. He was moral and loyal to Blanche. Legend recalls that when Louis was on his deathbed, his friend had slipped a naked woman into his bed to warm and heal him, this being a tradition of the times. Louis refused the woman, declaring that he would not engage in an activity that could tarnish his soul. Such was the love between Louis and Blanche.

Early in November, Blanche was preparing for Louis's arrival. She had been yearning to see him and was overjoyed that he was coming home. She dressed in her most appealing gown and delicately deco-

HOLDING HER HEAD HIGH

rated her hair and face in a romantic fashion. She excitedly gathered all of her children, and too impatient to wait, they rushed on horseback to meet him. After traveling a long way, they saw his caravan in the distance. Blanche's heart jumped in anticipation of seeing him again, touching his face, and falling into his embrace. Louis IX, twelve years old, was thrilled about reuniting with his father and rushed ahead to greet the entourage. He was halted and told to return to his mother. Blanche must have sensed that something was amiss. She climbed out of her carriage and ran to Louis's retinue. She threw herself upon them and raged with an indescribable, inconsolable grief. *How can he be gone? He can't possibly be gone. How can he be gone? No . . . no . . . no.*

'Mad with grief—most phrases seem inadequate to describe Blanche's despair, for the chroniclers affirm that she would indeed have killed herself on the spot if they had not stopped her. Hers was an impulsive, absolute nature. This loss, so unexpected, tore at her innermost being, her every fiber. Louis had been her all, her tender spouse, her children's father, her still young lord and king. His death was hers as well. The violence of her grief overwhelmed her entourage.[4]

The Widow, the Queen

Her husband was dead. Blanche was now alone in the world that had previously been a partnership. How could she continue? How could she ever *care* to continue? Riding the ripples to the depths of her soul through the dark, black hole of despair, Blanche once again reached an emotional crossroads. She had to choose. She had to choose life or death, defeat or rebirth. As a queen, as a mother, she had to proceed through the arduous, daunting pain and choose life. Kahlil Gabran says, "The self same well that is filled with our laughter is also filled with our tears."[5]

Blanche knew that for the sake of her children, for the sake of her country, she had to find the inner strength to face the awesome tasks that lay before her. It was her duty. So, summoning her strength, her

God, and somehow her spirit, she turned her entourage back toward home and a new life.

Once again destiny forsook desire. Blanche was powerless over everything except her response, through which her depth of character prevailed. At the age of thirty-eight she was the widowed mother of six children ages twelve, ten, seven, six, four, and one, and she was currently four months pregnant with her seventh living child, her twelfth pregnancy. She was also now a single mother and the sole ruler of France.

Thus Blanche's life as a single mother and the ruling queen had begun. There was no time to grieve because her duties besieged her. Blanche did "not allow the woman in her to overcome the queen."[6] She had to hold her head high. All of her attention was on protecting her son's crown. There was no time to spare. Brilliantly accomplished in the short span of three weeks, the majestic ceremony took place. Louis VIII had died on November 8, 1226, and the coronation of her son, Louis IX, as king took place on November 29. Louis may have been wearing the crown, but Blanche was the ruling queen. According to Regine Pernoud in *Blanche of Castile*, some historians who claimed that Blanche was simply the regent were incorrect, because, "Louis had specifically left the administration of the kingdom in Blanche's hands."[7]

How did Blanche rule the country of France with seven children? She was disciplined and devout. Weary as she must have continuously been, she awakened before anyone else in the castle and dedicated that time to God in morning prayer. She was a pious woman and related to the Cistercians, admiring their vehement principles and meekness of character. She would in subsequent years establish two convents for the Cloistered Cistercian nuns.

A book entitled *The Mirror of the Soul*, most likely written by a nun, was given to Blanche. It was dedicated to her with the following inscription: "Most noble and puissant Lady Blanche, Queen of France by the grace of God, I send you this book, called *The Mirror of the Soul*, which I have caused to be written for you."[8] The book represented the belief, one that Blanche must have constituted, that as you look into the mirror to appraise, value, and remedy your physical appearance, you should also hold the mirror up to your soul as a means to purity and remove sin. Blanche, as a faithful, self-sacrificing servant of God, most certainly reflected upon the inner voices of her soul, purging anything inconsistent with God's will. As queen and as a Christian, Blanche was generous and charitable. Always aware of the misfortunes of others, she gave bountiful gifts to the poor, the monks and cloistered nuns, the lepers, and the hospitals. There was a daily bread line in the palace courtyard.

Blanche, the Mother

Blanche kept a tight rein on her children. Piety was to supercede all other virtues. In this respect Louis IX provided an introspective look at Blanche's influence. One day during her morning prayers, the abiding monk asked Blanche to come to the window. As she glanced out upon the beggars, sick, and homeless in the daily bread line, she saw a young man handing out coins to the less fortunate. To Blanche's amazement and admiration, this young man was her son, the king, in disguise. When young Louis was questioned about his actions, he replied:

> Friar, those people are true soldiers of the realm. They fought for us against our enemies. They are the ones who keep France in safety and peace. If truth were told, we have not paid them all the wages they deserve.[9]

Louis "looked upon the poor and humble as the incarnation of Christ himself."[10] Of course, Blanche was proud of her son's compassion. He was exhibiting heavenly inspired traits.

Blanche also ran a tight ship regarding the education of her children. She was intent on preparing Louis for his future with the best studies and tutors. She insisted that his tutors be not only brilliant but pious as well. And Blanche didn't leave Louis's training to others. Elusive was not a word in her vocabulary. She was ever present and persistent. She insisted that prayers be part of their daily routine. They went to mass each day and attended the singing of vespers.

Blanche's actions were not insincere but were representative of the deeply ingrained beliefs she held. She believed that God was her protector, her companion, her priority; it was He who gave her the fortitude to continue, providing the light for her path. These sentiments and passions were reflected in the acts of her son. Louis IX would draw upon these principles throughout his life, and he would later be named a saint.

Children are watching, and they learn to cope as they have seen their parents cope. Life is a workshop and tools are a necessity. Blanche, as mother and father, provided these tools admirably, focusing on the influence and necessity of faith.

The Lioness

Blanche's devotion to her God and her children were not her only tasks. She was queen of France, not ceremoniously but literally. She didn't rely on others to make decisions or set her agendas. She made all the decisions herself. She had to maintain the character and complexion of the country for her son. Fortunately Blanche, unlike most women of her day, had not just been educated "appropriately for a girl"[11]; she had been educated with her husband. She had ruled beside him and had been privy to Louis's administrative decisions. This act, too, was unusual for women of that time. Thus, Blanche was no wallflower and was empowered by faith, intelligence, education, and will. A lioness. She would protect her family, her country, her people. That's why Louis left her in charge.

Blanche's days were also filled with her duties as administrator and ruler. She had to be wise, patient, and strong. Enemies were on the prowl, constantly watching her for signs of weakness. Opportunists were looking for chances to steal her throne, to attack the country. She had to incessantly assess deceptions, deciphering who in her realm was her enemy and who was her ally. Loyalty was like a dandelion, dissipating with a breath. Wars existed within the court and without, and upheavals were constant. She ruled astutely with the prudence of a woman. More than once she dismantled conspiracies without warfare. She directed situations with finesse, succeeding with brains instead of blood.

The lioness in Blanche was summoned again, this time in defense of her son, Louis IX. He found himself caught in an uprising in Orleans. He had locked himself inside a castle and had no means of escape. Trapped! Blanche took quick action. Knowing she was well loved in Paris, she rode feverishly through the streets on horseback, as she had done for her husband years earlier, and appealed to the people. They didn't disappoint her, willingly rushing en masse to rescue her son and their king. Louis was treated to a warm and tender homecoming. The people lined the streets shouting their affection for him.

Blanche would call on the people many times through the years. When her enemies schemed against her, she made alliances with the free towns, obtaining their pledges, their allegiance to her and her son. Blanche's actions set a precedent for future kings, who mirrored her tactics centuries later. Brave Blanche would leave her children behind when necessary, personally visiting the battlefields.

During one such visit it was inhumanely cold. She ascertained that they were immobilized, men and horses, by the cold and that they would soon be mercilessly attacked. So she ordered that trees be chopped down, whether walnut or apple, and brought to the army. Huge bonfires were made. The men and horses were able to warm themselves and were victorious. Blanche's common sense and tenacity saved the day.

Blanche was also a deft administrator who made many earnest and wise decisions. One such decision was when she took it upon herself to end the senseless war that had continued for an agonizing twenty years, the war that had claimed the life of her husband. This conflict, this plague, had permeated all the powers of Western Europe. Blanche's actions proved the most successful. She had witnessed that the violence of bloodshed had produced no tangible results. Thus, she instigated, sought, and provided peace through negotiation. Being wise, prudent, and resourceful, she was a queen worthy of respect and admiration. She, who ruled her land; educated, loved, and nurtured her children; and honored her God was a self-sacrificing, hard-working single mother who happened to be queen.

Over the years, Blanche was proud of her children, who were well mannered and pious. Ironically, it was Louis IX, the king, who was the most humble and pious. Once, when visiting a Cistercian monastery that Blanche had established and named Royaumont, Louis and his brothers were observing the monks. His brothers romped and played, but Louis insisted they respect the monks and do as they did. He said, "The monks now keep silence and so ought we." And, "The monks take no rest. Neither ought you."[12] These childhood sentiments were preludes to his lifelong, selfless devotion to his Lord.

BLANCHE, THE MOTHER-IN-LAW

Blanche loved all her children, yet her love for the king received the most attention. As Louis matured, Blanche realized she must find a noble wife for him. Surrendering her son to another woman must have broken Blanche's heart, but she yielded to duty, as she had always done. She chose Margaret of Provence for her son. A wedding had to be planned and the event entailed months of preparation. Finally, Margaret of Provence, age thirteen, arrived with fanfare and trumpets. After the wedding, it was back to business. The newlyweds were given no free reign. There was no time for fun and games because Blanche worked hard and expected the same of others. There was no time for personal pleasures or laziness when it came to the administration of a kingdom. Half measures availed her nothing! And perhaps passionate, strong-willed Blanche had a hard time letting go of her son. As Joinville wrote, "The Queen Blanche would not suffer more than she could help that her son bear his wife company, except it be at night when he did go to bed with her."[13]

BLANCHE, THE FORCE

Blanche of Castile was a powerful maternal force. She was a beacon of light for her children. Yet she also became a beloved queen. Pronouncements even from her foes deemed her a "magnificent queen." For eighteen years Blanche had ruled with frugality and dignity. She could balance a budget while battling barons. She could send in military reinforcements, even ride into battle herself, while diffusing uprisings from townspeople. She could educate her children as she adroitly handled the riotous university students. She could decipher threats, keeping plots of revolt in check, while planning weddings and making peace treaties. It had been noted that one could never tell where Blanche ended and Louis began, their works were so intertwined.

At the age of fifty-six Blanche hoped she could remove herself from the administrative demands and let Louis reign alone. Blanche was exhausted, yet there never seemed to be an appropriate or peaceful moment for such a transition. Threats continued to besiege France by foreigners like the Syrians and Genghis Kahn and the Golden Horde.

But her most despairing challenge was in regard to Louis's health. He was dreadfully sickened by dysentery and was bedridden with a raging fever. As the doctors practically pronounced him dead, Louis spoke the following profound words:

> Thus it comes that I, who was most rich and most noble in this world, exalted above all others by my treasure, my arms, and my alliances, cannot now force grim death or my illness to a truce, were it even for an hour. What then are all these worth?[14]

A sheet had been drawn over his head, and the court started to pay homage to the dead king. Blanche would have none of this! Instead, she sent for the relics of Christ's Passion (found by Helena Augusta!) and had them taken to Louis's bedside. Chroniclers say she prayed, "Lord God! Save the kingdom of France!" Suddenly, a sigh was heard from under the sheet as the king was regaining consciousness. He revived and Blanche was on her knees with gratitude to her Lord. She had the relics of Christ's Passion exposed in Saint-Denis on December 23, 1244. Passionate, pious, mother Blanche to the rescue again.

Blanche's joy was soon forgotten with the next wave of horrifying news. When Louis came to his senses, he announced that he wanted to take up the cross and fight for the Holy Land. The Moslems and Christians had been battling over the Holy Land for a century and a half. Louis's father, Louis VIII, had been forbidden by his father to take up the cross. He had allowed the pope to preach about it but had not endorsed it.

Blanche didn't believe her son's health was strong enough for this arduous undertaking. This decision would also mean that Blanche, in his absence, would once again be the sole ruler of France. The kingdom could become restless while he was in the Holy Land, not to mention the discontent that would arise when so many of the nation's funds were spent on the mission.

Blanche yearned for another way. She reminisced about how Francis of Assisi had handled the battle over the Holy Land. He had walked through the gateway of Islam and into the midst of flying arrows, crying, "I am Christian! Take me to your Master!" Stunned, the fighters did just that. The sultan and the monk visited for several days. As Francis departed, the sultan cried out, "Pray for me, that God may deign to discover to me that faith and law which please Him most!"[15] But this sort of pilgrimage was not to come to fruition for Louis IX, and he was determined to carry the cross into the Holy Land and reclaim it for the Christians approximately eight hundred years after Helena Augusta and Constantine.

Months of preparation preceded the military journey into the Holy Land—an undertaking that Blanche continued to believe was not in the best interest of Louis, her, or their country. Yet Blanche conceded to her son's wishes. This insured Louis's ability to follow his heart, for he couldn't even entertain the thought of going unless he knew his mother would so capably rule the country in his absence. The vulnerabilities were great when a king left the country for so long a time, on such a costly venture that all of the country didn't deem realistic. When the day came for Louis's departure, Blanche's heart was filled with trepidation and torn with sorrow. She couldn't let him go. Distraught, she insisted on accompanying him for three days. According to the Minstrel of Rheims, Louis finally said this to his mother:

> "Mother, most sweet, by that allegiance that you owe to me, I bid you return henceforth. I leave my three children for your wards, Louis, Philippe and Isabelle. I leave the realm of France, for you to govern, be." Then weeping the Queen did answer him: "Fairest son, how can my heart suffer that we be sundered? Truly, if it break atwain it be harder than stone for never has son to mother better than you to me" then swooning she fell, and the King did lift her again and kiss her, and weeping took his way. And the King's brothers and their ladies took their leave of her and wept. And she swoon anew and long lay senseless. When she recovered she said, "Sweet son and fair, I shall see you nevermore, my heart hath told me." And she spake true, for she was dead ere he returned.[16]

Oh my, Blanche watched her son go off on a venture, knowing within her heart that she would never see him again. The heartbreak she must have endured! To make matters worse, her other sons were going with Louis. Blanche was powerless to change the situation. How did she manage to cope? Once again, for the third time in her life, Blanche had to reach through overwhelming grief and persevere.

Thus, at the age of sixty, Blanche was left alone to rule France and to raise her grandchildren, just as she had done twenty-five years earlier when Louis VIII had died so suddenly. She was now a single grandmother and mother. As she had done before, she was to maintain the safety, dignity, and well-being of her country. She simultaneously had to supervise the development of the character of her grandson, a future king. She, who simply wanted to retire into an abbey, was beholden to her son's whims and wishes and to the duties that were demanded of her. These were situations she did not choose but that she chose to accept. She reached deep into her soul, relying on her love and trust in God. She must have felt His grace. She held her head high.

Blanche's daughter Isabella matured into a radiant young woman. She was described by her biographer, Sister Agnes of Harcourt, with the following words: "She was the mirror of innocence, a model of pertinence, a rose of patience, a lily of chastity, a fountain of mercy."[17] Isabella was special and adored by all. She could have married the holy Roman emperor's son, but she chose to be God's bride. Blanche proudly allowed Isabella to follow her heart. Since she had never been able to choose her own life, it must have given her great pleasure to allow her daughter to choose her destiny.

BLANCHE, THE JUST

As the queen of France, Blanche had always been respected, and even when Louis had taken over more of the duties, there was very little distinction between the two of them. People would always address Louis and Blanche together, both in paper and in person. Blanche was always concerned for the well-being of the less fortunate. It was noted that "she did take care that the common people be not trodden down by the rich, and gave evenhanded justice."[18]

Blanche's keen sense of humanity encompassed a wide spectrum. The Jews and Christians had continued to have communication with one another and debated the Scriptures. In AD 1200, however, the bishop of Paris forbad it. During the great debate of Talmud, Blanche intervened and protected all the Jews. Sadly, all dialogue between them had ceased by the fourteenth century.

Blanche also consistently reached out to the poor, the sick, the prisoners, and the frequently emancipated serfs. She was outraged when she heard about peasant men, women, and children being jailed and bodily thrown on top of each other. They were smothering in insufferable heat. She tried to mediate the situation but to no avail. So she took the matter into her own hands and, always protective of the underdog, she gathered her men, mounted her horse, and accompanied them to investigate.

Upon arrival, a furious Blanche grabbed a cudgel—a short, thick stick used as a weapon—and beat on the cellar door, freeing the peasants. They must have been shocked when they saw their queen standing with a cudgel in her hand. Once they were freed, Blanche took the unfortunate souls under her wing until they were able to manage for themselves. She had been powerless over her destiny, but she sought to help others who were powerless over their destinies as well.

News from the Front

News from the crusade was not good. Louis's army had been massacred. One of Blanche's sons was killed and her other children were prisoners of the sultan. Louis became once again sickened with dysentery and was so weak that he had to be bodily carried. Blanche loved her son immeasurably, and yet she would have rather he died than be guilty of sin. She was reported to have stated,

> Most humbly did the Queen disclaim such falseness and did add this, saying, for which she may be well praised, that were her son the King, whom she loved above all mortal creatures, sick to death, and she be told that he could be made well by lying with a woman other than his wedded wife, she would rather he die than he offend his Creator even once through mortal sin.[19]

He recovered, and on May 8, 1250, Louis and his brothers were freed. Blanche was desperate for him to come home, but he stayed behind to free the Christians in the Egyptian jails. These actions were heroic, and yet it was Blanche's diligence that made it physically possible. It was Blanche who sent the money and arranged for the barons to be paid overseas. It was Blanche who dealt with the tedious and grueling daily requirements of ruling the country. During his crusade, Louis was admirably benevolent. As disaster upon disaster manifested for him, he would quote St. Paul: "Who shall separate us from the love of Christ? Shall tribulation, or distress, or persecution, or famine, or nakedness, or peril, or sword?" (Romans 8:35). Everyone admired Louis's piety and bravery, even his enemies.

At the age of sixty-four Blanche was exhausted. She was void of strength physically, mentally, and emotionally. She reportedly collapsed into a bale of hay. She was immediately taken to her bed. Her last wish was that she be able to do upon her death what she yearned to do while she was living. She asked to wear the habit of the Cistercian nuns. Even if for a day, Blanche wanted to choose for herself, and she chose to honor her God. She knew that when she took the habit she would no longer be the ruler but under the submission of the mother superior of the convent of Maubuisson. These actions represented the yearning that must have lain passionately dormant within her heart. However, Blanche had always foregone her personal desires for duty. She had performed brilliantly with kindness, faithfulness, dignity, intelligence, and honor. Blanche had truly been a magnificent queen, a generous mother, a single mother. Now she wanted to be simply a child of God. She asked to lie on a straw pallet as she started to pray the liturgy known as the recommendation of the soul:

Help me, ye saints of God; fly hither, ye angels of the Lord;
Receive my soul and bear it before the All high . . .

She died at three o'clock in the afternoon on November 26 or 27, 1252. She was dressed in her royal gown, but they put on her head the Cistercian nun's veil, and then they placed the crown on top of the veil. Her remaining sons, who had returned from Jerusalem, carried Blanche from Melun to Paris. She was buried at Saint Denis. Her son King Louis IX was not there. Her heart had sincerely spoken: she was to never see her beloved son again.

The common people protected and paid homage to their queen, who lay in state, highlighted by the shimmering of innumerable candles. Mathew Paris observed, "She left France inconsolable."[20]

Word was sent to her son. As king, Louis emulated his mother's charitable nature and Christian virtues. Regine Pernoud stated the following:

Blanche's son earned his renown as a justice-giving king, a true friend of the poor and lowly, for his friendship was seen not only to consist in alms-giving, but in royal decrees, in practical measures designed to let the poor be heard, to listen to those to whom the high and mighty would not listen. It was a milestone in the history of government administration.[21]

As a single mother, Blanche must have done something right. Louis IX was a loving, kind, and just king who, when faced with adversity, would pray unceasingly. He was immortalized as a saint.

Blanche of Castile. She was a queen, yet she was a woman. She was a woman like any other woman. She lived over eight hundred years ago, yet her challenges mirror our challenges today. Blanche had no choice over many major aspects in her life. She didn't choose to be a queen. She didn't choose to leave her parents. She didn't choose the man she married. She didn't choose to rule France. She didn't choose to be a single mother. She didn't choose her son's crusade. She didn't choose to rule alone in her old age.

Blanche was powerless over the life cards she was dealt, but she was not powerless over the way she played them. This is the essence of Blanche's greatness. She took lemons and made lemonade, pulling herself up by her own bootstraps with faith, prayer, and inner fortitude. She made the best of every situation she encountered. She faced her demons with God's grace and defeat with defiance.

Her foundation was built upon God's guidance, and she sought His strength through prayer and meditation. With every lack of choice, Blanche held her head high. She was a respected, adored queen; a loving, loyal wife; a devoted, nurturing single mother; an intelligent, cunning administrator; a faithful servant of God. She was a steward to the less fortunate, those who also could not choose their own fates. She considered others' woes. She was strong and brave and protected the defenseless. Blanche was a lioness. Her attributes didn't simply manifest inside her. She struggled, she wept, she despaired. Her character was formed by one challenge after another. One by one, she found within herself the resolution to overcome adversity.

Life Lesson: Choose God's Greatness

The message of Blanche of Castile speaks boldly to us today. When we're dealt life cards we don't like, we have a choice: Do we choose defeat or do we choose God's greatness? Do we succumb to despair and depression, or do we take the bull by the horns and make the best out of the situation? God is great and fills our spirits and our consciousnesses with His greatness. However, He must be able to trust us. We must be willing to use our God-given gifts of greatness for His will. We have to be willing to serve others, make selfless decisions, and exhibit responsibility to our fellow men. Blanche defined God's essence of choosing greatness. She chose greatness as His will.

We will always be faced with situations that are out of our control, but our responses are within our control. We can make gratitude our attitude. We can discern where the lesson of the problem lies, seek to learn from it, amend it, and hold our heads high. All ability, wisdom, and strength lie within the problem. All it takes is willingness to see the solution. All it takes is the courage to choose God's greatness.

At her grief, the common people sorrowed much,
for she had ever a care that they be not fleeced by the rich,
and did well defend that right.

—Chroniclers of France

CHRISTINE DE PIZAN

Resilient Single Mother

AD 1365–1429

SNAPSHOT	Recognizing, as she stood in court, that the men's rudeness and ridicule was an effort to get her to relinquish
MOTHER MOMENT	Advising her son not to believe the contemptible, erroneous perspectives written about women
CHALLENGE	Disrespect and poverty after becoming a widow
STEWARDSHIP	Lifting her children and women to higher ground
SCRIPTURE	These are they who have come out of the great tribulation; they have washed their robes and made them white in the blood of the Lamb. Therefore ... he will lead them to springs of living water. And God will wipe away every tear from their eyes. (Revelation 7:14,17 NIV)

CHAPTER FIVE

Turn Tribulations into Triumphs

*If you would reflect well and wisely, you would realize that those
events you regard as personal misfortunes have served a useful purpose
even in this worldly life, and indeed have worked for your betterment.*[1]

—CHRISTINE DE PIZAN

The French Court. Exciting and insidious. Intricate and passionate.
Intrigue and scandal. Power and greed resembling J.R. and the Ewings
or *90210*. The same confused, beautiful people. Except they were
laden with clothes, smelled of garlic, and attended church because
it was the "in" thing to do. Christine de Pizan lived approximately
two hundred years after Blanche of Castille. She lived in the palace
court and read her books in the Louvre in Paris.

Although Christine lived more than six hundred years ago, she
feels incredibly modern to me. I feel as if I am able to reach out and
touch her. I relate to her struggles, emotions, and determination to
overcome adversity. When I was researching Christine, I was amazed
that we would be wrestling with the same exact issue. I felt as if she
were a sister or a best friend, sitting in my room, advising me how to
cope with certain situations. Christine was funny, intelligent, outspoken, resilient, dramatic, and a five-star general for her cause. She is the
poster child for single mothers.

CHRISTINE'S MISSION

Christine was utterly disgusted and shocked by the way she was treated as a woman. Thus, her life's mission was to educate and rescue women from similar fates, and she didn't just want to educate the women but also the men. One fabulous aspect of Christine de Pizan is that she was a writer. From her very own words, which are fluid and amazingly contemporary, we are enlightened about her life, and we reap the rewards of her knowledge. Against the background of the Middle Ages a modern woman, a medieval feminist, emerges.

Christine de Pizan was a woman before her time. She was a revolutionary with a survivor's spirit. As challenges were thrown her way, or as she would say, "When Fortune's wheel dipped to drag me to the ground,"[2] Christine held on and rose to the occasion. Her challenges, and her breadth of spirit in dealing with them, would prove to benefit not only her children but the many women of her day and subsequent centuries. Christine was an outspoken visionary for women in a time when women were not allowed to dream. She was the Susan B. Anthony of medieval times.

When Christine's king, her father, and her husband died, she became a twenty-five-year-old widow with three children, her mother, and a niece for whom to care. Her fortune fell from a darling, pampered young damsel of the court to a forgotten, fragile foe left to scrape and crawl for survival. She refused to remarry and thus tackled all of her problems on her own as a single mother in a man's world and court. Destitute and disillusioned, it took her ten years to crawl out from under her burdens. But resurface she did with vigor and valiance. She did it with her wit, her determination, her sense of purpose, and her pen. She became the first female professional writer of the Middle Ages.

Timeless Scenario: Girl from middle-class family enjoys life among higher class. Girl marries boy father chooses. Girl and boy are in love. Girl and boy have three children. Boy dies. Girl is single mother and sole provider. Girl is spurned by society. Girl loses friends and money. Girl has never worked. Girl is desperate and destitute. Girl finds her voice and self-respect. Girl finds a vocation and succeeds. Girl becomes a beacon for her children and all women.

HOLDING HER HEAD HIGH

Family Life

Christine was born in Venice, Italy, in AD 1365, but she moved to France with her family when she was a teenager. She was not royalty; she was not a queen. Yet her father worked for the king and, thus, Christine lived at the court. They were comparable to a modern-day, middle-class family. Her mother was a Venetian, and her father, Thomas de Pizzano, was a court physician and astrologer from Bologna. Her father and grandfather were counselors of the Venetian Republic.

An educated family, Christine's father and grandfather both graduated from the University of Bologna. Thomas had an esteemed reputation coupled with the fact that he had a gracious heart. His expertise was highly sought, and during his career he received employment invitations from King Louis I of Hungary and King Charles V of France. He chose to work for Charles V of France because he was a king who had a reputation as a humanist. Thomas de Pizzano traveled to the king's court, and Charles V was so enthralled with him that he wouldn't even let him leave to retrieve his family. His family eventually did journey to France, and Christine arrived at the splendid court and was royally received by the charming King Charles V at the Louvre.

Contrary to the times and to Christine's mother's opinion, Christine's dad encouraged his daughter to be educated. She lamented later that she took these studies for granted. At the age of fifteen Christine was married to a man whom her father had chosen, Etienne de Castel, a young nobleman from Picardy and a graduate with the title Master of Law. So he was called Master Etienne de Castel. Thomas knew that when Christine married Etienne, she would continue to be surrounded by educated men. Etienne's confidants were intellectuals who became France's first humanists. They cultivated Latin prose and read Patrarch and Boccaccio and Salutati. Happily for Christine, she actually loved Etienne. He was a talented courier, and he was the king's secretary and notary. They were blissfully married and had three children. According to Christine, these were the happiest times of her life.

On September 16, 1380, their beloved King Charles V died at the age of forty-four. Things changed drastically for Christine and her family. Her father lost his income, his pensions from the kings were suddenly withdrawn, and his salary was cut.

Christine commented, "Now the door to our misfortunes was open, and I, being still quite young, entered in."

Her father, after losing everything, became ill and died a few years later, at the very hour he had predicted (he was an astrologer), sometime around 1385. He was genuinely missed and mourned by many. Christine immortalized her father's character with her words, ". . . among which there was nothing blameworthy save, perhaps, his excessive generosity to the poor to the detriment of wife and family."[3] It was revealed after his death that his savings were nonexistent. Christine would later write, "I consider not at all praiseworthy for married men whose duty it is to provide for their families, who could fall into poverty after their death as a result of their prodigality."[4] Thus, she would in time advise, "I deem prudent saving a wise practice in youth, as it provides comfort in old age."[5]

Becoming a Single Mother

Etienne was now the master of the house, and his job led him on travels with King Charles VI in the autumn of 1390. While he was away from his wife, children, and home, he got sick and died at the age of thirty-four. Christine was devastated emotionally. She wrote,

> And I, at twenty-five, was left with the responsibilities of three small children and a large household, I had good reason to be filled with bitterness and longed for his sweet company and my vanished happiness, which had lasted but ten years. Seeing a vast wave of tribulations about to rush upon me, I desired death rather than face living. And remembering my troth and the love I had pledged him, I wisely resolved never to have another. I had fallen into the valley of tribulation.[6]

Christine was in the depths of despair, even contemplating suicide. (She would later comment, however, that had her husband not died, she would never have discovered her studious life that gave her such pleasure.) She contemplated entering a convent to isolate herself and escape her troubles, but she came to the resolution that it would not benefit her children. As she looked into her children's faces with pity, she decided to trust in Christ's mercy and innately in herself. She decided to hold her head high. She, too, like Helena and Blanche, did not succumb to the darkness. She persevered and etched her way into the history books. She became a revolutionary icon, a beacon of hope for women. Instigated by her tribulations, she became their voice, their guide, and their protector. She chose to fight and not relent to the seemingly hopeless times; to wait for the miracle—a miracle which proved to be a talent God would help her find within herself.

She wrote of this time later with the ballade XI, part of which appears here:

Alone Am I

Alone Am I and alone would I be
Alone by my lover left suddenly,
Alone am I, no friend or master with me,
Alone am I, both sad and angrily,
Alone am I, in languor wretchedly,
Alone am I, completely lost doubtlessly,
Alone am I, friendless and so lonely . . .

Alone am I, on any street or hearth,
Alone am I, whether moving or at rest,
Alone am I, more than any thing on earth,
Alone am I, by all others cast aside,
Alone am I, so cast down to abide,
Alone am I, who such hot tears have cried,
Alone am I, friendless and so lonely . . .[7]

Christine had now lost her kind king, her revered father, and her beloved husband. She was left completely unprepared for all the shocking and tumultuous tasks that lay before her. "Troubles surged upon me from all sides, as is the common lot of widows. I became entangled in legal disputes of every sort."[8]

Her husband left her no trade upon which to lean. He had not been a tradesman, and he was not a farmer; thus, she could not provide for herself by, say, cultivating the land. She was beset by troubles financially and was shocked by the lack of chivalry and the betrayal from her friends. She was dismayed at her lack of knowledge regarding her husband's affairs, making it almost impossible to assess and cope with the situation. She wrote,

> For it is customary for married men not to discuss financial matters in detail with their wives, a practice that often leads to great problems, as I have learned from experience, and does not make any sense at all when a woman is not stupid but prudent and wise in her dealings.[9]

She was prohibited from inheriting the property that was her husband's. She would have to appear time and time again in court to challenge unjust acts, only to find herself belittled and ridiculed by men. She invested her children's money with a man she thought she could trust, who was "tempted by the evil one." He said he had been robbed and disappeared without a word. She had to contend with a long illness and was besieged with shivering and unable to get out of bed. She watched as bailiffs came to carry away her precious belongings, stating, "I recognize that worldly goods are like the wind."[10] She also lamented, "What anguish when I look at my young children and poor relatives, and compared past days to my present misfortunes that cast me down and seemed beyond my power to redress. In those days I pitied my family more than myself."[11]

Lack of funds prevented Christine from pursuing all of her cases of injustice in court because she was unable to pay for the court fees. Yet she was able to defend some of her rights because she had cases in four different courts running concurrently in Paris. She writes of her experiences in court, which seem amazingly modern. She explains that she would debate in court, then wait for hours, and be the victim of annoying remarks, sly glances, and belittling jokes "from men bloated with wine and the flesh of ease."[12] Yet Christine was savvy and wise and observed the nuances of the game at play "when I realized that the ridicule to which I was being subjected was an attempt to force me to relinquish."[13]

Christine's Resilience

Christine, though at times shaken and depressed, exhibited stamina, besides the fact that "what happened to me was against all reason."[14] Christine's situations were steeped in history, taking place six hundred years ago, and yet I marvel at how relevant and everlasting her situations are. I, quite frankly, have found restitution in her words and wisdom.

In one such situation Christine found herself the victim of gossip. She exclaimed,

> Thus, I marveled at how such tales could arise, spreading from mouth to mouth that would repeat, "I heard it was so." And I, knowing my innocence, was sometimes distressed when the story reached me, and other times would smile and say, "God and he and I know that these rumors are without foundation!"[15]

I have told my own daughter this particular truth on many occasions: "God, you, and I know the truth, and that's all that matters." I was having a particularly hard day recently, and as I read this particular quote of Christine's, I marveled at the fact that her perspective on such events mirrored mine. Ironically, at that moment, I had needed to be reminded of this everlasting sentiment, and her words refreshed my soul. In regard to gossip, she also wrote the following words in her book *The Tale of the Rose* that deals with slander:

> *For in this mortal life there's not*
> *A man who might be loved by all,*
> *Nor one whom all consider good.*

That's Envy's doing, who attempts
To harm high fame; a worthy man
Should pay no heed, but just do good
For honor will win out, I say . . .

For slander, when one ponders it,
Is like a lance or javelin
That kills the man who launches it
As well as him at whom it's aimed . . .

But we may feel assured
That there exist a judge so sure
He knows the inside and the out,
He knows it all and sees it all,
He'll render up what each deserves
Of good or ill, that's sure to be . . .[16]

Christine was determined and defiant. After her unsettling times she would write, "Deprivation makes one more sensitive to the plight of others . . . to the needs of others than does abundance, and that humankind is misguided to expect true felicity except in eternity." She also learned the virtue of patience, writing, "Our Lord Jesus Christ suffered to be tormented in every part of His body in order to teach us patience."[17] During her trying experiences, Christine took an action, one that I teach my daughter, and exercised a coping skill. She picked up the pen and started to write her first ballad through her tears.

Where can they flee? In France
They find only
Empty hopes
Deadly counsel
Treacherous words
Prodding them to damnation
No one espouses their concerns,

Seeming help turns to harm
And princes are deaf to their pleas.[18]

CHRISTINE, THE WRITER

Christine's tribulations lasted for approximately ten years. Repeatedly, though at times overcome with trepidation, Christine attacked each situation with stoicism and defiance. She held her head high and walked firmly in her faith in God. As a single mother she exhibited a sense of retribution and survival. As she emerged from the drama of simply trying to overcome adversity, she decided that perhaps she had a gift for writing. She had no one to support her family and no other means of employment; so she started to support her family with her pen.

Her first form of employment as a writer was as a copyist and a corrector in a manuscript workshop. Christine found within herself the flame of righteousness and was determined not to let others have the satisfaction of extinguishing it. Through all her turmoil Christine turned within herself, listening to God's voice within her, and found her talent. She came to the realization that "if you would reflect well and wisely, you would realize that those events you regard as personal misfortunes have served a useful purpose even in this worldly life, and indeed have worked for your betterment."[19] She put her flow of emotions into her pen and found both her purpose and an opportunity as a single mother to provide for her family. She commented, "It would appear that when you see yourself as so unfortunate, you forget the gifts with which you have been blessed."[20] In her writings she found great pleasure and an outlet for her woes. "Fortune could not assail me to the point of depriving me of the company of the poet's muses."[21]

Christine had always been surrounded by men who not only relished education and challenged themselves with continuous education, but encouraged Christine to follow suit. This was an immense gift for a woman of her time, and now she was prepared to launch into the realm of self-education. Christine reflected, "Does not Aristotle say that the wise man leads the ignorant, as the soul governs the body?"[22] However, even though her familial men had the sense of enlightenment to acknowledge and thus not discriminate against a woman's natural capacity for learning, this was not the case for the majority of men in medieval times. She retorted, "One day, a man criticized my desire for knowledge, saying that it was inappropriate for a woman to be learned, as it was rare, to which I replied that it was even less fitting for a man to be ignorant, as it was common."[23] So Christine read voraciously in French, Italian, and Latin as she studied the histories of the Hebrews, Assyrians, and famous rulers of antiquity such as the Romans, French, and Bretons. She also gained insights from her study of science and poetry. She believed that learning had enduring qualities and that, as a writer, she could express her opinions in a permanent, everlasting fashion.

Fortified with self-education, she began to write. As she said, "Then in order to pass the time and also to cheer myself somewhat, I began writing love poems expressing others' feelings."[24] She was an early *femme de letters* in France and the first female professional writer. She was not only a talented poet and a social commentator, she was also an enterprising woman. In order to instigate interest in her works, she sent her writings to nobles. I believe the conduit for success is talent with a sense of self-promotion; one cannot preclude the other, in my experience. She recounts that the gifts were accepted joyfully, though she credits this response to the fact that they had been "written by woman, a phenomenon not seen in quite some time."[25] She dedicated copies of her works to the prestigious men and women of the day, and they rewarded her generously. Thus, due to her talent and entrepreneurial ways, she found an instrument through which to provide for her family: her wit, her knowledge, her life experiences, her political opinions, her pen.

THE REALIST

Christine's writings were not of a romantic nature but of a realistic nature. She was called the poet of love's *ending* instead of love's *beginning.* Her writings were unique in that they represented a realistic point of view of the Middle Ages and that of a woman. They were also revolutionary because she understood the value of externalizing the inner drama, and she took the bold step of writing about her life, which was a rarity during her time and which also provided invaluable insights into medieval times.

In her times of despair, Christine realized that she indeed had many virtues in her life. First and foremost were her children. She reflected,

> Do you not have children who are good looking and endowed with good sense? Your firstborn is a daughter who entered the noble order of the Poissy to dedicate her life to the service of God, contrary to your own wishes but in response to God's call to her? In the flower of her youthful beauty, she loves the life of contemplation and devotion so well that you often derive great comfort from speaking about her and from those sweet letters she writes in her young innocence, full of good sense and wisdom, consoling you and exhorting you to despise this world and worldly success.[26]

Her daughter had entered the Dominican convent of St. Louis in Poissy. (This Dominican convent may have been dedicated to Blanche of Castile's son, Louis IX, St. Louis.) The current king's aunt was an abbess there and his sister a nun. Christine wrote delicate, delightful words about her daughter and a refreshing visit to her abbey entitled "The Tale of Poissy."

> *That I had desire*
> *To go out to play, so I wished to see*
> *A daughter that I have, to speak truly,*
> *Beautiful and refined, young and well-schooled.*
> *And gracious*
> *As everyone says; she is religious*
> *At an abbey rich and precious,*

Noble, royal, and most delicious. . . .
Then she whom I love greatly and hold dear
Came towards me, and very humbly
Knelt, and I kissed her face
Sweet and tender,
And then hand in hand, without delay, we went
Into the church to pay reverence to God;
We heard mass, and wanted to take
Our leave thereafter,
But the ladies pressed us strongly
To take refreshment and led us
To a cool, bright, and lovely spot nearby . . .[27]

What is striking within this poem is the happiness that it exudes. This visit with her daughter reflected the great love she must have felt for her as her own words describe, "I kissed her face, sweet and tender."

Christine instructed women how to teach their daughters by writing,

Instruct them in wisdom when they are young making sure that the mother herself sets a good example of integrity and learnedness, for if the mother loves foolishly, she will hardly be an example for their daughter. The daughter should also be protected from bad company and raised in accordance with strict rules which she respects, for the discipline exercised over children and young people prepares them to live upright lives for their whole lifetime.[28]

Christine admonished men who complained that they had daughters instead of sons, writing,

And let us suppose that all sons were good, nevertheless, one usually sees the daughters keep their fathers and mothers company more often than the sons, and the daughters visit them more, comfort them more, and take care of them in sickness and old age more frequently.[29]

Of her son, she wrote,

Do you not also have a son who is fair and well mannered? Despite his years numbering no more than twenty, from the time he began his studies, scarcely could anyone be found surpassing him in natural aptitude for grammar, rhetoric, and poetic language, nor anyone of subtler understanding. And truth of what I say is obvious and can easily be verified.[30]

One of her earliest writings was "The Moral Teachings and Proverbs a.k.a. Christine's Teachings for her Son, Jean Du Castel." She wrote the ballad for her son Jean.

> Son, I have no great treasure
> To make you rich, but a measure
> Of good advice which you may need
> I give it hoping you'll take heed . . .
>
> Never serve an evil master,
> For you would only court disaster
> By wickedness to gain his aid,
> So avoid such service like the plague.
>
> Would you long life and victory lure?
> Teach your heart it must endure;
> It's by endurance that one gains
> Rewards and comfort for one's pains.
>
> If Fortune gives you as rewards
> That over others you are lord
> Among your subjects then be not
> Dangerous nor too proud thought.

Always be truthful in your word;
Speak little, to the point be heard,
For too much talk in any guise
Makes others think one far from wise.

Another's wealth do not envy,
The envious in this life may see
The flames of Hell and feel its pains,
A burden heavier than chains.

Never believe all the false blame
Of women that some books proclaim,
For women can be good and sweet;
May it be fortune such to meet.[31]

Christine's words eloquently describe how she held her head high. There is no doubt that through her painful years Christine defined a moral and astute sense of purpose. She advised her son about the value of education, to avoid ill influences and a false sense of security, to be honest and not to envy money. She had obviously learned that money was fleeting and misleading. And of course, Christine commented in her ballad to her son about the virtues of women and encouraged him not to believe all that is written in books about them.

Christine's eventual fame and reputation as a writer led to a golden opportunity for her son. The Earl of Salisbury was so taken with Christine's works that he offered to take her son Jean back to England to work as a page in his household and be a companion for his son of the same age. After much reluctance, devastated at the thought of being separated from her son, she finally relented. Two years later the Earl of Salisbury was executed because of plotting to kill King Henry IV in revenge for the death of Richard II. Henry IV, respectful of Christine's talents, invited her to live in England. He offered her generous amounts of money. She had no desire to do this, so she slyly dodged answering his requests forthrightly until her son was safely returned home to her. She writes,

As the prospect did not tempt me in the least, I feigned acqui-
escence in order to obtain my son's return. To get straight to
the point, after laborious maneuvers on my part and the expedition of some of my works, my son received permission to
come home so he could accompany me on a journey I have yet
to make. Thus, I rejected an opportunity for both of us,
because I cannot believe that the faithless person can come to
any good.[32]

Christine established a code of values for her son, because words
are powerful but actions are essential. He witnessed his mother
decline a handsome amount of money, money that they needed,
because she did not approve of the king's values. Christine's actions
were worthy and she commented, "How happy I was to be reunited
after those three years with my beloved child."[33] Jean eventually
entered into the service of the Duke of Burgandy. (Her other son
evidently died, because he disappeared from the history books.)

FIGHTER FOR JUSTICE

Christine was a defiant fighter for justice for women. She was
motivated by her motherly desire to protect women from the enormity of slander that they were enduring. Her concern spanned all
social classes. She argued that women were so sheltered by their
fathers and husbands that they were left destitute and unable to
cope in the world should something unforeseen happen. Her mission became to aid these women and arm them with knowledge. In
The Treasure of the City of Ladies Christine sought to help widows
through her experiences:

Dear Friends, we pity each one of you in the state of widowhood
because death has deprived you of your husbands, whoever they
may have been. Moreover, much anguish and many trying problems afflicting you, affecting the rich in one manner and those
not rich in another. The rich are troubled because unscrupulous
people commonly try to despoil them in their inheritance. The

poor, or at least those not at all rich, are distressed because they find no pity from anyone for their problems. Along with the grief of having lost your mate, which is quite enough, you also must suffer three trials in particular which assault you whether you are rich or poor.

First is that, undoubtedly, you will find harshness and lack of consideration or sympathy everywhere. Those who honored you during the lifetime of your husbands . . . now will pay little attention to you and barely even bother to be friendly. The second distress facing you is the variety of lawsuits and demands of certain people regarding debts, claims on your property, and income. Third is the evil talk of people who are all too willing to attack you, so that you hardly know what you can do that will not be criticized.[34]

The following words were Christine's possible remedies for the three problems:

Turn toward God, who was willing to suffer so much for human creatures. Reflecting on this will teach you patience, a quality you will need greatly. It will bring you to the point where you will place little value on the rewards and honors of this world. First of all, you will learn how undependable all earthly things are. The second remedy is to turn your heart to gentleness and kindliness in word and courtesy to everyone. You will overcome the hard-hearted and bend them to your will by gentle prayers and humble requests. Third, in spite of what we just said about quiet humility in words, apparel, and in countenance, nevertheless you must learn the judgment and behavior necessary to protect yourself against those only too willing to get the better of you. You must avoid their company, having nothing to do with them if you can help it.[35]

Christine could speak from the heart because she had been a victim of all these experiences. These were Christine's wounds, and she yearned to spread hope to other widows and single mothers—to help them hold their heads high—in the face of trouble.

The Enlightener

Christine also wanted to enlighten men to women's virtues and potentially alter their attitudes toward them. She wanted women to play bigger roles in the outcomes of their own lives. She called for them to not wither away from adversity but to "take on the heart of a man,"[36] a medieval precursor to our modern-day saying, "Don't be a victim." This concept was unheard of during her time, and for centuries to come. She was a feminist who loved men. She proclaimed that all of the slanderous remarks written by men about women were not rational. In her writings, she argued that innately within all men and women is a great capacity to love one another. She was baffled as to why women are considered incapable of facing the same challenges as men.

To demonstrate that women were worthy of respect, Christine listed many women throughout history who ruled in their husbands' absences. The women of note were Nicola, the empress of Ethiopia; Queen Fredegonde of France, who governed after her husband's, King Chiperic's, death; Charles IV's queen, Jeanne; King Louis VIII's queen, Blanche of Castile; the Duchess of Anjou; Louise of Savoy; and Margaret of Austria. All of these women served as regents and/or administrators after their husbands' deaths, either for themselves or as regents for their sons. And they were all single mothers! Christine wrote, "My Lady, I can truly and clearly see that God—may He be praised—has granted that the mind of an intelligent woman can conceive, know, and retain all perceptible things."[37]

Christine was curious as to why women were not allowed to study as men do. She rallied that women need only equal opportunities to show their equal capabilities. And in true Christine fashion, she questioned the irrational paradox about why men would want to limit women's knowledge when an educated woman makes a better companion. Her controversial and groundbreaking ideas spread throughout Europe and were admired by many kings. The

Duke of Milan tried to persuade Christine to return to her homeland and his court, but she remained faithful to France.

One of Christine's passions was to rebuke the overwhelming sense of disdain and disrespect for women. She entered into one of the most famous *Querelles* or quarrels, of the Middle Ages. It was the scholastic debate over the book *Romance of the Rose*.

The book was begun in 1230 by Guillaume de Lorris and was continued until around 1275–80 by Jean de Meung, who was the misogynist (woman hater) of the two authors. It was about the seduction of a lady. The lady was represented as a prize rose in a garden. Christine, one of the few women who read the book, rebuked the book and its immorality in her poem "Letter to the God of Love" in 1399. She was the only woman who had the courage to argue against such an immensely popular work. Two men joined her in her rebuttal. She was distraught that men would write so vehemently about women. She was alarmed that men were infamously defining the character of women, women who had no resources with which to defend themselves. Why were men representing the soul and character of women? They were not women. How did they know? Why would men write so harshly about the women to whom they owed their very existence? She questioned whether they had ever cared for their mothers, sisters, wives, or daughters. Why were all women being stereotyped in such a vulgar way?

COURAGE OF CONVICTIONS

Christine was a woman on a mission. She was considered a radical in a world that accepted the demoralizing of women. Against strong opposition Christine exhibited the courage of her convictions. She engaged in a three-year literary debate. She eventually gave her account of the three-year, controversial debate to the queen of France to read. Giving her accounts to the queen once again represented Christine's tenacity, spunk, and her unwillingness to let the undefended be unprotected. The men of the *Querrelle* were quite taken aback that Christine would present her case to the queen. It shed an embarrassing light on their prejudices. Christine lobbied that *Romance of the Rose* not be used as a teaching aid, and obviously she forbad her son to read it. Christine was not going to let such absurd prejudices against women be unopposed. In 1404 she wrote her rebuttal in her book *The Book of the City of Ladies*:

> I tell you that, in spite of what you may have found in the writings of pagan authors on the subject of criticizing women, you will find little said against them in the holy legends of Jesus Christ and His Apostles; instead, even in the histories of all the saints, just as you can see yourself, you will find through God's grace many cases of extraordinary firmness and strength in women. Oh, the beautiful service, the outstanding charity which they have performed with great care and solicitude, unflinchingly for the servants of God! Should not such hospitality and service be considered?[38]

In the book she expressed and defined all the examples of strengths and redeeming qualities that the misogynist writers had insinuated all women lacked. She defeated every argument of women's inferiority with wit, wisdom, and advice. She beseeched all women to disregard men's interpretations of women and rely on their own self-knowledge. A scandalous thought! Why should women's moral fiber and reputation be defined by men? Do men know women's hearts or struggles? Christine had the courage and the audacity to challenge men on their dastardly assertions. Men could not ascertain women's character honestly or truthfully. She was the lone voice for women in a crowded world of chauvinism.

MEDIEVAL "DEAR ABBY"

In 1405 Christine wrote *The Treasure of the City of Ladies*. She finished the book when she was forty years old. This book encompassed an array of advice on the subjects of etiquette and survival. In her true democratic style, she wrote to all levels of society, from royalty to peasants, widows, spinsters, prostitutes, and nuns. Her advice to women had a psychoanalytical aspect to it, embodying many characteristics of a medieval times "Dear Abby." She contemplated issues of the day with a wide perspective. She addressed in her writings an admonishment of vices, such as envy, extravagance, and hypocrisy, and she applauded women who exhibit constancy, wisdom, and the willingness to defend themselves. She had zero tolerance for idleness. One of her recurring themes was that women should align with one another. They should unite, refrain from gossip about one another, be tolerant, and embody sisterly love.

Like a mother hen, Christine warned that adultery was a losing proposition for all concerned and that ladies should refrain from extramarital affairs, acknowledging that the law did not protect women from the reprisals of jealous husbands. With her keen eye and wisdom, she preached the evils of men who would promise anything for love: secrecy, discretion, affirming that courtly love was a disaster waiting to happen. She prophesized that they will brag the moment their conquests were brought to fruition and leave the woman and her reputation to suffer the consequences. Once again, it is important to weigh Christine's words against the medieval times. Sexual affairs were exceptionally risky for women during these times because women were likely to get pregnant, then be abandoned and left to suffer the consequences. Then she would be alone to provide for the baby with a tarnished reputation for life. The child would suffer as well, as it would be abandoned, raised in destitute conditions, or suffer the consequences of infanticide.

Deeply dedicated to preventing women from being victimized by society, she shared her woes of widowhood, hoping to enlighten women to the events they were likely to incur and prepare them for the misfortunes they would experience. She gave accounts of her life, earnestly sharing her experiences. She warned that one should get a lawyer, an old one, who knows all the tricks! However, she should weigh the situation carefully so that the costs of litigation do not surpass what success could bring. In regard to marriage, Christine states,

If in married life everything were all repose and peace, truly it would be sensible for a woman to enter it again, but because one sees quite to the contrary, any woman ought to be very wary of remarriage, although for young women it may be a necessity or anyway very convenient. But for those who have already passed their youth and who are well enough off and are not constrained by poverty, it is sheer folly, although some women who wish to remarry say that it is no life for a woman on her own. So few women trust in their own intelligence that they excuse themselves by saying that they would not know how to look after themselves.[39]

Obviously Christine thought this was nonsense, because women *did* know how to take care of themselves; they were simply being brainwashed by society and by men. She advised women that they should be aware of their surroundings and circumstances. She said that women should know how their estate was run and the details of its management so that they might be prepared to take over if they needed to someday. Christine was speaking from experience and her lack of knowledge in regard to her husband's estate. She also spoke freely about the issue of budgeting money, once again due to her own experience and her father's lack of prudence. She stated that women should divide their expenditures into five categories: 1) giving to the poor, 2) paying their debts and household expenses, 3) paying their staff and servants, 4) putting some aside for gifts, and 5) spending the remainder on their own clothing and jewels.[40]

HER BODY OF WORK

Christine finished *The Treasure of the City of Ladies* by the age of forty. She had written twenty major works in poetry and prose. They included *One Hundred Ballads, More Ballads, Allegorical Poetry, The Book of the City of Ladies, The Treasure of the City of Ladies, The Book of the Duke of True Lovers, The Letter of the God of Love, The Tale of the Rose, The Book of the Deeds and Good Character of King Charles V the Wise, (Queen of France, Isabel of Bavaria), The Book of the Deeds of Arms and of Chivalry, The Book of Peace, Prayers to Our Lady, The Seven Allegorized Psalms, The Letter Concerning the*

Prison of Human Life, The Hours of Contemplation on the Passion of Our Lord, The Poem of Joan of Arc.

Christine added to her list an unusual book for feminists of the Middle Ages—*The Book of Feats of Arms and Chivalry.* In this book she shared the knowledge she had compiled from her experience with soldiers and the battlefield. She included various tips, from campground choices to prevention of attack on one's own castle. Henry VII was so impressed with her volume of advice that he had it translated into English by William Caxtin eighty years after Christine wrote it. He then had it printed for the English men-at-arms.

One of Christine's greatest passions resonates around her desire for peace. Peace for marriages, family, and her country. She was greatly distressed by the French Civil War and wrote *The Book of Peace.* She finished it in 1413, lamenting, "a poor voice crying in this kingdom, desirous of peace and the good for all of you, your servant Christine, who prays that she may see the day when peace comes."[41] Christine proved that she was capable of predicting political events. She warned ten years before Agincourt that if civil war erupted in the nation, France would be vulnerable to foreign attack. In 1418 this happened. After the Burgundians took over Paris, Christine sought refuge in the royal abbey of Poissy.

A FINAL TRIBUTE

Once Christine was in the convent, her works declined in volume. She wrote prayers for bereaved women and her final work, a tribute to Joan of Arc. Christine was the only contemporary to write about Joan of Arc, who epitomized all that Christine admired. She relished her female heroism, her dignity, her triumph over adversity in French politics, and her desire for peace. She was living proof that a woman could achieve great things. In "The Poem of Joan of Arc," she wrote,

> *When I reflect upon your state,*
> *The youthful maiden that you are,*
> *To whom God gives the force and strength*
> *To be the champion and he one*

To suckle France upon her milk
Of peace, the sweetest nourishment,
To overthrow the rebel host;
The wonder passes Nature's work!

That is, if God, through Joshua
Performed so many miracles
In conquering those places where
So many met defeat—a man
Of strength was Joshua. But she's
A woman—simple shepherdess—
More brave than ever a man at Rome!
An easy thing for God to do! . . .[42]

CHRISTINE'S INFLUENCE

Christine's works were prevalent in many lands, including France, Portugal, and England. She held persuasive powers, redirecting the attitudes and perceptions regarding women and their place in society as a whole. One of the first books William Caxton, the first English printer, printed after the Bible was one of Christine's books. He glowingly described her as "the mistress and mirror of intelligence."[43] Her fame and reputation spread throughout the region. Her literature was read by a diverse society: royal families, dukes, queens, princesses, and merchants' daughters. She regained the respect that had been lost with the death of her king, father, and husband, but this time it was on her own accord. She approached the end of her life with a foundation of people who sought to protect her and relished her prose, poetry, and social perspective. The legend of her work and word of mouth of her advice permeated all realms of society.

Christine's influence was undeniably vast and valuable. Women read her works for one hundred years after she wrote them. She attributed her success to God, "so that you will give thanks to God, the source of all good, Who has given you these blessings and many others. It is not Fortune who bestows these gifts but His, solely out of His grace, and to whom He pleases."[44] After retreating to the abbey at Poissy, many years after she had originally contemplated escaping there, she died in 1429. Christine's accomplishments, virtues, and teachings, however, live on forever.

Christine was a rebel, a visionary, a revolutionary, a daughter, a wife, a child of God, a mother, a single working mother, a survivor. Her defiant qualities were not her own but thrown onto her via circumstances. She was quite content as a wife and mother. After her misfortunes, anguish, and great sorrow, she held her head high and opted to fight fire with fire. Maturing as a result of her pain, she laid the groundwork that would serve as a shining example for her children and magnanimously benefit women. Christine's revolutionary writings were always rooted in a deep sense of humanity, salt-and-peppered with wit and wisdom. She cared deeply for the spiritual, emotional, mental, and physical welfare of her children and for all women. She tried to rally women to find their inner strength so that they might survive adversity. She knew how to enlighten and instruct, even scold, in a way that was not offensive, and she had the courage and tenacity of an army of knights. She documented brilliantly in her writings that women were not insignificant. She accentuated that women were equally as intelligent and inherently as good as men.

As a single mother Christine made brave decisions despite her desire to deflate. Through her darkness and doubts she rose to meet the foe head on, displaying an unwillingness to let defeat capture and enslave her soul. She did a great service for her children, serving as an example as she deftly demonstrated how to handle times of crisis. She heeded God's call of purpose in her life. She taught her children that worldly things do not matter but that piety, morals, education, and character do matter. I believe through hard times, and because of hard times, our children's characters are enriched.

LIFE LESSON: TURN TRIBULATIONS INTO TRIUMPHS

From a woman who lived in the Middle Ages more than six hundred years ago, we glean that it is through the most difficult times that we learn the most. A blissful, trouble-free life does not always warrant a bountiful spirit ready to face the world. Challenges create courage. Bravery perseveres even when fear is prevalent. Christine exuded valor and endured her indignities nobly. She found her inner strength to carry on and turned her path of hardships into an avenue to avenge herself, her children, and all women. Goodness reigned from her grueling misfortunes. With faith and a zealous desire to right the wrongs inflicted upon her, she recognized the purpose of her despair. She found her God-given talent and used it to raise the feminine conscience. She was a visionary of her trials. She turned her tribulations into triumphs and held her head high, and you can too.

So whatever difficulty you are facing, question why and seek the reason God has given it to you. There is purpose in pain. Be determined to trounce the problem and twist it to honor God, your children, and you. When you do, you will touch everyone you encounter with your triumph.

Christine, by trumping trials with triumphs,
became the visionary for all such women.

—JANINE TURNER

CHapter six

Colonial and Revolutionary America—Setting the Stage

1700s

The abandoned, single mother, pregnant with child,
was punished by a public whipping of thirty lashes.

—PURITAN RULE OF CONDUCT

America. Grand and glorious! Adventuresome spirits render grueling awakenings. Danger and disease. Survival of the fittest. Puritans and Quakers. Christ and Christians. Human frailty versus religious rigors. Women stifled and children suppressed. Who will rise to victory?

Queens had ruled Europe for centuries. These queens had proven that their intellect could rival men's, and they could rule their countries with just as much cunning and perseverance as kings. Women in Colonial America could expect no equality with men, however. It was conveniently assumed that women were weak and inferior to men intellectually and physically. The irony was that within the male's household he was surely privy to numerous examples of women's mental sharpness and physical stamina. Women as a whole did not really question this assumption of inferiority. They may have individually challenged the idea from time to time, but generally it wasn't a topic of discussion.

Life and survival took up the majority of time otherwise devoted to the luxury of demanding equality. Women were busy surviving cold winters, starvation, sickness, childbirth, and infant mortality. Who had time to wear a banner and walk the streets? Also, the enormity of the challenge must have loomed like an elephant in a log cabin. Without the protection of her "sisters," she was a loner and likely to get thrown out of the house for even daring to think such a thought.

Religion played a big role as well. Women were to be subservient, especially if they were Puritans. Life was tough on Puritan women. Quakers were much more liberal, and to the horror of the Puritans, female Quakers were even allowed to preach. These Quaker women created havoc in the Puritan regions, and many of them were hung. Thus, women may have randomly spoken, yearned, yelled and screamed, but the collective consciousness for the feminine cause would not emerge until the nineteenth century.

The Harsh Life

Life was tough on the Revolutionary-era, colonial woman. It is only with the knowledge of what their restrictions and sometimes terrors were that I could fully understand some of the decisions these women made.

Most girls were forced to marry early in life. In fact, men who had sex with a girl under the age of ten were punished by death. (I guess that meant if a man had sex with a girl who was eleven, it was justifiable.) Girls married young and rarely had a say in who they were marrying. Even if they did, how could a girl that young really know who she was marrying? In most cases, it was a financial burden for a family to provide for the children as they reached puberty. Boys were expected to work the fields, and girls were expected to marry. When a girl married, her husband assumed all claims to her money, lands, and children. A single woman or a widowed woman could own land, but the married woman could not own land or be in charge of her estate. Her husband could also spend her money, if she had any, as he pleased. A married woman had no right to her previously owned land, her belongings, or her dowry.

If a woman decided she wanted a divorce, she was fighting an uphill battle. Divorce was most assuredly granted to a man if the woman had been adulterous. However, a woman was rarely granted a divorce if the man was adulterous. Cruelty or violent abuse was not considered grounds for a divorce unless a woman could prove he was trying to kill her. But how was a woman to prove this when lawyers were expensive and a woman had no money?

If the woman couldn't obtain a divorce, then sometimes she simply left her husband. If a woman was, by some miracle, granted a divorce for abuse, she was rarely given the right to financial support. Whether she secured a divorce or left her husband, she would tragically lose her rights to her children. The children could not come with her because the man had automatic rights to the children. They were considered his entities and property. Thus, if a woman was miserable or beaten, or if her husband was a drunkard or a loser, she had absolutely no ability, no resources, to claim her children. She, not to mention her children, was consequently stuck in an intolerable situation if she couldn't bear to part with her children, and what mother really could? Men knew this paradox captivated a mother's heart.

To ponder this scenario is haunting. To make matters even worse, married or not married to the mother, the father could do as he wished with the child. If he wanted to sell his child as an indentured slave, send him off to another family, or assign him to an apprenticeship, he could do so without the mother's consent. The father had total legal authority over his children. If the woman became a widow and then remarried, she lost the independent authority over her children to the new husband.

A woman who was abused and ran away or divorced would most likely be forced to live in an almshouse. She could only stay there until she was well. So what was a woman to do after she was kicked out and had no place to live? She wasn't allowed to be educated; so how could she work and provide for herself? These women were in a terrible bind. Many women ended up returning to their husbands. If a woman who left her husband couldn't succeed in getting a divorce, then she couldn't remarry. In this case, sometimes she simply became a common-law wife to another man.

In 1725, for example, Benjamin Franklin's common-law wife, Deborah, married a man later revealed to be a bigamist. He rushed off to the West Indies, and she was not able to divorce him. The procedure was laden with gigantic hurdles. Thus, she simply moved in with Benjamin Franklin. She was never able to legally marry him.

FAMILY LIFE

Women had big families, which were considered a form of wealth because children were assets. With no available knowledge of birth control, every act of intercourse was apt to produce a baby. Women's childbearing spanned twenty years, and each pregnancy and birth threatened her life. One of the many reasons women breast-fed was because it provided a rudimentary form of birth control; women were told to refrain from sexual activity during the time they breast-fed because it was believed it would damage their milk. Then again, a woman was hesitant to bond with her baby for the first few months because 10 percent of children died in their first year.

The Revolutionary-era mother had little time on her hands to dote on her children. She had to milk the cows and churn the butter, cook the meals and clean the house, spin the wool and fetch the water, wash the clothes, make the soap to wash the clothes, and make the candles. Fetching the water, of course, meant going to the well or river, and washing the clothes meant using a bucket, home-made soap, and a rock. Her exhaustion was wrought with heart-break. She had to endure wicked winters with no heat and little food, resulting in sweeping disease and death. There were rarely doctors, and if they did show up, they brought razors to bleed the patient and emetics to cause them to vomit.

The Puritans valued education; so a 1647 Massachusetts law mandated that every town of fifty or more families had to support an elementary school. Boys and girls attended these schools, though at different times for different reasons. Girls could receive an education but mostly in the summer and evenings when the boys were not in attendance. Colonial law demanded that parents teach their children to read and train them in a vocation. If they didn't obey, the parents could lose their child. Mothers routinely educated their daughters, and a great deal of the education revolved around household duties. The older girls were in charge of the younger children and many of the household duties. Boys could go on to college. Girls could go to finishing school where they were taught handwriting, French, music, and needlework. The southern colonies had fewer schools. The wealthy southerners had tutors, the middle class could learn from their literate parents or siblings, and the poor were unschooled.

OUT-OF-WEDLOCK PREGNANCY

Out-of-wedlock pregnancy resulted in big problems for the woman and the child in the 1700s. The child and woman were branded for life, and the child was not entitled to an inheritance from his biological parents. Most of these children born out of wedlock were sold into servitude until the age of eighteen. Then they were released into the world.

If the out-of-wedlock pregnancy occurred in the Puritan sect, life could be especially hard. Forty percent of these pregnancies occurred among female servants; 60 percent occurred among girls of middle or upper class status. Two-thirds of the women married the fathers, but one-third didn't. Many women were unduly influenced or raped. Regardless of class, the majority of the time they were left alone to carry the burden, as was the child.

Out-of-wedlock pregnancy was a crime in the Puritan New England area. Even if the man and woman were subsequently married after the woman became pregnant, they were still prosecuted. They had to pay a fine, appear in front of a congregation, and appeal for forgiveness. The abandoned, single mother, pregnant with child, was punished by a public whipping of thirty lashes. After the child was born, the mother was allowed to care for the baby and even breastfeed the baby until it was weaned. After the child was weaned, the town owned the baby. They most often would sell it into servitude.

In the case of Susanah Durbin, the town authorities arrived to take her baby after weaning. Allowing the mother the opportunity to wean made the separation cruel and desperate. Before they took the child, the authorities often stripped him of his clothes and took him naked believing that even the baby's clothes were tainted by the mother. Susanah must have been devastated. She was taken to court because she attempted to see the child after he had been taken from her. Tragic.

If the new mother could not provide for the child, she could go to an almshouse, but they could still take the child without her consent and sell it into servitude. Many women would protect the father and not tell. The woman was often in fear of the man's potentially vehement abuse if she reported him. Midwives would hover during childbirth because it was believed that the woman would reveal the father's name during the delirium of the pain. If revealed, the father could be made to pay child support, but only until the child reached the age of six.

INFANTICIDE

With the horrors of out-of-wedlock pregnancies, it is not surprising that infanticide was frequent. The single mother had three choices: fall onto the mercy of her employer, her parents, or her lover. If the mother was deserted, she might choose to abandon the baby. She would choose to leave it where it could be found and potentially nurtured, or she would kill the baby by drowning it or abandoning it in the woods. When the dead babies were found in wells, ponds, or the woods, it was almost impossible to discover who the mother was. Most women who were caught were either frantic, fraught with fear, or single women steeped in poverty. Infanticide was considered a mother's crime.

The man was rarely held responsible, even if the cause of the infanticide was due to his neglect of the mother and child. For example, in 1786 a twenty-seven-year-old tavern maid, Elizabeth Wilson, was accused of killing her twin babies, even though she testified that the father had murdered them by stomping them to death. He did this after she said she was going to take him to court for child support. Elizabeth was hung anyway, and the father was never taken to court.

New Horizons

After the American Revolution, horizons eventually brightened for women and children. The prevailing attitude was transitioning into a belief that children were the future of the new country. The mother's value was emerging due to the perspective that they were now nurturers of the new American spirit. They were responsible for imbuing their children with dignity and character. Mothers were to shape their religious views, appreciation of the classics, and sense of humanity.

Another contributing factor for the transformation in regard to the rearing of children was due to John Locke's and Jean-Jacques Rousseau's new philosophies. The prevalent thought of the times had been that children were born wicked and must be treated with harsh discipline. It wasn't until the new philosophies came along that perceptions started to change. Locke and Rosseau philosophized that children were not innately bad. They believed that children were blank slates and needed nurturing and love to evolve into healthy adults. Their influence was enormous, and by the end of the century the collective thought that children were born depraved was almost resolutely rejected. At last, the mother was emerging as an essential element in the evolution of familial bonding.

"My mother was the most beautiful woman I ever saw. All I am I owe to my mother. I attribute my success in life to the moral, intellectual and physical education I received form her."

—President George Washington

RACHEL LAVEIN FAWCETT

Spirited Single Mother

1729–1768

SNAPSHOT	Walking through the town of her imprisonment with her head held high— her red skirt billowing in the wind
MOTHER MOMENT	Rachel and Alexander working collectively and happily in the business she established
CHALLENGE	Abused by husband and society
STEWARDSHIP	Inspired her boys with resolute spirit
SCRIPTURE	Do not judge, or you too will be judged. For in the same way you judge others, you will be judged, and with the measure you use, it will be measured to you. (Mathew 7:1–2 NIV)

chapter seven

Define Your Own Destiny

We must make the best of those ills which cannot be avoided.

—Alexander Hamilton

Early 1700s. Hot. Steamy. The island of Nevis. Paradise and cesspools. Natives and aliens. Rich and poor. The native people are surrounded by an eager influx of fortune-seeking foreigners. Random religious people are surrounded by rowdy, restless sinners. A melting pot of perversion. God save the innocent!

Rachel Lavein Fawcett was a beautiful, intelligent woman caught in a tragic situation during times that were not kind to women. She wasn't a queen, or rich, or noble, or a slave, or a pioneer. Yet she produced one of our great Americans, Alexander Hamilton. Through wretched conditions, she somehow instilled qualities of dignity, tenacity, and character in her son. If Alexander had not become a man of such international acclaim and intrigue, Rachel would have fallen into obscurity.

As it so happens, Rachel's life with all of its blemishes provides us a glimpse into the realm of another day and time when women were thrown into hopeless, defenseless positions. Rachel was a victim who defiantly rose to empower herself, and consequently, in an inherent way, her son.

So often parents don't think about how the consequences of their actions will mark their children. They are myopic in their views. Rachel's mother, her husband, and her lover didn't consider the repercussions of their selfishness and how it would resonate in the lives of Rachel and her children. Sometimes these actions are malicious and premeditated, and sometimes they are just misguided moments. Rachel's mother, perhaps, miscalculated. Rachel's husband was malicious. Rachel's lover and common-law husband was negligent. Nevertheless, Rachel's life shows that it's through the most difficult times that we learn the most, and it's how we deal with defeat that carves character out of stone. The key is learning to define your own destiny.

Timeless Scenario: Girl is born into dysfunctional family. Girl is forced to marry boy. Boy is physically, emotionally abusive to girl. Girl is put in jail. Girl escapes jail but not boy's wrath. Girl lives with different boy. Girl and new boy have two sons. New boy is a drinker and abandons girl. Girl is single mother in town where she was slandered and imprisoned. Girl is left penniless. Girl holds her head high. Girl exemplifies resolute character and provides for her sons.

The Confusing Facts

What I found interesting about researching Rachel is the diversity of facts. Both the names Lavein and Fawcett were spelled three different ways. I chose to use Lavein and Fawcett. Different interpretations yielded different biases, and certain renditions were highly judgmental. None of the versions I read dealt with Rachel from the perspective of a woman or as a single mother. After educating myself about the laws and restrictions women encountered in the 1700s, I felt an immense sense of compassion for Rachel. She was truly a victim of circumstances beyond her control.

Rachel's Childhood

Rachel Lavein Fawcett was born in 1729 on the island of Nevis. Her mother, Mary Uppington, was British, and her father, John Fawcett, was a French Huguenot, a sugar planter, and a physician. The sketchy records indicate that young Mary and the much-older

John lived together as common-law man and wife, finally marrying in 1718 after bearing two children. Eventually, Mary and John had a total of seven children.

The island of Nevis was a small island in the West Indies that was nine miles long and five miles wide. It was a beautiful island with the feeling, as recorded in 1745, of "a kind of perpetual spring."[2] Nevis had been a sugar plantation haven, and people had flocked to the island in the early eighteenth century like the gold rushes of the wild West. By the time Alexander was born, though, the sugar exports had fallen from one hundred thousand hundred-pound barrels in 1707 to fewer than twenty-five thousand barrels in 1755. The island had somehow peaked in its productivity, and yet it didn't prevent the influx of nefarious gamblers who were hoping to bet their all and get rich quick. Like a wild day at the stock market, men would carouse the town in splendor one day and be in prison for debt the next. The Reverend Hugh Knox, a contemporary of Alexander Hamilton, described the island as filled with ". . . rakes, night rioters, drunkards, gamesters, Sabbath breakers, church neglectors, common swearers, unjust dealers."[3]

On this Fawcett plantation with breathtaking views of reflective white beaches outlining the aqua Atlantic Ocean and volcanic mountains, the statuesque, ebony-haired Rachel spent her childhood. She had the fortune of an education bestowed upon her and obviously the aptitude for it. She was taught French literature and the classics of Greece and Rome.

It was not all bliss, however, because Rachel lost five siblings to an epidemic common to the tropics, and a terrifying hurricane devastated the island. Rachel must have wondered why she was spared. Her mother and father proved incapable of handling the stress. In 1741 Rachel's mother, rumored to possess an ineffable charm, somehow managed to win a Leeward Islands agreement of separate maintenance. Mary left her husband and took Rachel with her. She couldn't, however, under the conditions of the agreement and laws of the time, remarry while John was alive. This was a rare feat for those days, for divorce within the British Empire was almost never accomplished. What took place for such an unusual document to be granted? What did Rachel witness? The channels of history don't reveal these facts. However, Rachel was taken from her home and her father at age eleven and accompanied her mother to the island of St. Croix, capital of the Danish Caribbean islands. Rachel's mother was now a divorced, single mother. They lived near Rachel's sister, Ann, and her husband, James Lytton, in the small society of Christiansted for five years.

FORTUNES AND FORTUNE HUNTERS

In 1745 Dr. John Fawcett died and left everything he had, including his money and his property, to sixteen-year-old Rachel. Technically he was leaving it to Mary until Rachel either married or turned twenty-one. Rachel was, in her son Alexander's words, "a woman of great beauty, brilliancy and accomplishments."[4] Sixteen-year-old Rachel was now rich and, consequently, a target for money-grubbers on the island.

Certain renditions paint Rachel's mother as ambitious and manipulative. Perhaps this was the case when it came to Johann Michael Lavein. Mary thought she had found a rich man for her daughter. Johann, an older, insidious man, presented himself to be a sugar plantation owner. In reality, he had already proved disastrous with money and had lost much of his capital on a failed minor St. Croix plantation. Alexander wrote, "A dane fortune hunter of the name of Lavein came to Nevis bedizened with gold and paid his addresses to my mother, then a handsome young woman having a snug fortune."[5]

If this was the reason for facilitating the marriage, then Mary was drastically misguided in her judgments. If only she had seen behind the disguise. His flashy clothes, bought with his last dime, seduced Mary. Seemingly only Rachel saw the hypocrisy of his character. She didn't want to marry Lavein, who was twelve years her senior. Yet Mary, believing he was the right choice for Rachel, for the obvious wrong reasons, ignored her daughter's premonitions and willingly thrust her sixteen-year-old daughter into the hands of this deceitful man. Thus, in accordance with the times, Rachel was forced to marry a man she didn't love, she didn't choose, she didn't want. As Alexander wrote, "In compliance with the wishes of her mother . . . But against her own inclination."[6]

Bound in marriage, beautiful, bright Rachel was sent off to a plantation, ironically named Contentment, with her evil husband. In the same year that her father died, 1745, at the age of sixteen, she was ripped from her mother and sent away with a strange man she feared. Who really wants to contemplate what occurred next? It's a situation that seems foreign to the majority of women today. Young Rachel was forced to sleep with a man she didn't love and found repulsive and vulgar. The following year she gave birth to a son, Peter. Rachel had to watch in vain as Lavein spent all of her savings and lost one plantation after another. In light of his soon-to-be-revealed, documented, spiteful words, it may be safely assumed that he was verbally, emotionally, and physically abusive. Rachel found him insufferable. In Alexander's words it was "a hated marriage."[7]

RACHEL REBELS

Rachel endured this despised position for five years. At the age of twenty-one, she reached into her resources of inner strength and summoned the courage to rebel. One version tells of Rachel running away; the other says she threatened to leave and take the baby. Either way, Rachel was a young girl with absolutely no resources. Lavein had spent all of her money, and she had no protection from the courts. The law stated that she would only be granted a divorce if it could be proven that her husband had tried to kill her. Even if she could prove that, she had no money to hire a lawyer. Thus she would never be granted a divorce. She had no rights or claims to her lands or her belongings, and worst of all, she had no rights to her child.

The situation must have been really bad for Rachel to take such a risk. When she rebelled against her manipulative, abusive husband, he, with injured pride, had her thrown into prison, stating that she had "shown herself to be shameless, rude and ungodly and had . . . completely forgotten her duty."[8] "Completely forgotten her duty" is a veiled way of saying she was no longer consenting to sexual relations with him. For this crime she was sent to prison.

RACHEL IN PRISON

Rachel was taken to the ominous, dark Christiansvaern, the Christiansted fort that was also the town jail. Among blacks, who were being whipped and castrated, local drunkards, and thieves, she was the only woman—seemingly the first woman ever imprisoned in Christiansted. The law stipulated that the only way a woman could be thrown in jail was for "twice committing adultery."[9] However, when Lavein had Rachel jailed he did not list adultery. Her "errors" were that she was refusing to live with her husband. Most assuredly, Lavein would have listed adultery if such an act had occurred.

Rachel was imprisoned without a trial or obvious justification. The horror must have been unbearable for the twenty-one-year-old Rachel. She was imprisoned in a dark, cramped, filthy jail cell for several months, eating salted fish. The only ray of light was what could penetrate the wooden slats. Lavein had hoped that after several months in this prison, Rachel would submit to his whims and that "everything would be better and that she, like a true wife, would have changed her ungodly mode of life and would live with him as was meet and fitting."[10] He expected her to come back to him a broken, malleable young woman. But he was betting on the wrong horse!

Lavein had miscalculated Rachel's inner strength. He had underestimated her intelligence and her sense of self-preservation, her determination to define herself and hold her head high. Rachel's mother used her charms and finesse on the fort's commandant, and Captain Bertram Pieter De Nuilly released Rachel. Upon release, she didn't run to Lavein, much to his fury. She fled to find safe haven with her custodian, the island's highest-ranking officer.

Powerless, traumatized, and most certainly fearing for her life, Rachel knew she was up against insurmountable odds in regard to her son, Peter. She feared her husband, and any action in regard to getting her child would subject her to him and force her to return to him. She was also the victim of so much slander that the chances of winning in a male-dominated court, against those who had already unjustly thrown her in jail, were nil. Not to mention, she would have to fight the pre-existing law stating that the father always retained the rights of custody of the children. And she had no money. Thus she was forced to leave Peter with Lavein. She escaped with her mother, sailing back to Nevis.

Rachel was a survivor, though, and she was not broken. Hamilton revealed that by witnessing his mother's indomitable spirit, the seeds of revolutionary fervor were planted. Commenting upon his mother's plight, he wrote, "'Tis only to consult our own hearts to be convinced that nations like individuals revolt at the idea of being guided by external compulsion."[11]

RACHEL AND JAMES HAMILTON

Upon her return to Nevis, Rachel met James Hamilton, eleven years her senior. She was twenty-one and he was thirty-two. He has been described as handsome and gentle. He was of noble Scottish lineage—the fourth son of a Scottish laird, a descendent from a ducal line who had married the daughter of an "ancient Baronet." Rachel must have been attracted to his meek nature, the antithesis of her former husband.

After seven years of cohabitation, Rachel and James were considered to be common-law husband and wife. Rachel could not marry James, however, because she had not been able to obtain a legal divorce from Lavein. There are some statements that Rachel and James were married after Lavein had obtained a divorce. One such statement was by Alexander himself: "A marriage between them ensued."[12] This, however, could not have actually been true, because in the divorce decree that Lavein eventually obtained, he made sure that it stated she could never remarry. Rachel and James may have tried to marry and were shocked to find that they were unable to do so. Nevertheless, Rachel bore her first son with James in 1753, and Alexander was born on January 11, 1755.

Meanwhile, like one of the plots from *General Hospital*, Lavein was intent on ruining Rachel. His vindication never subsided throughout his lifetime. Lavein had spiraled from plantation owner to plantation worker to janitor. In 1759 he decided he wanted to marry another woman, and he sought Rachel for a divorce. He behaved like a spurned lover and spewed forth venom. He, who had squandered all of Rachel's money, abused her in every way, and imprisoned her without warrant, was determined to humiliate her.

In the divorce decree he alleged that she had "shown herself to be shameless, rude and ungodly" and had "completely forgotten her duty and let husband and child alone and instead gave herself up to whoring with everyone" and that she had been "twice guilty of adultery."[13] Rachel had been living with James and had given birth to two children, yet this doesn't constitute "whoring with everyone." The papers were filed in court and made public for all to read on the island of St. Croix. Rachel, who had been drifting from island to island, had never returned to St. Croix and certainly couldn't have received the summons. So she was not present at these hearings, either out of fear or ignorance of their existence.

Rachel was not able to defend her honor, so the court ruled against her. After dissolving the marriage, it claimed that Rachel would have "no rights whatsoever as a wife to either person or means."[14] It also stated that Rachel's children with Hamilton were denied "all rights or pretensions" to Lavein's possessions. The most damaging ruling, the one with everlasting repercussions, was that Lavein was free to remarry but Rachel was not. Thus Rachel could never marry James Hamilton. They were nevertheless considered a common-law husband and wife. On October 1, 1758, they were present at a christening and listed as godparents, "James Hamilton and his wife."[15]

RACHEL'S LEADERSHIP

Through these hardships and her ability to ride the waves of controversy with a proud defiance, Rachel was teaching her boys how to persevere with mental toughness and resiliency; how to define themselves, rather than submitting to someone else's definition. They would desperately need these skills later in life. Rachel was the one who has been credited with the education of the boys and instilling a love for books and study. Alexander proved to be the one who was most inclined toward her persuasions. His grandson, Alan McLane Hamilton, later wrote,

> Hamilton's father does not appear to have been successful in any pursuit, but in many ways was a great deal of a dreamer, and something of a student, whose chief happiness seemed to be in the society of his beautiful and talented wife, who was in every way intellectually his superior.[16]

Rachel taught the boys French and enrolled Alexander at the age of five in a small Hebrew school. As a little boy, he stood beside his teacher on a small table and recited the Decalogue in Hebrew.

Rachel had been taught the art of accounting, which proved fortunate, because once again she was strapped with a partner who was inept at providing for the family. James was lazy and drank to excess. Consequently, Rachel stepped in to oversee the books and attempted to make James's business a success and solvent. James went bankrupt, however, and essentially became a drifter, going from job to job as a chief clerk on plantations or in counting houses.

RACHEL, SINGLE MOTHER

In 1765 James had to follow the demands of his current job by taking Rachel and her two sons from the island of St. Kitts back to Christiansted. Rachel was now forced to return to the island of her captivity and her deranged husband. It was an act of great courage and mental toughness for Rachel to return to the island where she was to face the demons that had tormented her. It was there that she had lived with a barbaric husband, had been unjustly imprisoned, and had been privy to indefensible slander. She accepted the mission with muster and showed her true colors by walking through the town in her billowing red skirt, holding her head high.

Once again this island didn't warrant good times for Rachel, for shortly after their arrival James deserted Rachel and her boys. After he had completed the deeds required of him by his job, he simply left the island. Rachel was never to see or hear from him again, nor was Alexander. At the age of thirty-six Rachel was an abandoned, single mother, and her boys were fatherless. Incredulously, James walked away from his paternal, parental duties physically, emotionally, and financially.

There are no documents or journals detailing Rachel's emotions during these times. Yet one must assume the disappointment that Rachel must have endured and the absolute dismay and sadness the boys must have felt. Never stooping to defeat, Rachel, now a single mother, once again rose to the challenge. She proved to her boys the breadth of spirit that lived within her and showed them how to survive challenging times.

Always resourceful and obviously intelligent, Rachel rented a house at No. 34 Company's Lane next to St. John's Anglican Church and opened her own store. As a merchant she bought goods from her landlord, reselling them to planters and ships' captains. Rachel gave the boys more financial security than James had ever done. Alexander worked by her side, thriving in the interchange of business. With pride and preparedness Rachel provided for her family in a type of work that was rare for a woman and even rarer for a woman to succeed in. With her experience in accounting, she kept neat and accurate books and always paid her bills on time. She also never accepted money from her relatives, determined to sustain herself and her children on her own.

Her accomplishments gleam brighter in the context of the times and place. Rachel managed to not only succeed as a single, divorced, slandered, abandoned mother in the 1700s, but to regain stature and respect. She accomplished this in a chauvinistic world on an island where her good name had been seriously blemished. She succeeded in business admirably in the face of incredible odds. The boys must have found a solace in her ability to provide for them. They surely appreciated and respected her spirit, love, and devotion. Rachel held her head high. With an appetite for challenge and an aptitude for resolution, she was a woman of fortitude and depth. She demonstrated to her sons that one is able to survive and thrive through adversity. She taught them that, even through dire circumstances, the human spirit is irrepressible.

RACHEL'S DEATH

The boys would have to draw upon her example because Rachel contracted yellow fever and died three years after their father deserted them. She was thirty-nine years old. Due to the expense of the doctor, Rachel had suffered with only a nurse for about a week. She was burning with fever when the doctor was called. He took a razor to the already-dehydrated Rachel's arm, bled her, and gave her an emetic, inducing her to vomit. Alexander contracted the fever as well. In Rachel's only bed, she and Alexander suffered together under these horrific conditions. Together they struggled with the raging fever, vomiting, and diarrhea. Alexander won the battle but Rachel didn't. He was lying beside her when she died.

Within an hour of her death, before the midwife even had time to wash Rachel's body or console her sons, the judge arrived to take inventory of her belongings. It was ten o'clock at night. By the glimmering light of candles, they walked around notating her few possessions, sealing off her home as the shocked and sickly Alexander and his brother watched in numbed silence. The lack of compassion is utterly mind boggling and almost unfathomable. The only belonging the judge and clerk left unsealed was the washbasin to cleanse Rachel's dead body. They even documented the feather bed upon which Alexander and his mother were lying.

Rachel had very little—a few bowls, a few pieces of china, and approximately two skirts. She did have, however, a bevy of books. The judge advanced the money so the boys could have a pair of shoes. Aware of Rachel's death, James, the boys' father, didn't return to console or provide for them. At the funeral, thirteen-year-old Alexander, standing by his mother's grave, heard the merciless words from the local Church of England curate, "Man that is born of woman has a short time to live and is full of misery" (Job 14:1 NIV).

Rachel died without a will, and her belongings were auctioned off in the yard behind 34 Company's Lane. A guardian, exhibiting the only goodwill gesture bestowed on Alexander, bought all of Rachel's books and gave them to him. The devastation of the boys was only deepened by the unrelenting revenge of Lavein. He returned before the probate closed, heaping insults upon their mother and filing with the courts to prevent the boys from inheriting a single thing. There wasn't much, yet he insisted that everything belonged to his son and her first son, Peter. The court complied with Lavein, and Alexander and his brother were left orphaned, penniless, and humiliated.

With the interminable void left by the death of their mother and the abandonment of their father, the boys went to live with their cousin, who shortly committed suicide and was found in a pool of blood in his bed. In his will, he left nothing to the boys. Thus, the boys were separated. James was taken in as an apprentice, and Alexander went to live with a wealthy merchant, Thomas Stevens, who was the father of his best friend, Edward Stevens.

Why relay such a story? How is this most upsetting finale to Rachel's life uplifting? Rachel's story is complex and is one I had initially contemplated not including. And yet, in light of the times when she lived, and even in modern times, I find her resolve and spirit stimulating and inspiring. Rachel's life wasn't easy. As a matter of fact, none of the women in this book experienced easy journeys. Yet Rachel's life seems to have ended so abruptly and disappointingly.

Through her fortitude and insatiable ability to withstand adversity, during times that didn't bode well for women, Rachel proves to be a remarkable woman. She endured a marriage against her will, abuse, imprisonment, slander, and abandonment. However, Rachel routinely found an inexhaustible inner strength, resiliency of spirit, and an intellectual prowess. Bravery is borne out of fear and the ability to conquer it. Rachel exemplified bravery, a woman's bravery in a man's world. Her life did end abruptly, yet she had left her indelible imprint on her boys.

Rachel's Ongoing Influence

The most supplicant of Rachel's two sons was Alexander. His intellectual aptitude mirrored hers. Rising like a phoenix from the ashes, Alexander not only survived but also became one of our country's most brilliant and influential forefathers. Children watch, listen, and learn, and it was due to Rachel's influence that Alexander was educated. She taught him how to read and write in French, shared with him her appreciation of the classics of history and philosophy and the love of books. She was reported to have one of the largest libraries on the island, thirty books. She also taught Alexander the art of survival and the dignity of self-respect. He observed his mother fall to the bottom, pick herself up again, and venture forth with her head held high. He was privy to the circumstances around him, and with the sharp eyes of a child he absorbed her valiant efforts to never be extinguished by the oppressions of life. These characteristics proved vital tools for Alexander as he weathered the seemingly insurmountable indignities he encountered throughout his lifetime.

Alexander Hamilton became one of America's leading politicians, statesmen, financiers, and military officers. In 1775 he joined the New York militia company called the Hearts of Oaks. Hamilton achieved the rank of lieutenant, while studying military history and tactics on his own. He led successful raids and won the interest of Nathaniel Greene and George Washington for his proficiency and bravery. He joined Washington's staff in March 1777 and served for four years, essentially as Washington's chief of staff. He led an infantry regiment that took Redoubt #10 of the British fortifications at Yorktown, one of the last battles of the Revolutionary War.

Hamilton was one of America's most renowned constitutional lawyers, proposing the United States Constitutional Convention in 1787. He was one of the two leading authors of the *Federalist Papers*, which was the single most important interpretation of the Constitution. He was the first secretary of the Treasury from 1789–1795. His policies included the creation of a national debt, federal assumption of the state debts, the creation of a national bank, and a system of taxes through a tariff on imports and a tax on whiskey that would pay for it all. His ideas were not entirely appreciated at the time but would later be applauded, utilized, and applied, building a strong economy, military, and country. It is his face on the ten dollar bill.

It is to his mother's credit that America benefited from the visionary and intellectual contributions of Alexander Hamilton. If Rachel had dissolved into a puddle of pity and ineptitude, who would have been his example, his guiding force? His father had abandoned him, never to be seen again. It was Rachel who laid the foundation of his character. It was she, beautiful, raven-haired, spirited, intelligent Rachel—wife, lover, mother, single mother—who prevailed over the challenges of humanity and lit the lanterns of life. She sparked the flames of passion and became the beacon upon which her sons measured their destinies. She was a victim of abuse and abandonment, yet she taught her boys how to survive the instabilities of life.

Life for women is unpredictable, and the men we love may sometimes become abusive and intolerable. Situations may be bleak and our minds vulnerable to the psychological torment. Others may simply want to bring us down. But Rachel Lavein Fawcett is a stalwart example of overcoming incredible odds by not allowing anyone or anything to crush her spirit.

Life Lesson: Define Your Own Destiny

Rachel held her head high and walked through the town where she had been unjustly imprisoned and labeled a whore. She didn't let the judgments of others define her self-worth. By her courageous example we learn that only we are capable of defining ourselves. Others are only successful in this attempt if we let them. Don't let them! Hold on to the flame of goodness, joy, and self-worth that abides in your soul, and never give anyone permission to extinguish your flame.

You are a child of God, and your children are your gifts from God. Show your children the dignity of self-worth. Help them walk through life with pride. No one else has walked in your shoes or theirs. No one else has the right to judge. Only God is the judge. People tried to rob Rachel of her spirit, but she would not let them have it. Hold on to your dignity and your self-esteem and do not give it away. Define your own destiny. Take God's hand, walk with Him, and hold your head high.

> *A woman of superior intellect, elevated sentiment,*
> *and unusual grace of persona and manner.*
> *To her he was indebted for his genius.*[7]
>
> —JOHN, SON OF ALEXANDER HAMILTON

ELIZA LUCAS PINCKNEY

Revolutionary Single Mother

1723–1793

SNAPSHOT	Eliza praying over her indigo seeds as she planted them for the first time
MOTHER MOMENT	Standing on the front porch with her daughter as President George Washington honored them with a visit
CHALLENGE	Left alone to run her plantation and her children
STEWARDSHIP	Enriched South Carolina and reared Revolutionary War heroes
SCRIPTURE	When a prophet of the LORD is among you, I reveal myself to him in visions, I speak to him in dreams. (Numbers 12:6 NIV)

chapter eight

Dare to Dream

Only a fool knows no fear; only a coward runs from the battle.[1]

—FAVORITE MAXIM OF COLONEL LUCAS

Pre-revolutionary America. Rich. Virgin. Varied. Patriotic and industrious. Religious and rowdy. Electrified atmosphere. Promise. Men, dressed in tri-corn hats and tights, gallop the plantations. Women join side-saddle—long gowns billowing over the horses' flanks. The pulse of a new country is quickening. The British are coming!

Eliza Lucas Pinckney was a South Carolina wonder. Her unrelenting dedication was fearsome, whether it was to her father, her crops, her husband, her children, or her country. Eliza's personality was one of fiery ebullience. As a single mother, she warranted brave, distinguished sons who decorated our country in its infancy, as did Eliza.

Eliza is an example of how accomplishments early in life, even before the birth of children, can resonate throughout the subsequent generations, influencing and shaping our children's character. As a young girl, she was given extraordinary responsibilities. At the age of sixteen she single-handedly ran her family's plantations because her father had to return to the army. Undaunted, Eliza embraced her challenges and met every task with enthusiasm. Her unbridled tenacity yielded great riches for her home colony of South Carolina. She earnestly sought a rich cash crop in indigo and her dreams were unparalleled. Eliza carried this fresh perspective with her throughout her life, even through the loss of her child and her husband.

Eliza, as a single mother, diligently nurtured her children, who amplified her resolve. Eliza teaches us to dream. I was impressed with the breadth and earnestness of her early accomplishments. I was also compelled by her revolutionary fervor and sacrifices. She was a great American. Even though she lived in the early 1700s, her life struggles are universal.

Timeless Scenario: Girl solely manages farm. Girl wants to succeed. Girl cultivates a crop. Girl refuses to marry boy her father chooses. Girl marries boy she chooses. Girl and boy are in love. Girl and boy have children. Girl and boy lose a child. Boy dies. Girl is demoralized. Girl rebounds. Girl raises American patriots. Girl loses everything in the war. Girl relishes treasure in her children. Girl loves her country.

ELIZA, THE EARLY YEARS

Eliza was born in 1723 on the island of Antigua in the West Indies. Her father was a major in the army of His Majesty, George II of England. Eliza's mother was delicate and always fighting fatigue and illness due to recurring bouts of malaria. There is no portrait of Eliza because all of her possessions were destroyed by the British during the Revolutionary War. Aspects of her life are represented through entries in her journals and letters. Eliza's great-granddaughter, Eliza Lucas Rutledge, thankfully saved them from some deranged person who wanted to burn them. Due to the size and coloring of Eliza's dresses, she is thought to have been a petite brunette.

Eliza's father had inherited three plantations in South Carolina: a 2,950-acre plantation named Waccamaw, a 15,000-acre plantation on the Combahee River, and a 600-acre plantation named Wappoo. When Eliza was fifteen years old, her father decided that the plantations needed his supervision in order to yield profitable revenue. Thus he, his wife, Eliza, sixteen years old, and her younger sister Polly, three years of age, embarked on the journey to the colonies.

To understand Eliza is to experience her youthful, visionary spirit.

She was always enthusiastic about life and ready for an adventure. Once she arrived in South Carolina, she embraced her new home with vigor. At a young age, Eliza assumed most of the duties of the house, because her mother was incapacitated the majority of the time. She and her father were very close, and she was eager to please him. Eliza's father was a botanist, and Eliza shared his love for plants and flowers. They would walk through the fields and dream. They grew rice, cotton, and corn. Eliza wrote, "I was very fond of the vegetable world. My father was pleased with it and encouraged it."[2]

Colonel Lucas taught Eliza the aspects and disciplines of managing a plantation. They studied the soil and the weather. Eliza was also fortunate because her father recognized her intellectual capabilities and encouraged her education. Ironically, her father didn't want Eliza to practice the femininities of the time. He detested it when she did embroidery. She was not, however, sent to London for a superior education, as were her brothers. This proved fortunate for South Carolina, as Eliza's common sense, vision, and tenacity yielded immense success with her horticultural enterprises.

In 1739 Colonel Lucas had to return to army duty in Antigua due to the impending war between England and Spain. He had to wrestle with the decision about whether to take his family back to Antigua with him. His problem was financial. He had mortgaged his plantation to provide for his family. If he left his plantation unattended, he might lose everything. He decided his family must stay, yet his sons were in England, Polly was a mere child, and his wife could barely get out of bed. This left the burden of success entirely on Eliza. He must have had enormous confidence in her abilities for, after a heart-to-heart talk with her, he decided to leave the financial future of three plantations and the family's care in her hands. In addition he left her in charge of eighty-six people besides children, including paying their wages. This was an immense burden for a young girl of sixteen. She understood both the gravity and responsibility of the situation, and she relished the challenge. Eliza was bright, capable, and compelled. She responded by saying to her father, "I am strong enough for any responsibility you may ask me to carry."[3]

Thus her father was off, leaving Eliza in charge of over five thousand acres of plantations. Eliza thrived among her self-imposed disciplines. She awakened at five in the morning and read before breakfast. After breakfast she spent an hour on her music. Then she studied French and shorthand. After that she would tutor Polly and several slave children. In those days, one wasn't to tutor slave children, but Eliza insisted and turned a deaf ear to the criticisms she received. During the afternoon, she would look after her mother and manage the house, practice her music again, write letters to her father and brothers, and order goods from London. She pickled pork, sent peach trees to her cousin in Boston, wove shrimp nets, and shipped eggs to her father.

These chores were coupled with her dedication to the plantation. She walked the grounds on a daily basis and managed the progress. At sixteen she was not recognized as an authority on the plantation, but she eventually won respect due to her prevailing wisdom and continual presence. She was so busy that she exclaimed, "I hardly allow myself time to eat and sleep."[4] She did allow time for her faith and frequently visited her church, praying at St. Phillip's Church and always setting Sundays aside for the Sabbath. It was here that she learned that she should not worry about "borrowing tomorrow's trouble"(see Matthew 6:34). She wrote to her brother about Charles Town, "Charles Town . . . is a neat pretty place . . . the streets and houses regularly built; the ladies and gentlemen gay in dress . . . people of a religious turn of mind."[5] She would occasionally sneak in a social day, Tuesdays, to visit with friends and do embroidery.

Eliza, the Visionary

Eliza was very interested in trying new crops. She was fascinated with new plants and had amazing foresight for such a young girl. She planted a large grove of oak trees because she envisioned that South Carolina was going to need them in the future to build ships. Demonstrating a prophetic sensibility, she wrote of their potential benefit in the future "when oaks are more valuable than they are now, which you know they will be."[6] She also noted that two-thirds of the profits from the oaks were to be given to charity.

Eliza also experimented with fruit trees and planted a fig orchard. In a letter she reported,

> O! I had like to forget the last thing I have done a great while. I have planted a large fig orchard, with design to dry and export them. I have reckoned my expense and the profits to arise from these figs, but was I to tell you how great an Estate I am to make this way, and how 'tis to be laid out you would think me far gone in romance. Yr. Uncle I know has long thought I have a fertile brain at scheming, I only confirm him in his opinion.[7]

She experimented with ginger, but to her disappointment it turned out poorly. Her experiments were varied and extensive. She planted different plants in various soils. Her enthusiasm had to be peppered with patience and salted with determination, as gain in agriculture was a slow process.

Eliza had a dream to experiment and succeed with the indigo crop. Others in South Carolina had tried and failed. The indigo dye was immensely popular, and England purchased all of its indigo from France. If Eliza could succeed in growing indigo in South Carolina, it would greatly benefit not only her father but also her colony.

Eliza did enjoy a few friendships. One such friendship was with Mr. and Mrs. Pinckney. Eliza was charmed by Mrs. Pinckney and intellectually stimulated and admired by Mr. Pinckney. He would bring her books, such as *Plutarch's Lives* and *Virgil's Georgies*, books about tilling the land and growing trees. He also enlightened her to shorthand, providing her an easier way to document the records. Charles Pinckney endearingly called Eliza "the little visionary." In reply Eliza wrote, "What he may now think whims and projects may turn out well by and by—out of many surely one may hit."[8]

It must be duly noted that Eliza's dream would never have come to fruition had it not been for the diligence and sacrifice of the slaves. She was powerless over the existence of slavery, the dark blight upon humanity; nevertheless, she fought for justice in her small way. She insisted that they have sick houses; nursery houses, that they be supplied with a healthy diet of food and supplied warm blankets and essentials. Eliza would personally tend to the sick and tutor the children.

A common comment about Eliza was that even men didn't work as hard as she did. There was much surprise when she showed up to oversee the men as they were to slash and box the pine trees. During the harvest of the rice crop, she would save the rough rice for the cattle and the other for table rice. The rice crop was a cash crop for Eliza and helped her pay the bills. She would send her father shingles and lumber, salt meat, barrels of rough rice, corn, peas, and eggs preserved in salt. Her journal entry in July 1739 read,

> I wrote my father a very long letter on his plantation affairs . . . on the pains I had taken to bring the Indigo, Ginger, Cotton, Lucern. And Cassada to perfection, and had greater hopes from Indigo . . . if I could have the seeds earlier next year from the West Indies, than any of ye rest of ye things I had tried . . . also concerning pitch and tar and lime and other plantation affairs.[9]

Pursuing Her Dream

In 1739 Colonel Lucas sent his daughter some indigo seeds from the West Indies. Eliza was thrilled. However, she knew absolutely nothing about the plant. She didn't know when to plant or when to harvest or any of the delicacies of the seedlings. Ready for an experiment, she tucked in the first seeds herself, then knelt and prayed over them. The seeds sprouted but were burned by an early frost. Despondent, Eliza would go to the woods to cry. She had no support because her mother was preoccupied and didn't understand Eliza's pursuit of a man's world. Polly, her sister, was so much younger she couldn't comprehend the burdens that overwhelmed Eliza. However, she would always be cheered by nature and the birds, often stimulated and inspired by the mockingbirds.

Eliza's father was worried about her, and as was customary for the times, he wrote of his intentions for her to marry. He had chosen two older, wiser, wealthy men who could provide for her needs. Uncharacteristically for the times, Eliza hotly responded,

The riches of Chile and Peru put together, if he had them, could not purchase a sufficient Esteem for him to make him my husband. As to the other gentleman you mention, Mr. W., you know, sir, I have so slight a knowledge of him I can form no judgment, and a Case of such consequences requires the nicest distinction of humours and sentiments. But you give me leave to assure you, my dear Sir, that a single life's my only Choice; and, if it were not, as I am yet Eighteen, hope you will put aside the thoughts of my marrying yet these two or three years at least.[10]

These shockingly brave sentiments from a young girl in the mid-eighteenth century revealed the substance that resonated within Eliza. These virtues would prove to be her ally when she became a single mother later in life.

In the spring of that same year, Eliza took the remaining indigo seeds and planted them. To her dismay, once again the crop failed. She wrote to her father, "We had a fine Crop of Indigo Seed upon the ground . . . the frost took it before it was dry. I picked out the best of it and had it planted, but there is not more than a hundred bushel of it come up . . . I am sorry we lost this season."[11]

In addition to her distress over the indigo, Eliza was worried about her father, who was engaged in England's war with Spain. She would not hear from him for lengthy amounts of time, and she worried that he'd been wounded or killed in battle. Adding to her consternation was the inconsistency of the environment and weather. She had to contend with too much or too little rain, worms or insects in the crops, unexpected frosts or devastating heat, and droughts. All of these variables were in addition to the tasks of managing the plantation's daily affairs.

The more people negated her indigo dream, the more passionate she became. She again planted seeds, her third try, in May of the next year, 1740. The seeds were growing nicely this time until a freak September frost attacked in the middle of the night. Eliza rushed to save some of the plants and managed to save enough seeds to plant half an acre the next year. Unlike her counterparts in South Carolina, she refused to quit the vision of a successful indigo industry. She wrote, "I have no doubt indigo will prove a very valuable commodity in time if we could have the seeds from the East Indies in time enough to plant the latter end of March that the seed might be dry enough to gather before our frost."[12]

In early 1741, two years after her first effort, and now her fourth attempt, she planted her half-acre of seedlings. These seeds yielded a nice, though modest, crop. Eliza's father sent an expert from the West Indies to teach her how to cultivate the crop and turn it into dye. The expert her father provided proved to be a disaster, however. Secretly harboring a desire for her efforts to fail, he intentionally added too much lime to the process to destroy her crop. (He didn't want France to lose her most valuable export.) She wrote, "He made a great mystery of the process. [He] . . . said he repented coming as he should ruin his own Country by it . . . [he] threw in a large quantity of Lime water as to spoil the colour."[13] At this point Eliza, having been subjected to this man's rude and chauvinistic behaviors, wrote, "I will have to pretend that I have a little patience, which I do not feel."[14]

In 1742 Eliza was still experimenting with the exact time to harvest, and she wrote to her father, "The Indigo stood till many of the leaves dropped." Later that year, the seeds he sent didn't even come up. "The last Indigo seed sent was not good. None of it came up. We shall save of our own to make a Crop next year."[15] In 1743 Eliza's sister was sent to boarding school. Eliza, now twenty years old, continued to manage a large assortment of activities. She enlarged her class of slave children and took immense pleasure in teaching them. She continued with her music, improved her French, and amazingly, educated herself in the law.

Industrious Eliza willingly provided her legal services to her neighbors. She wrote,

> Nor shall I grudge a little pains and application, if that will make me useful to any of my poor Neighbors. We have some in this neighborhood who never think of making a will 'till they come upon a sick bed, and find it too expensive to send to town for a Lawyer. If you will not laugh too immoderately at me, I'll trust you with a Secret, I have made two wills already. I know I have done no harm for I con'd my lesson very perfect . . . But after all, what can I do if a poor creature lies a-dying and their family takes it into their head that I can serve them. I can't refuse: but when they are well and able to employ a Lawyer, I always shall (refuse).[16]

Demonstrating an unrelenting determination, striving to achieve where others in her colony had failed, Eliza finally succeeded in 1744. She had seventeen pounds of indigo! She had achieved the planting and the harvesting. She had learned the proper way, from a different gentleman, to soak the indigo in the proper amount of lime for the appropriate amount of time and to drain, dry, and cube the indigo. She sent six pounds to England. The response was remarkable, "The Sample of Indigo sent here . . . has been tried and found to be better than the French Indigo."[17]

Eliza did it! Her hard work and perseverance had brought indigo to South Carolina. She had been tenacious and patient and after five years, from the ages of sixteen to twenty-one, she had produced a high caliber of indigo to send to England. Eliza, a teenaged girl, had persisted and accomplished this amazing feat that the colonial men had considered impossible and had relinquished all hope of achieving years earlier.

This triumph proved to be a great advantage for Eliza's father. Yet, Eliza gallantly didn't withhold her newfound discovery. She generously shared it with all of her fellow planters in South Carolina. A patriot, she wanted her colony to reap from the extraordinary benefits as well. Most of her 1744 crop had been saved for seed, and she shared it with her neighbors. By 1747, over one hundred thousand pounds of indigo were sold to England. Over the course of time, the colony sold a million pounds of dye to England every year. All of this was due to the vision and contribution of a young teenaged girl who, in 1739, left to oversee her father's plantation, was determined to yield an indigo success.

MARRIAGE AND MOTHERHOOD

The year 1744 was a busy one for Eliza. Her indigo was deemed a success, her father sent word that he wanted Eliza and her family to move back to Antigua, and she received a marriage proposal from Charles Pinckney. His wife, also Eliza's friend, had died recently. He had always been fond of Eliza and admired her spunk and enthusiasm for life, his little visionary. Now, he could not bear to see her leave South Carolina to return to Antigua.

Eliza had always admired Charles. He was one of South Carolina's most distinguished citizens. He was the Speaker of the Commons House of Assembly, was a colonel of the militia, and took an avid interest in his plantation. Eliza did not have a dowry to bring to the marriage, but this didn't matter to Charles. He had been Eliza's dear friend and mentor. Eliza said yes, having the great fortune of picking her own husband. She refused an expensive gown because she knew her family was incurring a huge expense moving back to Antigua. Eliza and Charles were married on May 27, 1744, when she was twenty-one.

The Pinckneys were very happy together, and Charles rarely left Eliza's side. They lived on his plantation, Belmont, and he built a townhouse for her in Charles Town. On Belmont they planted trees—magnolias, oaks, and mulberries—and Eliza continued to oversee the indigo on her plantation. Always industrious, she turned her attentions to silk.

Eliza's first child was born on February 25, 1746. They named him Charles Cotesworth Pinckney. Enthralled with motherhood, Eliza loved her baby with her famous enthusiasm and devotion.

She would order special toys from England, explaining to a friend, "To teach him according to Mr. Lock's method (which I have studied carefully) to play himself into learning." (This would be the philosopher John Locke noted earlier.) She notated all of his special developments: "Little Charles can tell all his letters in any book without hesitation and begins to spell before he is two years old."[18]

Eliza was expecting her second child in 1747. During her pregnancy, her beloved father died. Charles hid the letter from her, fearing her emotions would cause her to lose the baby. She accidentally stumbled across the letter and was so unnerved that, as Charles had predicted, the baby came early and died two weeks later. It was a little boy; ironically, the boy who was to carry her father's name.

After these tragedies, Eliza became ill and depressed. The robust, vibrant Eliza disappeared. Eventually, though, with time and faith in God, she recovered. Her faith, strong will, and resilient personality were triumphant.

A bouncing baby girl was Eliza's next baby born on August 8, 1748. They named her Harriott, and her little brother, Thomas, was born on October 23, 1750. Eliza was a loving, nurturing, and dedicated mother. She was also their educator and mentor. She savored motherhood in the same fashion she had relished running the plantation.

In 1753 the Pinckneys set sail to England. Charles was to negotiate on behalf of the colonies. An entrepreneur at heart, Eliza took to England three gowns made of her homegrown silks. One gown was for the Queen Mother, another was for the Lady of Lord Chesterfield, and one was for herself. They enjoyed the cultural and social aspects of England. America, however, was growing restless with the looming war between England and France. Eliza and Charles worried about the solvency of their plantations and thus made the inevitable decision to return to South Carolina. The boys had been in school in England for five years. The painstaking decision was made to leave the boys in England to prepare for the famous Westminster school. Eliza, heartbroken, grieved as she left her boys behind, yet she knew how the education would benefit them in the years to come. Charles was twelve years of age, and Thomas was eight. They were her young, darling boys.

ELIZA, SINGLE MOTHER

Upon return to South Carolina, Charles tragically contracted malaria and died shortly thereafter on July 13, 1758. Shocked and sorrow laden, Eliza was a widow at the age of thirty-five with three children ages twelve, ten, and eight. In a letter to her boys she expressed, "You have met with the greatest loss, my children . . . Your dear, dear father, the best and most valuable of parents, is no more!"[19] With a vast ocean between them, it must have been devastating not to be able to comfort her boys during this time. Eliza deeply mourned the loss of Charles, who had made her "for more than fourteen years the happiest mortal upon Earth."

Eliza was once again faced with enormous challenges. Now a single mother, she was responsible for her family's income in pre-Revolutionary America. Eliza's greatest resource had been her plantations. However, they had fallen into neglect during the years she and Charles were in England. She must have recalled her father's favorite maxim, "Only a fool knows no fear; only a coward runs from the battle." And within her own soul she would have to draw on the courage of the teenage girl who had said to her father, "I am strong enough for any responsibility you may ask me to carry."

Eliza chose never to remarry, so she wrote to her boys as both mother and father. She reminded them of the importance of the "dignity of human nature." She wrote them weekly letters, shaping their character as best she could. As a single mother, Eliza was now the one responsible for providing financially for their education. She returned to the disciplines of her childhood. She rented out her townhouse and lived with her ten-year-old daughter, Harriott, on the Belmont plantation and business properties. She tutored her daughter as she focused her attention on the much-neglected Wappoo indigo crops. The weather proved to be a nemesis and she wrote to her London business agent, "Drought had brought on financial difficulties . . . All that we make from ye planting interest will hardly defray ye charges of ye plantation."[20]

Due to her unrelenting drive and willingness to work diligently, she single-handedly put her boys through extraordinarily expensive schools in England: Westminster, Christ Church, Oxford University, and then law studies in Middle Temple, London. They also studied military science at the Royal Military Academy in Caen, France. Many of the finances were provided through the thriving indigo industry Eliza had so tenaciously birthed twenty years earlier. In her childhood she had laid the foundation for her sons' welfare and career, and through her indomitable spirit and never-faltering devotion, she was a stalwart role model. Spending all of the formative years in England, Eliza's boys could have easily sympathized with the British. The boys' devotion to America was certainly the culmination of the respect and love they felt for their mother. Charles and Thomas were to become American heroes.

American Patriots

Eliza was very close to her daughter, who was her constant companion. Harriott grew to be a charming young woman and married Daniel Horry in 1768. Eliza and her family longed for an end to the tyranny of the king. Her boys were well informed, as they could visit Parliament and be privy to the debates of the enemy. Eliza's son Thomas was so fiercely devoted to America, he was nicknamed "the little rebel." Charles and Thomas returned to America, and Eliza was proud of them as they volunteered to bear arms for the colonies against England in the South Carolina militia. They dedicated their lives to passionate campaigning for independence. They became rebel leaders as they spoke against the right of Parliament to tax the colonies and called on all colonialists not to buy English goods. Eliza and her family were getting ready to risk their lives, their fortunes, and their honor for what they believed was right: independence. They began to prepare for war.

During the war, Charles and Thomas rose in rank from junior officers to friends of George Washington. They endured capture, imprisonment, and life-threatening injury. Their wives were subjected to the ravages of war as well. Charles had married in 1773, and Thomas, most assuredly a romantic, decided to get married in the middle of the war in 1779.

In the spring of 1779 the English started their advance to South Carolina. In May the troops attacked Thomas Pinckney's plantation. Eliza had thought this plantation would never be in danger and had moved all of her belongings and valuables to his home. The entire place was raided and demolished. Thomas reported to Eliza, "They took with them all the best horses they could find, burnt the dwelling house and books, destroyed all the furniture, china, etc., killed the sheep and poultry and drank the liquors."[21]

In 1780 Charles was taken prisoner during a battle in Charles Town. In the Battle of Camden, Thomas's leg was badly hurt by a musket ball, and for weeks he fought for his life. Eliza was living with her daughter at Hampton Plantation. One day, after fighting the English at Georgetown, Colonel Francis Marion, the famous Swamp Fox, arrived at Hampton on his horse, hungry and exhausted. Eliza and Harriott rushed to fix him a hot meal as he slept. In hot pursuit, the enemy stampeded toward their house. Eliza rushed the Swamp Fox out the back door just as the English burst through the front door. He hid as the English soldiers ate his hot meal, meandered through Harriott's library, and then disappeared. With the girls' help, the Swamp Fox had outmaneuvered them again. Finally, on December 14, 1782, the English flag was no longer flying over Charles Town. And there was great rejoicing!

The revolution had not been without sacrifice for Americans, and this included Eliza. She wrote of the war, "Both my sons, their wives and infants were exiled . . . [my estate] was shattered and ruined . . . nor had I in Country or Town a place to lay my head . . . all was taken from me, nor was I able to hire a lodging."[22] Harriott had lost her husband, and Charles had lost his wife.

Eliza's Successful Sons

After the Revolution, Eliza's boys continued to serve their country in its infancy. Charles Pinckney became a delegate from South Carolina to the Federal Constitutional Convention in Philadelphia in 1787 and participated in the drafting of the Constitution of the United States. Thomas Pinckney became the governor of South Carolina. They both were instrumental in getting the federal constitution ratified by the South Carolina Convention in 1788. Thomas presided over the convention as well.

He followed in his mother's footsteps. Eager to improve the quality of cattle, he began crossbreeding his cattle with imported breeds. He also built dikes to hold back seawater so rice could be more adequately cultivated.

Charles Pinckney was extended the prestigious invitation of serving as either Washington's secretary of state, his secretary of war, or to serve on the Supreme Court. Charles felt his obligation was to his state, however, and he declined the opportunities. Eliza was proud of both Charles's honorable invitations and his commitment to South Carolina.

In 1792 Thomas was appointed by George Washington as minister to Great Britain. Thomas achieved many diplomatic successes. One such victory was when, as special envoy to Spain, he negotiated a treaty that established commercial relations between the two countries. He settled boundary disputes regarding the Spanish territory bordering the United States, and he solidified the right for the United States to have the freedom to navigate the Mississippi, as well as having the entitlement to utilize New Orleans as a port of entry. Meanwhile, Charles became the minister to France, a major general, and the Federalist candidate for president two times.

Wow! The contributions Eliza's sons made to our country are mesmerizing. The contribution Eliza made as a single mother to nurture and guide their greatness is monumental. Eliza's teenage triumphs with indigo laid the foundation for her children's inspiration, determination, and successes. Her bravery, exhibited during the emotional depths of her life, were witnessed by her children and whispered into their spirits. Eliza's courage, love, and loyalty to her children, her colony, and ultimately her country served as motivational momentum, propelling her sons to higher ground.

During the last years of her life, Eliza lived with her beloved daughter, Harriott. Eliza had lost all of her material possessions during the war. Her home had been desecrated during the British invasion, and everything in her home had been demolished. Her cattle had been killed to satisfy the British soldiers' appetites, and the beautiful oak trees she had lovingly planted had been chopped down and used for firewood. Her Charles Town home had been confiscated as well. Eliza, who had shared her dream, her vision, and her fortune with others to make her colony prosper, was now bankrupt. She had no money to restore her property from the ravages of war. She was rich, however, in dignity, reputation, and accomplishment. No one could take that away from her. Eliza also had the most valuable asset, and truly the only one that matters—love. She loved her children and grandchildren, and they loved her. She was proud of her children and reveled in their character and accomplishments. She surely took pride in her participation in the nurturing of those traits. As William Rose Wallace said, "The hand that rocks the cradle rules the world." How different the hue of our country would have been had Eliza not found the fortitude to carry the torch when her husband died.

Eliza's Death and Legacy

In 1791 President Washington visited Eliza at her daughter Harriott's home. He commended her for her contributions to her country and applauded her for the brilliancy of her sons and her family's bravery during the war. In April 1793 Eliza, battling breast cancer, traveled to Philadelphia to visit a doctor renowned for his knowledge of cancer. She died in Philadelphia at the age of seventy on May 26, 1793, in the presence of her granddaughter.

On May 27, 1793, Eliza's funeral was held in Philadelphia in St. Peter's Episcopal Church. President Washington, at his request, was a pallbearer. She was buried in Philadelphia. One of her final comments was, "I now see my children grown up, and blessed be God! See them such as I hoped."[23] What a blessing for a woman who blessed so many.

Eliza was an extraordinary visionary, planter, patriot, single mother. She suffered overwhelming challenges when her father, her baby, and her beloved husband died. She, however, held her head high and met those challenges for her children, her colony, and her country. She was self-sacrificing whenever the call of duty demanded it, whether it was as a teenage girl given the responsibility to cultivate a plantation, in the demands of providing for her children as a single mother, or as a patriot fighting for her country.

LIFE LESSON: DARE TO DREAM

Eliza teaches us that positive, life-enriching dreams are the visions of God in our hearts to use the gifts He has given us. He has planted the seeds of inspiration within us. We simply need to muster the courage to manifest them. Eliza dreamed but she also recognized the sacrifices needed to accomplish her dreams. The road less traveled that Eliza journeyed was filled with heartache, disappointment, and unquenchable determination.

All dreamers who have manifested their visions have done so with much toil and labor. We, as single mothers, have a special and unique journey. Like Eliza, for whatever reason, we have arrived to greet our fates as both mother and father. This is not a burden. It simply means we have an added helping of God's sweet blessings. He walks with us as our Partner and our children's Father. Why would God give us a dream and then abandon His cause? He would not and He does not.

Another message we may glean from Eliza is that the actions of our lives reflect upon our children. As we accomplish our missions, our children are watching. We owe it to them to teach them that attaining our dreams is our destiny. In response, they will learn that attaining their dreams is their destiny. Eliza's resiliency with indigo rewarded not just her and her colony but eventually, and unknown to her at the time, her children. Eliza didn't realize the far-reaching benefits her indigo endeavors would bequeath, but God did, because God sees eternity in perspective.

So dare to dream. Teach your children how to dream. Teach them how to listen to the inner voice of God, beckoning their talents to awaken. Clasp hands with your children and pray for knowledge of His will. Assure your children that they are unique and special. Dream together and reach for your God-given destinies.

*I find it requires great care and attention to attend
to a Carolina estate, though but a moderate one and
to do one's duty, and make all turn to account.*[24]

—ELIZA PINCKNEY

ISABELLA MARSHALL GRAHAM

Benevolent Single Mother

1742–1814

SNAPSHOT	Isabella, the only calm harbor for a sinking boat, quoting Scripture as she holds her baby with one arm and her three children with the other
MOTHER MOMENT	Thrusting her hands toward the heavens, saying, "I wish you joy, my darling!" as her daughter takes her last breath
CHALLENGE	Death of her husband
STEWARDSHIP	Tirelessly dedicated her life to widows and orphans
SCRIPTURE	"Let the LORD be glorified, that we may see your joy!" (Isaiah 66:5 NIV)

CHAPTER NINE

Put God First

*Art thou my Husband? Art thou the Father of my
fatherless children? Wilt thou be the stay of these orphans,
and their and my shield in a strange land?*

—ISABELLA GRAHAM

Widows and orphans. Poverty and disease. Mysterious illnesses and maddening, misguided medical techniques. Pony express and inaccessibilities. New York City in the 1700s. An era on the brink of enlightenment.

Isabella Marshall Graham was a woman who lived, like Rachel Lavein and Eliza Pinckney, in the mid-eighteenth century. Isabella leapt off the page of my research papers with her intensity of faith. She had every reason in the world to curl up into the fetal position and spend her days in the darkness of depression. But she did not. Isabella chose the Light. She chose to reach for her Savior from her bottomless pit of despair. She relished God's Word, and with a fervent, passionate fire of faith, she walked in His grace.

Isabella had to be included in this book due to her unlimited and unrelenting hope, coupled with her tenacious determination to hold her head high. She reached out and helped others who were suffering as she had suffered. She had immense empathy; and she not only felt it, she acted on it. It's lovely to sit on the sofa and cry for another's sorrows, but it's courageous to get up and pound the pavement from dawn until dusk as Isabella did. She prayed with the overwhelmed, she fed the hungry, she provided for the destitute. Isabella didn't just talk the talk, she walked the walk. If she had been a Catholic, she most assuredly would have been named a saint.

My pastor, Dr. John McKellar, told a humorous yet pointed tale of two boys fighting over who would get their mother's first peanut-butter-and-jelly sandwich. As they wrestled on the floor, the mother interceded and said, "Boys, boys! Now, is this the way Jesus would act? What would Jesus do?"

The older boy guiltily responded, "He would give his brother the first sandwich."

To this, the younger boy replied, "That's right! That's right! Okay, now, *you* be Jesus!"

That sums up the majority. Everyone wants someone else to be Jesus. In fact, the majority of people rely on others to be Jesus. Very few actually mirror Jesus' acts of passion, purpose, and selfless concern for others. And yet, Isabella was such a reflection. So as we proceed into her life, hold on to your hat, for Isabella was a firestorm of faith.

Timeless Scenario: Girl born to middle-class family in Scotland. Girl finds God at age seventeen. Girl falls in love with boy. Girl and boy get married. Girl and boy have children. Boy dies. Girl is extremely grieved. Girl must provide for her children and ailing, penniless father. Girl moves to America. Girl is fiercely dedicated to God. Girl commits her life to her children, widows, and to the less fortunate.

Isabella's Tragedies

Isabella Marshall Graham was born on July 29, 1742, in the shire of Lanark, Scotland. There are not too many details regarding her youth. She was raised in the Church of Scotland. At the age of ten she was sent to boarding school, where she resided for seven winters. It was during her lonesome times at boarding school that Isabella confessed her faith in God. She was seventeen years old.

Upon graduating from school, Isabella fell in love and married Dr.

John Graham when she was twenty-three years old. She had experienced two advantages over her contemporaries at this point: she had been educated, and she was able to choose the man she married. John was a practicing physician. After a year of marriage, Isabella and John had a baby boy. Shortly thereafter, Dr. Graham was appointed as surgeon to the 60th Royal American Regiment. He was ordered to Canada, and they moved to Montreal. Isabella left her infant son with her mother in Scotland because the hardships of the trip would be too much for him to bear.

After they arrived in Montreal, she gave birth to her eldest daughter, Jessie. Around this time she received word that her baby son had died. This was the first of Isabella's many despairs. It is hard to imagine how Isabella felt, having to receive this news posthumously. The shock must have been paralyzing and the regret indescribable. There was absolutely no way to communicate and alter any decision or outcome.

With little time to adjust, John was transferred to Lake Ontario, where Isabella gave birth to her second and third daughters, Joanna and Isabella. Then once again they moved. On November 5, 1772, they relocated to Antigua (birthplace of Eliza Pinckney). In 1773 Isabella received word that her mother had died. How remorseful deaths were during these times—one couldn't hop on a plane for one last good-bye before a loved one departed. This was combined with the impossibility of being there for the funeral. The letters arrived too late, the bodies could not wait, and it would take too long to get there. Isabella, by the age of thirty-one, had lost a baby son and her mother. But the worst was yet to come.

In 1775 in Antigua, John became ill. Isabella recounted the utter horror and helplessness of the situation word for word in a letter to a family member. He was overcome by a putrid fever and languished in the cabin in a helpless state. With John seemingly recovering, yet not quite well, the island doctor gave him a potion of some sort. This medicine induced a fit of hiccups that didn't abate for days. Isabella sat beside her husband helplessly. After a tormenting fight, he eventually died.

Isabella was besieged with grief. She held on to him and kissed him over and over again. She recalls how she was haunted and kept thinking she was hearing his footsteps coming up the stairs. She wrote, "But oh, the pangs I felt upon my first awakening. I could not for some time believe it was true that I was indeed a widow, and that I had lost my heart's treasure—my all I held dear on earth." She recounts how she didn't really believe John was dead, even though the doctor had pronounced him so. She was completely alone on a foreign island and knew nothing of the customs or trustworthiness of the people. She thought she saw color in his cheeks and made the doctor inspect him over and over again. She was bereft that she had let them bury him so quickly, which was not the tradition in Scotland. At the age of thirty-three Isabella was all alone with three children, the oldest only five years of age, and she was pregnant with another. She became obsessed that they had buried him alive. Those who cared for her finally had her husband's grave reopened so she could see there were no signs of life in his body. At this juncture, she finally accepted the reality of her husband's death. She dressed in widow's clothes and vowed to never marry again. And she did not.

ISABELLA, SINGLE MOTHER

Thus at the age of thirty-three Isabella was a single mother in a foreign country with three children and another child soon to be born. She was immobilized with grief, with fear, and was essentially penniless. All she had was two hundred pounds sterling. Worrying now about her children in the event of her own death, she wrote her father a letter regarding their lives and their upbringing should she die.

My only concern and prayer to God for them is that they may be taught early to love God and serve him; that they may fall into such hands as will carefully instruct them in the principles of morality and religion, and teach them the great, but too little thought of truth, that our chief business in life is to prepare for death. As to the polite parts of education, I Look upon them as of no consequence; that they may be as good Christians, perhaps better, without than with them; the perfection of their nature no way depends upon them. I am equally indifferent what station of life they may occupy, whether they swim in affluence or earn their daily bread, if they act properly, and obtain the approbation of their God, in that station where in he, in his infinite wisdom, sees fit to place them. Remember to give my love to all my dear children.

Soon after her husband's death, she gave birth to her son. This was surely an emotional event. With no reason to stay in Antigua, Isabella dispersed all her belongings and secured all her remaining money in the hands of Major Brown, requesting a safe passage to Scotland. She decided to journey back to her homeland and to the security of her father's love and comfortably affluent domain.

With a newborn baby, Isabella boarded a boat and journeyed alone across the sea to Ireland. This was not a common feat for a woman during the 1700s. She, with her God, was the sole keeper of her four children, all under the age of five—daughters Jessie, Joanna, Isabella, and her newborn son. They arrived safely in Ireland; yet they were vulnerable in regard to a safe passage to Scotland. Isabella didn't know who to trust or where to turn. They happened upon a boat that, unknown to them, didn't even have a compass. The boat encountered a storm and the passengers were all tossed violently to and fro for nine hours. The rudder and mast were ripped from the boat and everything on deck was plunged into the sea. The vessel eventually struck a rock in the middle of the night. Everyone on the boat was in complete chaos and panic, wailing and screaming. Everyone except Isabella. There she stood, calm and composed, holding her baby boy, consoling her weeping children. She soothed them with words of faith and that soon they would see their daddy. Passengers were writing their names in their pocketbooks so that their bodies would be recognized.

A young man entered the cabin and screamed, "Is there no peace here?" He was surprised to find Isabella stoically reciting Scripture and praying with her children. Soon the young man joined her and read Psalm 107 with her: "He maketh the storm a calm, so that the waves thereof are still" (v. 29 KJV). Miraculously, the boat came off the rock, and though filled with water, floated safely to a sand bank. When they arrived, Isabella promptly went to a private room to pray.

When Isabella finally reached Scotland, she expected to find her father in his ancient mansion. Instead she found him broke and in ill health. Isabella had hoped to find some peace and tranquility in her father's hands. Instead she encountered a man-child and, thus, she gracefully added him to the list of her dependents. Isabella had returned home without money or income except for her small widow's pension of sixteen pounds sterling. What did she do? She leaned upon Jesus, whom she dearly loved. She prayed, "Humble yourselves, therefore, under God's mighty hand, that he may lift you up in due time. Cast all your anxiety on him because he cares for you" (1 Peter 5:6–7 NIV).

I find those words soothing today. Faith is timeless. God answered her prayers and she eventually found a job. With her respectable education and fine mind, Isabella taught in a small school and provided modestly for her four children and her father. With a meek income, she did what she had to do. She rolled up her sleeves and dressed her children in homespun cloth, sold the butter she made, and fed her children on milk. They ate a breakfast of her homemade bread and porridge and a dinner of potatoes and salt. With her last few bits of savings, she was convinced to invest in muslins. Sadly, the ship carrying the muslins was captured and the items confiscated by the French.

Educated, humble, resolute, and pious, Isabella's services were eagerly sought. She was offered the opportunity to run either a boarding school or a boarding house. She turned to the Lord and for a day fasted and prayed diligently. She asked for "a light for her feet and a lamp for her path" (see Psalm 119:105) and for God "to lead her in the way she should go" (see Isaiah 48:17). She decided upon the boarding house in Edinburgh and teaching youth. She was so overwrought with the decision, however, she ended up in a fever for weeks. Making decisions as a single mother, having no one with whom to confer, can be insurmountably frightening at times. She rebounded, however, and trusted that God would provide her with the financial means to bring this job to fruition.

Isabella sold all her heavy furniture and packed up all her belongings. As she was sitting by the fire, contemplating how she was going to make this new adventure work financially, she received a letter that enclosed a sum of money. It was the money from the underwriters who had insured Isabella's muslins captured by the French. She had not taken out the insurance herself, but a friend had done it for her. Isabella now had the money to travel and begin her new job. The Lord had directed her path and had provided the means with which to do it. Look what God can do.

Isabella devoted her talents, time, spirit, and devotion to the new school. The gospel was a major part of the school's curriculum, and she prayed with the children morning and evening, showing them how to put God first in their lives. Her attitude was always one of happiness and cheer, and she encouraged the children to solve their problems within their own democratic world. Isabella taught with authority and tenderness, and the children were industrious, intelligent, and content.

Isabella, a single, working mother of four—really five, including her father—somehow found the time to also reach out to the less fortunate. Isabella empathized with the poor and observed that when they were sick they could not afford to provide for themselves, and yet when they were healthy they were self-sustaining. She thought of a resource that could provide for them, a way for them to help themselves. She formed a Penny Society. In this Society everyone would put a penny a week in the fund. This fund would then be used when one in the Society became ill. It grew into a self-sustaining organization and was later named The Society for the Relief of the Destitute Sick. Isabella had witnessed ill health, misfortune, death, and need in her own life, and now she was helping others learn to hold their heads high in the face of adversity.

Isabella was an intelligent, beautiful, loving, and tender mother. However, it was her unshakable faith that yielded the most power. She gave her life to the will of God and based all of her decisions on her unshakable foundation of faith. God's guiding light helped Isabella cope in an honorable way. Her faith was coupled with a willingness to work hard and be of service to others. She epitomizes what I would like to become.

THE AMERICAN DREAM

Isabella had always harbored a secret desire to immigrate to America. She believed that the Americans were pious people and that her children would flourish there. A gentleman by the name of Dr. Witherspoon visited in 1785 and encouraged Isabella's ambitions. She waited until her children had completed their courses in education and then, after much prayer, she arranged the trip. She chartered a small British vessel to carry them to New York and, once again, was wondering how she would pay for the expense of her travels. Before she departed she received a letter from a Dr. Henderson. He had been the young friend of Dr. John Graham, Isabella's husband, who had succeeded him as surgeon of the regiment when Dr. Graham had died. Within the letter was "two hundred pounds bequeathed to her by Lady Glenorchy, as a mark of her regard." Once again God had shown His grace and provided for Isabella. How many miracles happen to us daily and go without notice? God is listening.

Before her departure Isabella resolved her fears through prayer. She seemed to answer her own questions with the resolve in her faith. She expressed this in the following letter that she wrote before she set sail to America:

Edinburgh, March 1789

"Leave thy fatherless children, I will preserve them alive; and let thy widows trust in me"; Jeremiah 49:11. The Lord's promise, which he made to me in the days of my widowhood, and which I have made the subject of my prayers from day to day, taking the words in a spiritual sense. The Lord has done wonders for me and mine since the day I was left a widow with three orphans, and the fourth not born, in a strange land, without money, at a distance from friends; or rather without friends.

Hitherto he has supplied all my wants, and laid to hand every necessary and many comforts; supporting character and credit, making a way for me through the wilderness, pointing out my path, and settling the bounds of my habitation. For all these blessings I desire to be grateful to the God of providence, whose is the earth and the fullness thereof . . . The salvation and the life I have wrestled for is that which Christ has died to purchase, and lives to bestow—even spiritual life and salvation from sin. My God knows I have held fast this view of the words, seeking first the kingdom of God for my children, leaving temporals to be given or withheld, as may best suit with the conversion and sanctification of their souls. I have not asked for them health, beauty, riches, honor, or temporal life; God knows what of these consists with their better interests; let him give or withhold accordingly. One thing I have asked of the Lord, one thing only, and will persist in asking, trust in him for, and for which I think I have his promise—even the life of their and my soul. 1 Thessalonians 5:23 is my petition for me and mine; verse 24, my anchor of hope, preceded by Jeremiah 49:11.

In July 1789 Isabella once again exhibited her bravery and took on the majestic dangers of the sea. She traveled as a single mother, alone with her three girls. She had left her son in Scotland to finish his education. Isabella crossed the Atlantic to America and landed in New York on September 8, 1789. She was forty-seven years old. She opened her school on October 5, 1789, one short month after arriving in a foreign land. She opened with five children, and by the end of the same month she had fifty children enrolled. Her school was once again a success as she applied the same principles she'd had in her school in Scotland. Her school became so respected that even George Washington visited it.

Isabella's eldest daughter, Jessie, had made a profession of religion in Scotland, following in her mother's footsteps. She was married in New York to Mr. Hay Stevenson. Isabella's other two daughters, Joanna and Isabella, joined the church in 1791. She wrote,

This same day, for the second time, have my two daughters sat down at the redeemer's table among his professing people, and I have reason to think, given their hearty assent to his covenant. Glory! Glory! Glory! To hear the hearer of prayer. I seek first my four children and myself, first of all, "the kingdom of God."

In September 1791 Isabella wrote, "The Lord has made me a grandmother, assisted my poor weakly girl, and gave a son to her and my arms. There was joy that a man child was born into the world." Isabella's son became an apprentice in the merchant service. He was shipwrecked, and a friend helped him get to New York so that he could visit his mother. He was there for some months, but Isabella encouraged him to complete his duty. He embarked back to Greenock. As she watched her only son honorably depart, she was terribly saddened.

Isabella had the gift of writing, and she proficiently expressed her thought, faith, and devotions in her letters. A beautiful example of how she persevered as a single mother is eloquently expressed in the following letter:

October 3, 1793, New York
    He has taught me that I could not walk a moment alone. This is now my fixed faith; and in proportion as I keep it in sight, I walk safely; but I still forget, and still stumble and still fall; but I am lifted up and taught lesson after lesson; and I shall stumble and shall fall while sin is in me; but the last stumble shall come, and the last stripe shall be laid on, and the last lesson taught, and that which concerns me shall be perfected. O! then shall I look back, and see "all the way by which he has led me, to prove me and try me, and show me what was in my heart, that he might do me good in my latter end." I am often, even in this valley of darkness and ignorance, allowed this retrospective view; and am led. O say not one word of all that he promised has failed.

The Pain of Loss

In 1793 Isabella heard the grievous news that her son had been very ill of a fever and had consequently been subjected to epileptic fits. How tormenting it must have been to be so far away from her ailing son, with no source of communication other than a dubious letter. With no other resources at her disposal, Isabella wrote to him and begged for his return:

> Your mother and all your sisters are willing to follow his example; return to us, my son. We will watch over you, we will pray over you, and we will try, by every endearing method, to restore you not only to health but to comfort. Your sisters wish you to come; all your friends are willing to receive you; we will not upbraid you. Do, my dear, leave Greenock; come out to us by any way you can find, I will pay your passage here; or if you can get to any port in America, you can write me from that, and I will get you forwarded here; and, after you are here, if you still wish to follow the sea we can get you a berth in some trading vessel from this. All your friends here send best wishes, And now, my son, I commend you to the Lord. Oh, that he may bless this to you.
>
> Your affectionate mother, I. Graham.

The last letter Isabella received from her son was dated in 1794 from Demarara. He said that he had been taken by the French and retaken by the English. He had arrived in Demarara on the ship *Hope*. He said that should he not hear from his mother he would return to Europe. The helplessness Isabella must have felt. If only her letters could reach him in time. She heard later that he had ended up in a French prison and most likely died there. Isabella wept and prayed that "her great redeemer had taken care of him and would finally save her prodigal son."

In 1795 Isabella encountered a joyous time. Her second daughter was getting married. She then, however, encountered a disastrous time. Her eldest daughter died after struggling with a fatal sickness. Isabella was steadfast by her bedside. Her daughter sang a hymn of triumph about going to see her Lord until death silenced her voice. Isabella displayed great courage and bravery during these last moments, and when the spirit of her daughter left, she thrust her hands toward the heavens and exclaimed, "I wish you joy, my darling." She was joyous at the full salvation of her daughter, but afterward she became absolutely overcome with despair. She didn't bounce back in her usual resilient way, and she prayed to God, saying, "Why, O why is my spirit still depressed? Why these sobs? Father, forgive . . ." She reminisced about her daughter, saying, "She was my pleasant companion, my affectionate child; my soul feels a want. O fill it up with more of thy presence; give yet more communication of thyself." Once again Isabella had no husband with whom to grieve. Alone she faced her sorrows. She only had her God, and from Him she fervently sought solace.

Reaching Out to Others

In time Isabella revived, and she once again held her head high. She had always tithed a tenth of her earnings, and she aided in forming the First Missionary Society in New York. In 1797 she joined the committee that developed the Society for the Relief of Poor Widows with Small Children. It was organized to aid the widows and orphans after the epidemics of yellow fever in 1798 and 1799. Fliers were passed out and volunteers congregated at Isabella's house. She was elected the first directress and held the office for ten years. They started with 190 subscribers donating three dollars a year. She wrote,

> We have spent three hundred dollars this winter, and nearly all upon worthy objects. The poor increase fast: emigrants from all quarters flock to us, and when they come they must not be allowed to die from want. There are eight hundred in the almshouse, and our society have helped along many, with their own industry, that must otherwise have been there. The French, poor things, are also starving among us; it would need a stout heart to lay up in these times.

She also talks of the . . .

first monthly missionary prayer meeting known to have been held in the city of New York to pray for blessings for the missionary societies. The Dutch churches, the Baptist and Presbyterian have united so far as to officiate in each others' churches; they have collected about seventeen hundred dollars, and are looking out for two missionaries to send among the Indians, or to the frontiers. Many denominations came together to help finance this worthwhile society.

It is always heartening to see Christians unite for the better cause, no matter what denomination. Isabella's vigor and persistence in helping the less fortunate is inspiring.

In 1798 Isabella's daughter Isabella was married. She had finally done it. As a single mother, she had provided for all of her children throughout the years, not just monetarily but spiritually. At this juncture, Isabella's health was waning. She decided to close her school, and she moved in with her daughter. This didn't mean that Isabella became inactive in any way. As long as she was alive, God had a purpose for her life, a mission.

Isabella became determined to help widows find work. She had a keen sense of social service, believing that just giving money was not enough, because people had pride and wanted to work. She deemed that until an institution could be formed that would provide employment opportunities for poor women who were willing to work, the work of charity would be incomplete.

Isabella was well known throughout her community and was perceived as a sort of angel. People would walk out of their homes when they saw her approaching, because they wanted to receive her blessing. She once went on a vacation for two weeks, and her neighbors and acquaintances were worried and exclaimed, "We live in the suburbs of the city, where she used to visit, relieve, and comfort the poor. We had missed her so long that we were worried she had been sick; when she walked our streets, it was customary with us to come to the door and receive her blessing as she passed."

Isabella would always pray over the money they received, asking God for His direction. "I thank thee for this sum towards the relief of thy creatures; be with us this evening, and direct our determination as to the division of it. Amen." The Society received a charter of incorporation and a small amount of aid from the legislature of the state. Isabella fervently took over the execution of the plans.

The Society purchased a small house, and it was at this house that they received work for the widows. They opened a school, as Isabella was always looking out for the education of the children. Many of her former pupils volunteered to teach. Isabella selected certain widows and employed them to open day schools for children in distant parts of the city. She also established two day schools personally. Isabella, though supposedly retired, superintended one of the schools, and she had her daughter superintend the other. Everyone in Isabella's path was put to work!

Isabella was relentless in her pursuit of helping the less fortunate and shedding God's light. If she ever saw Christians who were sick or in poverty, she would visit with them. She visited the almshouses and taught the children about the love of God. Isabella was now elderly and in ill health, but this did not stop her. She would leave the house at eight in the morning, with only a few rolls of bread and an orange, and would not return until eight in the evening. She might have some soup on the days she visited the soup house established for the Humane Society.

In 1804 Isabella was asked to speak to a group of young ladies. She certainly knew how to rally the troops.

My Dear Young Ladies,

Everything new becomes matter of speculation and variety of opinion. An association of ladies for the relief of destitute widows and orphans was a new thing in this country. It was feeble in its origin, the jest of most, the ridicule of many, and it met the opposition of not a few. The men could not allow our sex the steadiness and perseverance necessary to establish such an undertaking. But God put "his" seal upon it; and under his fostering care it has prospered beyond the most sanguine expectations of its propagators. Its fame is spread over the United States, and celebrated in foreign countries. It has been a precedent to many cities, who have followed the laudable example. This fame is not more brilliant than just. The hungry are fed, the naked are clothed, shelter is provided for the outcasts; medicine and cordials for the sick, and the soothing voice of sympathy cheers the disconsolate. Who are the authors of all these blessings? Your mothers, ladies, the benevolent members of this so justly famed Society. . . . A great general, in ancient times, in search of glory, landed his troops on the hostile coast, and then burnt all his ships, they must conquer or die. You have, ladies, already embarked in this design; there is no remaining neuter now; your name and undertaking are in every mouth; you must press forward and justify your cause; and justified it shall be if you persevere; it cannot be otherwise.

The winter of 1804–1805 was especially severe, fuel was scarce, and the poor suffered tremendously. Isabella, now sixty-two, ventured into the cold and the darkest parts of New York City, visiting almost two hundred families either by foot or on horseback. If she found a Bible she would pray with them, and if they didn't have a Bible she would give them one.

Again Isabella was called to chair a new society, the Asylum for Orphan Children. She was still deeply involved with the Widows Society, but she felt compassion for the Orphan Asylum. She or one of her daughters or family members taught the children daily until funds were sufficient to provide a teacher. They purchased land and built a house for these children. Like the Energizer Bunny, Isabella would also visit the New York Hospital and pray with the mentally deranged. Additionally, she visited the female convicts at the state prison. Jesus was surely proud.

Isabella participated in many other societies, too, such as the Bible Society, the Magdalen Society, Lancasterian School, the Society for the Promotion of Industry Among the Poor, and Adult Schools. Many were duly impressed and awed by Isabella's strength and generosity of spirit. However, when one would pronounce words of idolatry toward her, she would say, "There is only one Savior," or "Get thee behind me, Satan" (see Matthew 16:23). Near the end of her life, she was asked if she had any doubts about entering heaven, to which she replied,

> My dear children, I have no more doubt of going to my Savior, than if I were already in his arms; my guilt is all transferred; he has cancelled all I owed. Yet I could weep for sins against so good a God; it seems to me as if there must be weeping even in heaven for sin . . .

ISABELLA AT PEACE

When Isabella was on her deathbed, she was surrounded by her beloved family, who adored her. When the doctor visited, he commented that she was actually looking better. Someone close to Isabella said the good doctor's drugs "would prove little avail against her ardent prayers to depart and be with Christ." Isabella would awaken at times and speak the words, "Peace . . . then peace I leave with you, my peace I give unto you" (see John 14:27). It was observed that Isabella, upon her death, looked as if she were truly "falling asleep in Jesus," because her countenance was so peaceful and younger looking. She died on July 24, 1814, at the age of seventy-two. Her favorite saying was that she was a "sinner saved by grace." Etched on her epitaph were the words,

> *The other mother in Israel;*
> *Who, like Enoch, walked with God;*
> *Like Abraham, Obtained the Righteousness of Faith;*
> *And, like Paul, Finished Their Course with Joy.*

Upon her death, poetry and hymns were found in her pocket. Two of them are as follows:

Into thy hands, my Savior God,
Do I my soul resign,
In firm dependence on that truth
That made salvation mine.

The Inward Warfare

Strange and mysterious is my life!
What opposites I feel within:
A stable peace, a constant strife,
The rule of grace, the power of sin!
Too often I am captive led,
Yet daily triumph in my Head.

Isabella Graham. The word I have for her is, "Wow!" She was not an Augusta, a queen, a famous writer, a mother of a famous son, or a famous horticulturist. Her children didn't become patriots, governors, or geniuses. She was an ordinary woman with extraordinary faith. She fell into pits of despair, clawed her way out, and climbed the next mountain. She did not succumb to the dark side, because she carried the torch of her Lord. She was a simple woman who exemplified great characteristics: love, faith, hope, charity, humility—the only characteristics that truly matter. Yet they are characteristics that are so hard to attain and maintain.

Isabella was on the treadmill of stewardship, and she didn't stop until the end. Perhaps she didn't reach the masses, but she reached the person who was right in front of her. She saw her needs, her heartaches, her inner desires. She looked at the widows and the orphans and recognized their hunger, their pain, their sufferings, and she offered them hope. She had felt their pain, and she believed she was alive to alleviate that pain. Mutual healing is the blessing of stewardship. You know that good, fuzzy feeling you get when you help a blind person across the street or give money to a homeless person? I believe that feeling is the essence of Jesus and the element that binds all humanity.

LIFE LESSON: PUT GOD FIRST

Isabella wore many hats. She was a single mother. She was the sole provider for her children, financially and emotionally. She was a schoolteacher. She was one of the first people to structure charitable activities with the foresight of institutional planning. She was a diligent disciple. In all of her endeavors, Isabella vehemently, passionately, and admirably put God first. He was first in regard to her desires for her children's welfare, in the curriculum with her school children, and in her charitable activities. She was unwavering in her determination to honor her God.

Isabella exhibited actions that emulated God's compassion. She would leave her house and pray over those in need for twelve hours a day. She reached out to people individually, not en masse. Never should the singular efforts of one person be underestimated. Candles are lit one flame at a time. She prayed over every person she met, and she breathed the spirit of God into their lives. Could anything be more valuable? God's works don't have to be spectacular; they only have to be sincere.

Isabella could die peacefully because she knew she had the love of her God, and she knew that she had lived her life for Him. She had represented Him with her head held high. Isabella was a single mother, yet her capacity for love and nurturing was that of an army. She managed to couple all of her charitable acts with the greatest blessing she had ever received, her children. She provided for her children financially, but more importantly she witnessed the true meaning of life. Her children adored her. They felt as if they were blessed to be in her presence. What better attribute could a mother imbue?

Isabella demonstrated a life built on the foundation of faith and the essence of charity. How hard it is for us to put God first today. We are so obsessed with speed, entertainment, self, cell phones, e-mails, news flashes, that we forget to look around and see who may be in need. And it may be something as simple as a smile or a hug.

Do we really see other people? We get so busy that we ease God out of our lives. We become so self-absorbed that the attribute of compassion gets tarnished. How often do we reflect about God throughout the day? It's very hard. And yet, putting God first is essential to spiritual health and a productive life.

My goal is to love God first and seek first His will for my life. It is scary to turn my will over to the care of God, but the irony of letting go is that God always has something better in mind than I could possibly imagine. God sees eternity in perspective. It doesn't happen, however, unless I quit trying to run the show. He can't get in unless I make room for Him.

So put God first and defy modern society. Show your children how to put Him first, and watch them reap the rewards of confidence and serenity. Actually *see* the person beside you. That person is a child of God too. Put God first and perform an act of His compassion. The result will be mesmerizing.

> *There is no remaining neuter now; your name and undertaking*
> *are in every mouth; you must press forward and justify your cause;*
> *and justified it shall be if you persevere; it cannot be otherwise.*
>
> —ISABELLA GRAHAM

ELIZABETH TIMOTHY

Resourceful Single Mother

?–1757

SNAPSHOT	Printing her statement about her new editorial status as a single mother, pregnant, and with six children wrapped around her legs
MOTHER MOMENT	Brilliantly editing and printing the paper in her son's name
CHALLENGE	Left alone to provide for her children and publish a newspaper
STEWARDSHIP	Used her newspaper to shape her children and her colony
SCRIPTURE	If someone forces you to go one mile, go with him two miles. (Mathew 5:41 NIV)

CHAPTER TEN

Go the Extra Mile

Elizabeth . . . managed the business with such success that she not only brought up a . . . family of children, but . . . was able to purchase of me the printing house and establish her son in it.[1]

—BENJAMIN FRANKLIN

Sail boats and ocean breezes. Burgeoning America. Horses and hot air. Flies and ink vapor. Hustle and bustle. Carriages crisscross. Clippity clop. Clippity clop. Messengers run by foot relaying all the news that is fit to print. Physical labor meets exhaustion. Deadlines loom.

Elizabeth Timothy exuded the revolutionary spirit that made our country great and made women relevant. Her life chronicles a single mother in the early 1700s. Upon her husband's demise, she took his business by the reins and became the first female newspaper editor and publisher on the American continent and one of the first female journalists in the world. She accomplished this feat solely on her own as a single mother, with six children by her side, and she did it even better than her late husband had done. Research doesn't provide much about the emotional realm of Elizabeth's life, or even her date of birth; it's rather dry in that regard. It does, however, give us a glimpse into her professional life.

Elizabeth's contributions to her family, her colony, her country, and the society of women were far-reaching and significant. Her intention was most assuredly not to become a woman of fame in the history books. Her intention was simply to feed her family, honor her contract with Benjamin Franklin, and maintain the newspaper business for her son. Without even intending to do so, Elizabeth was a hallmark pioneer for women in the journalistic world. She proved that women could do a man's job and that they could even do it better.

Timeless scenario: Girl meets boy in Holland. Girl and boy fall in love. Girl and boy marry. Girl and boy have seven children. Girl and boy move to America. Boy dies. Girl has hungry children. Girl is revolutionary. Girl takes over business. Girl surpasses all expectations.

ELIZABETH'S EARLY YEARS

There is an interesting tidbit of history that involves Elizabeth's life. In 1685 King Louis repealed the Edict of Nantes, which had promised religious freedom to French citizens. The result of this blunder was a mass exodus from France of citizens called Huguenots. Some of these Huguenots decided to sail for America, the land of religious freedom. Earlier in the century, in 1629, Sir Robert Heath had been the lucky beneficiary of King Charles's generosity in England. Heath was granted a vast amount of land, covering the area from Virginia to the boundary of Spanish Florida. Heath negotiated with the influx of Huguenots to colonize the "Carolana" region.

Elizabeth Timothy's future father-in-law was one of the Huguenots who left France. He, however, immigrated to Holland instead of America. He taught his son, Louis, to be a printer. During his apprenticing years, Louis met Elizabeth, a Holland native.

She had been educated in Holland, specializing in accounting business methods. Elizabeth and Louis courted, fell in love, and married in 1722. In 1731, in search of a better life and perhaps better weather, they sailed from Rotterdam, Holland, to Philadelphia in the Penn Colony. They sailed on the *Britannia of London* with their four children, Peter, Louis, Charles, and Mary, ages one to six.

Louis sought a job as a printer and found employment with the brilliant patriot Benjamin Franklin. Franklin encouraged entrepreneurship and inspired capable printers to branch out and represent his paper, the *Gazette*, in other colonies. With a desire to, perhaps, join fellow Huguenots and pursue better opportunities, Louis and Elizabeth journeyed to South Carolina after two years in Philadelphia. They moved to Charles Town, and Louis purchased the *Gazette* from the estate of Whitmarsh, a former employee of Franklin's.

Louis then entered into a business arrangement with Benjamin Franklin, who furnished the printing press and other equipment and paid one-third of the expenses, receiving one-third of the profits. The term was for six years. In 1733 Louis reopened the *Gazette* on Church Street, and in 1734 he Americanized his name to Lewis Timothy. They joined, as a family, St. Philip's Anglican Church, and in 1736 Lewis obtained a six-hundred-acre land grant. Land was vast and generous in the 1700s.

From Homemaker to History Maker

During Christmas in 1738, Lewis died unexpectedly in a tragic accident. Overnight Elizabeth's life was forever altered. She had been a wife and mother. Now she would either have to remarry, losing legal authority over her children in the process, or take over the helm of the newspaper business and become a working, single mother. Choosing the latter, Elizabeth stepped out of the anonymity of motherhood straight into the history books. She became the colony's first female printer, as well as sole provider for her six children. Then pregnant with her seventh child, Elizabeth took over the responsibility of fulfilling the last year of the six-year contract with Franklin and maintaining the integrity of the paper for her thirteen-year-old son, printing the paper in his name. Elizabeth's challenge was writing and editing a paper primarily read by men. Ironically, she was thrust into a man's world where women had no voice and were not even allowed to vote. Unabashed due to necessity, Elizabeth manned the printing press with her children clinging to her ink-stained apron skirts.

Clever and astute, Elizabeth must have known that society might balk at a woman being responsible for relaying the news to Charles Town. She wasn't going to be just a hired hand or partner; she was the editor in chief, the printer, the decision maker. She would handpick which articles were newsworthy, informative, and educational. She was in a powerful position to sway the readers' minds. Were men really going to read what a woman had selected for them to read? Elizabeth didn't adhere to pretenses; she simply printed the following statement and added a plea for an opportunity to provide for her family.

> Whereas the late Printer of this gazette hath been deprived of his life by an Unhappy Accident, I take this opportunity of informing the Publick, that I shall continue the said Paper; and hope, by the Assistance of my friends to make it entertaining and correct as may be reasonably expected . . . be kindly please to continue their favors and good offices to his poor afflicted widow and six small children and another hourly expected.[2]

Elizabeth, surely ridden with sorrow, had no time to waste as the sole provider of her six children's emotional, spiritual, physical, and financial well-being. And the stress may have affected her seventh child. The baby may have died of premature birth, because it didn't appear in any later documentation. Elizabeth prevailed, however, and with amazing aptitude and success. She always delivered the paper on time, even through more tragedies. She lost two of her sons to yellow fever in 1739, only a year after her husband had died. She experienced three crippling deaths in only one year. The magnitude of emotional turmoil is beyond comprehension. Her stamina and inner sense of fortitude must have been immense. She was essentially incapable of mourning for a lengthy time, because her remaining children had to be fed, and the paper had to be printed. She was their only hope. There was no one else to do it for her.

Respected Businesswoman

Elizabeth not only managed to defeat despair, she reigned victorious with her renegade ways. Her husband had printed the paper only once a week, but Elizabeth published the paper every Monday and Thursday. She must have been clever, inspired, and tenacious, indicated by the fact that she didn't need to print the paper more than once a week. She chose to due to her fervor, her desire to be respected, and the fact that two papers a week resulted in twice the amount of income. She physically printed it with the assistance of her son, because the printing process was tedious and laborious. The type was set by hand, one letter at a time, then locked in place, inked, and printed one sheet at a time on an antiquated hand-fed press. Elizabeth didn't print just for the *Gazette* either. She was also the official printer for the province. She printed books, pamphlets, and documents for the Assembly.

Elizabeth maintained this pace for eight years, 1738–1746. She could have easily chosen to maintain the status quo and print politically correct material, and she would have been excused from the choice due to her necessity to provide for her children. Yet, she did not shy away from the relevant, controversial, and socially conscious issues of the day. She went the extra mile and printed stories that dealt with the harsh treatment and punishment of slaves in South Carolina. She published stories about the 1739 yellow fever epidemic and she supported Eliza Pinckney's dream of indigo becoming the official crop of South Carolina. She even printed Eliza's "Instructions on the Cultivation of Indigo." Many of her articles were respected and reprinted, some by none other than Benjamin Franklin.

Benjamin Franklin had not been impressed with Timothy Lewis's business acumen, and in his biography he expressed that Timothy was ignorant in matters of account and that he never received satisfactory remittances. In contrast, Elizabeth proved to be quite the businesswoman. She promptly made her payments to Franklin. Duly impressed, Franklin wrote that Elizabeth

. . . continues to account with the greatest regularity and exactitude every quarter afterwards and managed the business with such success that she not only brought up a . . . family of children, but at the expiration of the term [of partnership agreement between Franklin and Lewis] was able to purchase of me the printing house and establish her son in it.[3]

Elizabeth didn't rest on her laurels after her son Peter took over the paper at the age of twenty-one in 1746. She opened her own book and stationery store on King Street, announcing in an ad in the *Gazette* that she sold pocket Bibles, spellers, primers, and books entitled *Reflections on Courtship and Marriage*, *Armstrong's Poem on Health*, *The Westminster Confession and Faith*, and *Watts Psalms and Hymns*. She operated this shop for a year.

Once again a strong, revolutionary, groundbreaking single mother produced a politically active son who participated in the birthing of America. In 1776 Peter served as secretary of the Constitutional Congress, which wrote the South Carolina State Constitution. He was also one of the founders of the Charles Town Library and belonged to the Charles Town Library Society established in 1748. Loyal and respectful of his father's friend Benjamin Franklin, Peter encouraged people to buy Franklin's lightning rod, and he even named his son Benjamin Franklin Timothy.

In Elizabeth's Footsteps

On April 2, 1757, Elizabeth returned to Charles Town after an absence, wrote her will, and died within a month. Her few possessions included two French Bibles and money totaling twenty-five pounds. She left to her children a large tract of land with three houses. Peter continued to run the paper until the British invaded Charles Town in 1781, when he closed the paper and moved his family to Philadelphia.

After the war, in 1782, in order to get his paper refinanced, Peter sailed with his two daughters to Santo Domingo. Disastrously, their ship sank during a violent storm and they all perished.

Ann Donavan Timothy, Peter's wife and Elizabeth's daughter-in-law, traveled back to Charles Town in 1782, and on July 16, 1783, following in her beloved mother-in-law's footsteps, resumed the publication of the newspaper in a building on Broad Street that still exists today. She named it the *Gazette of the State of South Carolina*. Her son, Benjamin Franklin Timothy, Elizabeth's grandson, succeeded as publisher nine years later in 1792.

Elizabeth as a businesswoman imbued qualities of strength, intelligence, and imagination. She unabashedly walked into a man's profession and proved that a woman could present the news and serve the community in an honorable and respectable fashion. She proved her accountability and earned high marks in the realm of business. She also yielded power and influence in a dignified manner, as her editorial words and decisions carried great weight. She admirably represented formidable authority over public opinion and the development of her colony. She accomplished all of these achievements with her babies in tow, during an era that was not conducive to a woman's management.

The times in which Elizabeth lived magnify her successes. They are accomplishments arduous to achieve even today. Elizabeth's strengths were sorely tested by the sorrows of losing her husband and two of her precious sons. Yet Elizabeth's endurance and talent, combined with love for her children, proved to be a powerful combination. Holding her head high, she conveyed through her publishing, editing, and printing her message of hope.

Elizabeth also made evident her compassionate sense of social consciousness through her newspaper that reached thousands of people. If she had faltered, relinquishing her husband's newspaper, she would have lost her voice and her platform of persuasion. Even though burdened by mouths to feed, she surely recognized this opportunity and met her mission with courage and competitiveness.

Elizabeth's example was emulated by future generations, evident in the actions of her daughter-in-law and her grandson. Someone always has to be first, and Elizabeth blazed a new trail for future female journalists. She maintained the dreams and dignity of her family, and she did it as a single mother. What lesson do we learn from Elizabeth's editorial life? I am impressed with her gutsy acquisition of a powerful position. Motivated by survival, she grasped the reins of leadership and rode through the battle of her life victorious.

Life Lesson: Go the Extra Mile

Elizabeth surpassed expectations, traveling the extra mile. She exhibited for her children the attribute that, when faced with a challenge, you don't just meet it, you greet it and respond at a higher level. I'm always refreshed and inspired by people who go the extra mile, whether it's someone taking my food order with a sense of humor or an employer who makes that one extra call on my behalf. Going the extra mile results in better business acumen, yes, but it also parlays into a better sense of humanity. As Jesus says in the Bible, "If someone forces you to go one mile, go with him two miles" (Matthew 5:41 NIV).

That's the jewel in Elizabeth's crown. She was a single mother with singular vision. She passed down to her children the legacy of working hard and exceeding expectations. She only had to print the paper once a week, but she printed it twice, doubling her efforts and doubling her persuasive impact. She passed down to her children the ingredients of success—how to be a winner.

Going the extra mile is the cornerstone of our great country. God is evident in life's details, and He is the instigator of the extra mile. So go the extra mile and experience the rewards of God's glory. Your children are watching. Put smiles on their faces and motivation in their hearts. Show them the way life should be lived. When challenged by life to go one mile, go two!

"We never know how high we are till we are called to rise;
and then, if we are true to plan our statures touch the skies."

—Emily Dickenson

ABIGAIL ADAMS

Visionary Wartime Single Mother

1744–1818

SNAPSHOT	Putting her pen down and walking away from her desk because she felt so much unrequited passion for her husband, John
MOTHER MOMENT	Watching her children suffer from the smallpox vaccine, she writes, "Every expression of tenderness is a cordial to my heart. Unimportant as they are to the rest of the world, to me they are 'everything.'"
CHALLENGE	Her husband was absent due to the Revolutionary War
STEWARDSHIP	The power and purpose of the stay-at-home mom
SCRIPTURE	As a mother comforts her child, so will I comfort you. (Isaiah 66:13 NIV)

CHAPTER ELEVEN

Champion Your Children

'Tis almost fourteen years since we were united, but more
than half the time we had the happiness of living together.
The unfeeling world may consider it light if they please, I consider
it a sacrifice to my country and one of my greatest misfortunes.

—ABIGAIL ADAMS

Full-throttle Revolutionary-era America. Boston Tea Party and Paul Revere. Declaration of Independence and Crossing the Delaware. Pivotal times. Defiant British versus courageous rebels. Random raids and bitter battles. Hear the fifes, flutes, and battle drums. See the ragged troops marching by windows where imprisoned wartime widows are enduring their own Valley Forge.

I recently visited the Portrait Museum in Washington, D.C. In this beautiful new building hang the portraits of our nation's presidents. Scattered among the presidents are a few select First Ladies, including Martha Washington, Jacqueline Kennedy, and Hillary Clinton. Glaringly absent, in my opinion, is Abigail Adams. As a matter of fact, one of my missions, after completion of this book, is to lobby for a portrait of Abigail in this museum.

Abigail was a rival to her husband, John Adams, in spirit, spunk, determination, intelligence, and well-defined opinions. She was the wind beneath his wings, and if she had lived during our generation, she would have *been* the wings, soaring as an eagle. Due to the constraints placed upon women at the time, Abigail was confined, but her words, visions, and passions took flight. They were heard and admired by her husband. He wrote, "I can do nothing without you." She would quote the English poet Edward Young, "Affliction is a good man's shining time." And that's what Abigail did best—she shone like a blazing sun throughout her lifetime filled with hardships, always rising to the occasion. She sacrificed her husband and her children's father to a cause in which she believed, enduring loneliness and hardships bravely and without complaint. She wrote to her friend Mercy,

> I had it in my heart to dissuade him from going and I know I could have prevailed, but our public affairs at the time were so gloomy an aspect I thought if ever his assistance was wanted, it must be such a time. I therefore resigned myself to suffer some anxiety and many melancholy hours for this year to come.

Yes, Abigail was a mother with a husband and father for her children, yet during the American Revolution, she was a virtual wartime single mother. And if Abigail had not displayed the strength, courage, and capabilities to manage their children, business, household, and farm without her husband, our country may well have been very different. John Adams was a brilliant, pivotal influence in the birthing of our great nation. However, he could not have done it without Abigail. She was a rebel, a patriot, a hero, a mother, a wartime single mother.

Timeless scenario: Intelligent girl meets intelligent boy. They respect and love one another. Girl marries boy. Girl and boy have children. Boy leaves woman due to work, war. Girl must make do without boy. Girl is lonely. Girl raises children alone with only letters to bide her time. Girl helps birth great nation due to her courage.

Abigail and John

Abigail Adams was born on November 22, 1744, in Weymouth Massachusetts. She was the daughter of a Congregational minister. She met John at the age of sixteen and was initially intimidated by the outspoken, brash Harvard graduate. He was taken with her superior intellect, and soon they became inseparable. John and Abigail were married in 1764. Then they moved to John's hometown, Braintree, Massachusetts. Their first daughter, Abigail, was born in 1765. Their second child and future president of the United States, John Quincy, was born in 1767. Their third child, Susanna, was born in 1768 and died two years later in 1770. Their fourth child, Charles, was born in 1770, and their fifth child, Thomas, was born in 1772.

John Adams was a successful, respected lawyer, and he became insatiably passionate about American independence. In fact, John was the thorn in the side of Congress with his relentless pursuit of a declaration of independence. Such a manifesto didn't come without sacrifices, and one of those sacrifices was John's absence from his home, his wife, and his children.

Abigail was an advocate of revolution as well, and though it meant the inconsolable void of John's presence, she encouraged him, writing, "You cannot be, I know, nor do I wish to see you, an inactive spectator . . . we have too many high-sounding words, and too few actions that correspond with them." Abigail had revolutionary, rebel blood running through her veins, and with the divine inspiration of envisioning free and independent colonies, she realized the time was ripe and must be seized. She quoted Shakespeare,

> *There is a tide in the affairs of men,*
> *Which, taken at the flood, leads on to fortune;*
> *Omitted, all the voyage of their life*
> *Is bound in the shallows and in miseries*
> *And we must take the current when it serves*
> *Or lose our ventures.*

With unabated enthusiasm she wrote to John, "A people may let a King fall, yet still remain a people, but if a King let his people slip from him, he is no longer a King. And as this is most certainly our case, why not proclaim to the world in decisive terms our own importance?"

He replied, "I think you shine as a stateswoman."

Abigail echoed her husband's sentiments in and out of her home: "I could not join today in the petitions . . . for a reconciliation between our no longer parent state, by a tyrant state and these colonies. Let us separate; they are unworthy to be our brethren." Regarding the dreams and visions for Americans, Abigail eloquently scribed,

> I am more and more convinced that man is a dangerous crea-
> ture, and that power whether vested in many or few is ever
> grasping . . . The great fish swallow up the small . . . and he who
> is most strenuous for the rights of the people, when vested with
> power, is as eager after the prerogatives of government. You tell
> me of degrees of perfection to which human nature is capable
> of arriving and I believe it, but at the same time lament that our
> admiration should arise from the scarcity of the instances.

John and Abigail were of like minds, and she deferred to his opinions with her critiques many times throughout the years. During their times apart she constantly wrote many verbose, insightful, intuitive, and politically astute letters.

ABIGAIL—VIRTUAL SINGLE MOTHER

In 1775 John was called to duty and Abigail was left behind to manage their four children. She struggled with expenses and shortages as she educated her children socially, intellectually, and morally. She had to negotiate the daily rigors of the farm, of which she knew little. In regard to her efforts she wrote, "Frugality, industry, and economy are the lessons of the day; at least they must be so for me or my small boat will suffer shipwreck."

Abigail missed John terribly and yet couldn't visit him in Philadelphia because the children needed her, always ill with one sickness or another. She wrote to him, "I miss my partner and find myself unequal to the cares which fall upon me . . . I want to say many things I must omit. It is not fit to wake the soul by tender strokes of art, or to ruminate upon happiness we might enjoy, lest absences become intolerable." She surely missed the sensuous pleasures of her husband as she passionately wrote,

Here, I say, I have amused myself in reading and thinking of my absent friend, sometimes with a mixture of pain, sometimes with pleasure, sometimes anticipating a joyful and happy meeting, whilst my heart would bound and palpitate with the pleasing idea, and with the purest affection I have held you to my bosom 'til my whole soul has dissolved in tenderness and my pen fallen from my hand.

Most dramatically she writes of her inability to write due to her passions,

I must leave my pen to recover myself and write in another strain. I wish for peace and tranquility. All my desires and all my ambition is to be esteemed and loved by my partner, to join with him in the education and instruction of our little ones, to sit under our own vines in peace, liberty and safety.

In 1777, as a virtual single mother of four, Abigail was pregnant again, and as the months wore on she watched the troops march incessantly down her lane. She wrote, "Not an hour in the day but we see soldiers marching." She yearned for John. Abigail had been ill, weak, and pale throughout her pregnancy, and toward the end of pregnancy she awakened in the night to a bout of horrible shaking fits. Desperate for John to be by her side, she had to endure her fears alone. She feared for the baby, and most surely she must have feared for her own life. Something was wrong, and in the countryside during an era when healthcare was negligent, naïve, and nominal, childbirth was a frightening and ominous event. Abigail went into labor, yet she labored in vain. Her baby girl was born dead. She wrote to John, "It appears to be a fine babe, and as it never opened its eyes in this world, it looked as though they were only closed for sleep." Abigail endured this event both physically and emotionally as a virtual single mother, alone.

Times were hard, and Abigail had to learn to be frugal. There were food and clothing shortages, and it was very hard to find someone to help her on the farm. She wrote, "Our money will soon be useless as blank paper." Determined to not only survive but succeed, Abigail wove her own wool and made her children's clothes. She found ways to provide food with the growing lack of bread, salt, sugar, meat, and molasses. She believed maintaining the homestead and the health, vitality, and moral integrity of her children was her duty not only as a mother but as a patriot. She wrote, "I believe nature has assigned each sex its particular duties and sphere of action, and to act well your part, there all the honor lies."

ABIGAIL, THE WRITER

Abigail had a sharp intellect coupled with valid and forward-thinking opinions. In regard to slavery she was passionate and empathetic, writing to John, "I have sometimes been ready to think that the passion for liberty cannot be equally strong in the breasts of those who have been accustomed to depriving their fellow creatures of theirs." And in regard to slavery that she witnessed, she said, "I wish most sincerely there was not a slave in the province. It always seemed a most iniquitous scheme to me—[to] fight ourselves for what we are daily robbing and plundering from those who have as good a right to freedom as we have."

On the subject of women, Abigail was an instigator, a lone yet valiant voice. She wrote to John hoping to impress upon him the importance and dignity of recognizing women's plight:

I long to hear that you have declared independence—and by the way, on the new code of laws which I suppose it will be necessary for you to make, I desire you would remember the ladies, and be more favorable to them than your ancestors. Do not put such unlimited power into the hands of husbands . . . If particular care and attention is not paid to the ladies, we are determined to foment a rebellion, and will not hold ourselves bound by any laws in which we have no voice, or representation.

It would be more than a century before the rebellion of American women found a voice in the right to vote. Abigail continued with her plight:

That your sex are naturally tyrannical is a truth so thoroughly established as to admit of no dispute, but such of yours as wish to be happy willingly give up the harsh title of Master for the more tender and endearing one of friend. Why then, not put it out of the power of the vicious and the lawless to use us with cruelty and indignity with impunity. Men of sense in all ages abhor those customs which treat us only as vassals of your sex. Regard us then as being placed by providence under your protection and in imitation of the Supreme Being make use of that power only for our happiness.

Abigail quoted a line from a poem written by Daniel Defoe that may be applied to many issues—women, slavery, government. It is universal in theme. "Remember all men would be tyrants if they could."

As a wartime single mother, raising her children primarily on her own, Abigail was molding the future of the country, future patriots. She was responsible for shaping her children's character spiritually, intellectually, emotionally. Yes, she had a communication with her husband via sporadic letters, but the daily routine and diligence was Abigail's to bear. She made the brave decision to take her children to Boston to be inoculated for smallpox, which was no easy feat. In that day, traveling meant taking everything from the bedding to the milk cow.

As every mother knows, a sick child is an all-consuming agony, so to willingly inflict a dubious inoculation on her children surely must have been an anxiety-ridden affair. She wrote, "I wish it was so you could have been with us, but I submit." As they sickened from the affects of the inoculation, her son Charles endured high fever and succumbed to a delirium that lasted for forty-eight hours. She wrote, "The little folks are very sick and puke every morning, but after that they are comfortable. Every expression of tenderness is a cordial to my heart. Unimportant as they are to the rest of the world, to me they are 'everything.'" Does that not sum it all up? Is that not the definition that drives every mother's heart? Is that not the essence of a mother's all-consuming affection and love? Abigail's children were her *everything*, and she singularly raised them for a lengthy period of time and through their most formative and vulnerable years.

Duty and Country

With the Declaration of Independence finally completed by an often divided, cantankerous, passionate, frightened, yet courageous Congress, John could occasionally find times to return to Abigail in Braintree. But he had been home for only a brief time when the Congress once again called him to duty. Adams was flattered when he was chosen to work with Benjamin Franklin and Arthur Lee to negotiate an all-important and consequential alliance with France.

Abigail was devastated. Joyous and relieved to *finally* have her husband home, she was demoralized to have to part with him again so soon. He would be journeying across the treacherous seas, living in a foreign land for an endless amount of time with a massive ocean dividing their love and communications. Previously they had been separated by just a few days' journey on horseback. Abigail immediately wrote a letter to Mr. Lovell, who was on the committee for foreign affairs, vehemently inquiring how he could . . .

> contrive to rob me of all my happiness. And can I, sir, consent to be separated from him whom my heart esteems above all earthly things, and for an unlimited time? My life will be one

continued scene of anxiety and apprehension, and must I cheerfully comply with the demand of my country?

Abigail begged John to let her accompany him on the journey, but he would not allow her and the children to endure the hardships and dangers. Thus Abigail would once again have to garner her strength, restrain her passions, and call upon her patriotism. This separation was even more painful, because this time she was not to part with just her husband but also with her eldest son, Johnny. He was only ten years old. Abigail had to relinquish her maternal protectiveness and acquiesce to the limitless opportunities, though dangerous, the travel would present for her son. When John and John Quincy bid their good-byes and disappeared over the horizon, she didn't know if she would ever see them again. Abigail remained at home with their other children, Abigail, Charles, and Thomas, now roughly ages twelve, seven, and five. Abigail wrote a parting letter to her son:

> You are in possession of a natural good understanding and of spirits unbroken by adversity, and untamed with care. Improve your understanding for acquiring useful knowledge and virtue, such as will render you an ornament to society, an honor to your country and a blessing to your parents . . . and remember you are accountable to your Maker for all your words and actions.

Within this one paragraph is an example of the responsibilities Abigail undertook to shape her children's character. It represents her willingness to reason maturely with her children, to place emphasis on the value and blessing of education, to reinforce their sense of responsibility to their country, to honor their parents, and to the necessity of living a prudent life worthy of God's favor.

In 1779 John returned home briefly, and within three months was summoned again to Paris. He was asked to be the Minister Plenipotentiary in Paris, and his mission was to negotiate treaties of peace and commerce with Great Britain. This task held great significance and potentially far-reaching effects for America. John and his comrades would brilliantly accomplish the desired results with diplomatic finesse that required an endless amount of time and immense patience.

Once again, Abigail had to rely on her resources and resolve to conquer the demons of sacrifice. This time she had to part with not only her husband but also two of her sons, John Quincy and Charles, who was nine years old. They would, once again, be separated by that vast and furious ocean that would conspire to prevent communications between Abigail and her husband and sons of such a tender age. Abigail, delving into her wealth of maternal treasures, wrote a brilliant letter to John Quincy. It is, in my opinion, comparable to any of the ingenious treaties composed by her husband.

> It will be expected of you, my son, that as you are favored with superior advantages under the instructive eye of a tender parent, that your improvements should bear some proportion to your advantages. These are the times in which a genius would wish to live. It is not in the still calm of life, or the repose of a pacific station, that great characters are formed. The habits of a vigorous mind are formed in contending with difficulties. Great necessities call out great virtues. When a mind is raised, and animated by scenes that engage the heart, then those qualities which would otherwise lay dormant, wake into life and form the character of the hero and the statesman.

Wow! Abigail Adams. I find her words immensely powerful and poetic. Not only did her words inspire her sons, they also must have inspired her husband. They most certainly inspired women, mothers, and her country. Her words may describe her husband's valor, but they most assuredly reflect her own brilliance and gallant heroism. Three short months after John's return home he was gone again. Abigail wrote of her despair, "My habitation, how disconsolate it looks! My table I sit down to it. But I cannot swallow my food

. . . My hopes and fears rise alternately. I cannot resign more than I do, unless life is called for."

John was not without feelings of despair and loneliness either. His sacrifices were indeed courageous and great. John Adams was a genius. Consider his forward-looking aspirations for his sons and future generations: He wrote,

> I must study politics and war that my sons may have liberty to study mathematics and philosophy. My sons ought to study mathematics and philosophy, geography, natural history, naval architecture, navigation, commerce, and agriculture in order to give their children a right to study paintings, poetry, music, architecture, statuary, tapestry, and porcelain.

The Pain of Separation

Abigail endured one of the most bitter winters in forty years. They never stopped writing, though the letters would sometimes arrive months late or never arrive at all, having fallen victim to that vast, conquering ocean. If trouble was foreseen, letters were routinely tossed into the sea. They were always in danger of falling into treasonous hands or the wrong hands, resulting in heavy consequences or embarrassments.

Abigail wrote of the war, the deaths of family members, and the intensity of weather. She continued to write her motherly exhortations and was alarmed by her family members' move to Holland. She only heard months after the event had taken place and was worried about the dark, dank weather. She tried not to complain but to present an even composure. She wrote, "I am not suddenly elated or depressed. I know America capable of anything she undertakes with spirit and vigor." Of independence and her husband's successful pursuit of it she wrote,

> My whole soul is absorbed in the idea. The honor of my dearest friend, the welfare and happiness of this wide, extended country, ages yet unknown, depend for their happiness and

security upon the able and skillful, the honest and upright discharge of the important trust committed to him. It would not become me to write the full flow of my heart upon this occasion.

Abigail wrote of her desire for her husband and her loneliness on Christmas Day 1780. He would not receive it for almost six months.

How fondly can I call you mine, bound by every tie which consecrate the most inviolable friendship, yet separated by cruel destiny. I feel the pangs of absence sometimes too sensibly for my own repose . . .

There are times when the heart is peculiarly awake to tender impressions, when philosophy slumbers, or is over-powered by sentiments more comfortable to nature. It is then that I feel myself alone in the wide world, without anyone to tenderly care for me, or lend me an assisting hand through the difficulties that surround me. Yet my cooler reason disapproves the ripening thought, and bids me bless the hand from which my comforts flow.

Abigail felt a connection to her lover, her companion, her intellectual muse. Wherever she was she felt his nearness. She wrote, "The busy sylphs are ever at my ear, no sooner does Morpeus close my eyes, than 'my soul, unbounded flies to thee.'"

The presence of John Quincy was requested to accompany and translate for Francis Dana on a trip to Russia. John Quincy, having lived in Paris with his father over the years, was fluent in French. It was a 1,200-mile journey. John Adams thought the trip would be beneficial for John Quincy. (The experience did serve him well in his future presidency.) John allowed John Quincy to accompany Francis Dana. Russia by horseback! Abigail, of course, was ignorant to this decision until after the trip commenced. We can only imagine her concerns and fears. Charles, however, missing his mother immensely, was sent home. Charles's journey was not taken lightly, as this was no easy feat. Charles, a young boy traveling alone, encountered numerous hazards crossing the wartime seas.

John and Abigail Adams were separated for over three years during these European episodes. His accomplishments in Paris and Holland were remarkable, and to quote David McCullough, "As time would tell, the treaty that he, Franklin and Jay had made was as advantageous to their country as any in history. It would be said they had won the greatest victory in the annals of American diplomacy." Over the course of nine years, John and Abigail had been separated during such remarkable events as the First Continental Congress, the arduous undertaking of achieving a written declaration and unanimous vote declaring independence, the alliance with France, the peace treaty with England, and of course, ultimately, the victory of independence from England in 1782.

Abigail's Contributions

Abigail's contributions were no less remarkable than John's. The emergence of great thought, great ambitions, and a great country requires a great concert of sacrifices. There were many such instances of mothers and wives who birthed our glorious nation with their sense of duty, honor, and commitment. These contributions warranted loneliness, poverty, and even death. It was due to these women, however— these wartime single mothers, who manned the fort, kept the home fires burning, and nurtured the children—that our small yet spirited army could succeed. It's due to the partnerships of these women, who were willing to rise with the tides of opportunity and awaken the heroine within the hearts, that America could prove victorious.

Abigail, as one of these wartime single mothers, was not only a most brilliant example of endurance, sacrifice, love, and honor, but also infinitely dedicated to the principles of life, liberty, and the pursuit of happiness. Her stunning intellect and foresight, companionship, and moral integrity were the stepping stones of life upon which her children, and hence her country, could lay their feet and never falter. Her sacrifices and contributions did not only entail the Revolutionary era. They continued to buoy her husband and her country during John's years as vice president beside George Washington, and then as he became the nation's second president.

Abigail shined as a patriot, stateswoman, and First Lady, but she was hampered by ill health. Consequently, she and John continued to endure many separations until the final, irreparable separation: her death on October 28, 1818. She was seventy-three years old.

It is because of Abigail's pronounced dignity and talent with the pen that she lives on forever, and we have a wealth of knowledge and insight into the burgeoning growth and development of America. It's because of her tenacity that we, as a country, as women, as mothers, as single mothers, are able to absorb the Revolutionary era and relate to her challenges as a wartime single mother. She leaves her country a most remarkable record as a patriot and First Lady, wife of one president and mother of another. Abigail would be pleased to know that through the windows of her life we are able to comprehend and conceive not only the hardships and sufferings of our ancestors, but the resiliency of their spirit.

Life Lesson: Champion Your Children

Abigail was and is the champion of all mothers. We learn the immeasurable importance of a mother who stays behind to foster her children and the future of her country. She sacrificed many years without the loving, tender touch of her husband. She single-handedly bathed, fed, taught, disciplined, inspired, schooled, and tenderly cultivated the minds and spirits of her children. She was the 1700s' version of the stay-at-home mom, the stay-at-home, wartime, single mom. Like modern single mothers, she also had to provide for her children economically while protecting her homestead from the ever-present, imminently dangerous enemy. She had to contend with fear, loneliness, despair, sickness, and death. She was a champion for our country. She was a champion for her children. She stayed at home and raised her children, and did it with an inordinate amount of poise, pride, and purpose.

Abigail is an example of what fortitude and dedication reap. If you're at home with your child, don't underestimate your power.

There is no more meaningful job than etching the character of your child with the strokes of your devotion.

Abigail was a patriot. She was a mother. Like her, you have within your reach the future of our great country. Prepare their minds with the ladders of history and the platform of prayer. Champion your children to be all they can be—concerned contributors to society, humble servants for humanity, and noble citizens of their country.

It is not in the still calm of life, or the repose of a pacific station, that great characters are formed. The habits of a vigorous mind are formed in contending with difficulties. Great necessities call out great virtues. When a mind is raised, and animated by scenes that engage the heart, then those qualities which would otherwise lay dormant, wake into life and form the character of the hero and the statesman.

—Abigail Adams's letter to her son

chapter twelve

Single Mothers of Slavery—
Setting the Stage

1800's

*"Motherwit" is the collective body of female wisdom both formal
and informal, oral and written, spiritual and social—passed on
from generation to generation by African American females. It is the
strength of the total experience of black females, which has helped
them survive their diaspora experience in the Western World.*[1]

—Alonzo Johnson and Paul Jersild

Confederacy. Auction blocks and wicked ways. Sin and evil triumph. Flesh is ripped and spirits crumble. Cries ring out and injustice reigns. Husbands severed from wives. Children torn from mothers. Deep wounds yield magnificent pride. Remarkable resilience and beautiful souls. Who will save the children?

My next chapter is dedicated to Harriet Jacobs. Harriet was a slave during the 1800s, who, as a single mother, was so determined in both body and soul to break the chains of slavery for her children that she lived in an insufferable attic for seven years. I also have a chapter dedicated to Aunt Clara Brown, a pioneer single mother, who also endured the horrors of slavery. After being freed she dedicated her life to looking for her daughter, who had been ripped from her bosom on the auction block at the age of eight.

Slave Families

The family structure in the slave family was unpredictable and unprecedented. It could be inextricably altered at any time. Their lives were riding on their owners' whims. They could be sold in a moment's notice, and the whole family could be separated, never to reunite again. A woman might never see her husband again, a child might never see his mother again. And they were powerless to stop it. If a woman's husband wasn't sold, he could be killed. The sorrows and maddening injustices were deep. The single mother of slavery could be forced to work away from her children, leaving them in the protection of their grandmother or aunt. The family unit was diverse, but one fact emerges clearly: these single mothers were stoic and brave, loving and devoted. Survival of the children's spirits depended upon the fierce faith of these single mothers, single grandmothers, and single aunts. Their resiliency, their pride, their dedication, their boundless endurance was astonishing.

Faith was their rock of salvation. They survived their horrendous times by focusing not on the unbearable here-and-now but on the unbelievable hereafter. Can't you hear the wailing but joyful strains of the great old Negro spirituals that rose on the sultry night winds? Their children often had no shoes; so they sang, "I got shoes; you got shoes; all God's chillin got shoes!" Their circumstances were deplorable, and they had to walk for miles everywhere they went; so they pleaded, "Why don't you swing down, chariot—stop and let me ride?" They longed to be released from their bondage and go home to the Lord; so they reached out to Him in joy, singing, "I looked over Jordan, and what did I see? A band of angels comin' after me—coming for to carry me home!" It was primarily the single mother who heralded these choruses.

MOTHERWIT

Motherwit was learned wisdom, coupled with an unshakable faith that embodied the hearts and souls of the slave mothers and single mothers. These traits were indelibly pressed upon their children.

For instance, Frederick Douglass was born in 1817 in Tuckahoe, Maryland. He knew nothing of his biological father, and his mother was working on another plantation twelve miles away. Thus the primary responsibility of his childhood was left in the hands of his grandmother. She filled both the cabin and his soul with warmth and love. Frederick defines her as a "woman with great wisdom and strength."[2] He wrote, "It was a long time before I knew myself to be a slave,"[3] and he described his grandmother as one of "the greatest people in the world."[4]

Frederick's mother was no less valiant. She would walk twelve miles at the end of her plantation workday to see her son. When she found Frederick compromised, such as when his aunt Katy was punishing him by not feeding him all day, "she read aunt Katy a lecture which she never forgot."[5] Frederick witnessed motherwit in the actions of his mother. She wrapped her loving arms around him, defending her son and chastising her sister. Frederick wrote, "The friendless and hungry boy, in his extremist need—and when he did not dare look for succor—found himself in the strong, protecting arms of a mother; a mother who was, at that moment more than a match for his enemies."[6]

Harriet Jacobs rendered great strength and courage from her grandmother, as you will see in the next chapter. Her grandmother was a freed slave who exhibited a deep, resonating faith in God. She believed God would free her family to go "where the wicked shall cease from Troublin'."[7] Her grandmother, known as Aunt Martha, would raise her grandchildren and her great-grandchildren as a single grandmother and a single great-grandmother. Harriet was only able to withstand her plight in life, and subsequent seven years in a suffocating attic, due to the motherwit of her grandmother.

Aunt Clara Brown, as seen in chapter 16, exhibited great motherwit. She shared her graces from her divine Savior with others, singing her praises down the street. Strangers wanted what she possessed—an unstoppable benevolence and optimism. She also exhibited insurmountable faith as she searched for her daughter for over forty years. In the meantime, she became the mother and source of motherwit to innumerable people, whether black, white, slave, coal miner, men, women, or children.

The obstacles these women encountered and the distances they traveled, whether literal, spiritual, or emotional, are worthy of great admiration. The battles they fought were uniquely their own and incomparable in scope. It is the motherwit in these women that guided numerous generations through the storms of life and allowed them to hold their heads high.

> *Soon ah will be don' a-wid de troubles ob de worl' . . .*
> *Troubles ob de worl', troubles ob de worl'.*
> *Soon ah will be don' a-wid de troubles ob de worl' . . .*
> *Goin' home to live wid God!*
>
> —Traditional Negro Spiritual

Harriet Jacobs

Resilient Single Mother

1813–1897

SNAPSHOT	Harriet isolated in the attic, peering at her children through a tiny peephole
MOTHER MOMENT	Sitting with her two children by her feet, free at last in Boston
CHALLENGE	A sexually tormented slave
STEWARDSHIP	Determination to break the cycle of slavery and free her children
SCRIPTURE	He performs wonders that cannot be fathomed, miracles that cannot be counted. He bestows rain on the earth; he sends water upon the countryside. The lowly he sets on high, and those who mourn are lifted to safety. He thwarts the plans of the crafty, so that their hands achieve no success. (Job 5:9–12 NIV)

CHAPTER THIRTEEN

Don't Give Up Before the Miracle

The word contempt burned me like coals of fire. God alone knows
how I have suffered; and He, I trust, will forgive me. If I am permitted
to have my children, I intend to be a good mother and to love in
such a manner that people cannot treat me with contempt.

—HARRIET JACOBS

Hoop skirts and aprons. Blood and whiskey. Sorrows and horrors. Auction blocks. Sounds of whips breaking flesh and stillness harboring sin. Smells of cotton fields and tobacco. It's North Carolina before the Civil War. The horrific age of humans owning humans. The heinous age of slavery.

Harriet Jacobs's life story is one of awesome sacrifice based on her righteous, dignified determination that her children were going to be free. They were not going to experience the inhuman psychological cruelty she was experiencing. She was willing to manifest this expectation however life presented the opportunity. She was willing to give of herself, body and soul, in order to twist her children's future to favor. She was able to bring to fruition this magnificent triumph due to her selfless surrender of her physical and emotional being. Her tremendous undertaking was only possible because she had great love and wisdom from her aunt's and grandmother's motherwit. The foundation of Harriet's calling for a better life was her God. The springboard was her core belief in His grace.

Timeless Scenario: Young slave girl is in a very abusive home. Girl never wants her children to endure her pain. Girl chooses a father she can never marry but will yield a different life for her children. Girl escapes abusive home. Girl dedicates her whole life for a better life for her children. Girl succeeds after several decades.

HARRIET AS AUTHOR . . . AND SLAVE

The same year the Civil War began, Harriet Jacobs published the haunting account of her life. She was encouraged to write her book by two women, Amy Post and Lydia Maria Child. They had met and worked beside Harriet and believed that her story should be told to enlighten others to the wicked ways of slavery and to expose the unique sufferings of slave women. Lydia Maria Child wrote the foreword for Harriet's book, stating, "I willingly take responsibility of presenting them with the veil withdrawn. I do this for the sake of my sisters in bondage, who are suffering wrongs so foul that our ears are too delicate to listen to them." Lydia was hoping to salvage the lives of the free slaves by encouraging the reader, through Harriet's vivid rendition of her experiences, to never return a slave to the South. She wrote, "I do it with the hope that every man who reads this narrative will swear solemnly before God that, so far as he had power to prevent it, no fugitive from Slavery shall ever be sent back to suffer in that loathsome den of corruption and cruelty."

As Harriet's story unfolds, it's important to understand her history. Slave families of the South were unique because there was no structure. How could there be structure? Families were ripped apart as random family members were sold on the auction blocks, never to see their loved ones again. Untimely deaths met many children and parents due to hardships and abuses, and so children were often reared by their aunts and grandmothers. Quite frequently these matriarchs were mothers to many, and they were given the pseudonym of "aunt." Thus the slaves' lineages were tangled into the webs of the masters who caught them. Trying to understand their masters and who "belonged" to who is like trying to take that web and untangle its silks. However, in this case, it's essential to understand, so here we go.

Harriet's grandmother, known as Aunt Martha, was a "great treasure." She was the daughter of a South Carolina planter. When he died, he left Aunt Martha and her three children, one of which was Harriet's mother, free with enough money to go to St. Augustine. Their escape was during the Revolutionary War and proved unsuccessful. They were captured and carried back to the auction block and sold to different owners. Aunt Martha was sold to the manager of a hotel, where she proved herself invaluable, intelligent, and capable. She was a cook, a seamstress, a wet nurse. When her master died, Aunt Martha was kept by his surviving wife, but Aunt Martha's children, including Harriet's mother, were given to Aunt Martha's mistress's children. Aunt Martha's youngest son, Harriet's uncle, was sold for $720. Aunt Martha was given permission to bake crackers at night to sell, and she was determined to save enough money to buy her children back. She had saved $300 when suddenly one night her mistress asked to borrow it. Aunt Martha had no choice but to give it to her mistress. It was never returned.

Thus Harriet's mother was a slave in the household of her mother, Aunt Martha's mistress's daughter. Aunt Martha had nursed Harriet's mother and her mistress's daughter at the same time. As a result, Harriet's mother and her owner were the same age and best friends, contemporaries who felt like sisters. Harriet's mother died at an early age and, when she died, her owner/best friend/sister swore that no harm would come to her children while she was alive, and she was faithful to her word.

Harriet's father was a respected carpenter. He, too, had hoped to save enough money to buy his children someday. However, he died when Harriet was young, so it never happened. When her father died, Harriet was comforted by her grandmother's motherwit, such as, "Who knows the ways of God? Perhaps they have been kindly taken from the evil days to come." She had promised Harriet's father that she would be a mother to his children.

Thus Harriet was an orphan and grew up in her grandmother's

house. She was so loved and shielded, she never knew she was a slave until she was six years old. Her mother's mistress kept her word in regard to protecting her "sister's" children, and Harriet had fond memories of her.

> My mistress was so kind to me that I was always glad to do her bidding, and proud to labor for her . . . When she thought I was tired, she would send me out to run and jump; and away I bounded, to gather berries or flowers to decorate her room. Those were happy days—too happy to last."

She taught Harriet to read and spell, and Harriet remarked, "For this privilege, which so rarely falls to the lot of a slave, I bless her memory."

When her mistress died, Harriet had hoped she would be freed. She wasn't, however, and in true southern tradition Harriet was inherited by her mistress's five-year-old niece. The father of this five-year-old child was Dr. James Norcom, who had married the sister of Harriet's former mistress. Harriet's brother, William, had also been bequeathed to this family.

Meanwhile Aunt Martha's mistress had promised that when she died Aunt Martha would be freed, and when the mistress did pass away, her will gave freedom to Aunt Martha. Dr. Norcom, however, had no intention of honoring her will. He was too cunning to put Aunt Martha back on the public auction block, because this would publicly exhibit his disregard for his mother-in-law's wishes. He decided to sell her privately. The word quickly spread, and Aunt Martha's friends came to the rescue. Her inexhaustible dedication, honor, and goodwill came full circle. When the moment arrived for her to be sold, people gathered and shouted, "Shame, shame!" There were no bids, nothing but silence, except for a small, feeble voice that said, "Fifty dollars." It was the sister of her deceased mistress. She had lived under the same roof as her sister for forty years and had witnessed Aunt Martha's love and dedication. She knew her sister's wishes and *she* wanted to honor them. No one outbid her, so

Aunt Martha was a free woman for fifty dollars at fifty years of age.

Dr. Norcom, who tried to deprive Harriet's grandmother of her legal right to freedom, was Harriet's master. She had left her grandmother's home and was now living in Dr. Norcom's home. The sheltered days were over for Harriet as she witnessed the abuse her fellow slaves endured. She observed that Mrs. Norcom would do nothing to curb her husband's wrath. She "could sit in her easy chair and see a woman whipped, till blood trickled from every stroke of the lash." At her new home, Harriet would sleep in the protective bosom of Aunt Nancy, her mother's sister.

Sometimes there would be little time to eat. Harriet's grandmother recognized this and would always be waiting with some food for Harriet as she passed by the gate. Aunt Martha also left a new pair of shoes for Harriet when she saw Harriet walking in the snow with old, ragged shoes.

Harriet must have grown into a beautiful, young woman, because Dr. Norcom had a lifelong infatuation with her. He became absolutely obsessed with having her and would follow her around the house and hand her written notes. Harriet would pretend she couldn't read them and hand them back. He would order his food in a private room and insist that she stand close to him and swat his flies. When Harriet told Dr. Norcom that she would tell her Aunt Martha what he was doing, he threatened her with death. Harriet held her head high and drew upon some motherwit wisdom, saying to herself, "Like many a poor, simple slave before me, I trusted that some threads of joy would yet be woven into my dark destiny."

Harriet tried to stay within the sight of other people throughout the day so she could avoid Dr. Norcom's advances. When he succeeded in getting her alone, he would threaten her with a razor at her throat to try and get her to succumb. Harriet carried within her soul a quiet dignity and a moral code instilled into her by her grandmother. She was not one to lie down easily and acquiesce. She had witnessed what happened to a slave when she became pregnant by her master. She knew that children conceived by a master would be trapped in the same misery and mire as hers. With a fire burning as hot as the sun, Harriet did not want to bring a child into the world who would have to suffer the injustices she did. It was the never-wavering whisper of God in her ear that called her to higher ground. With God as her witness, if she were to birth children, they were going to be *free* children.

Dr. Norcom had been an active participant in extramarital affairs, causing the conception of eleven slave children. The mothers didn't dare tell who the father was, because the consequences were too hard to bear. Harriet recounts that "the secrets of slavery are concealed like those of the Inquisition." These actions were not unnoticed by Dr. Norcom's wife. She was overcome by a torturous jealousy, so they would quarrel, and the bitterness in the air was deeply felt.

Dr. Norcom, desperate in his unfulfilled pursuit of Harriet, ordered his four-year-old daughter to sleep in his room and then ordered Harriet to sleep in the same room to watch over his daughter. Harriet had always slept in the house with her Aunt Nancy, and this situation petrified her. Mrs. Norcom realized what was happening and took Harriet to live with her in her room. Harriet would awaken in the middle of the night with Mrs. Norcom standing over her, watching her breathe. On certain nights she would try to trick Harriet and whisper sweet nothings in her ear. She would pretend she was her husband to see if Harriet would respond. Harriet began to fear for her life and observed, "This bad institution deadens the moral sense, even in the white woman." She also commented,

> I would ten thousand times rather that my children be the half-starved pauper of Ireland than to be the most pampered among the slaves of America. I would rather drudge out my life on a cotton plantation till the grave opened to give me rest, than to live with an unprincipled master and a jealous wife.

Harriet's grandmother had an exchange of words with Dr. Norcom and tried to buy Harriet, but he claimed that she couldn't be sold because she was his daughter's property, and she was not of legal age to make decisions. This incestuous, insidious atmosphere is described in Harriet's words:

I can testify from my own experience and observation, that slavery is a curse to the whites as well as the blacks. It makes the white fathers cruel and sensual; the sons violent and licentious; it contaminates the daughters, and make wives wretched. And as for the colored race, it needs an abler pen than mine to describe the extremity of their sufferings, the depth of their degradation. Yet few slaveholders seem to be aware of the widespread moral ruin occasioned by this wicked system. Their talk is of blighted cotton crops—not on the blight of their children's souls.

Over the course of time, Harriet fell in love with a freed slave boy who wanted to buy her so they could marry. Harriet knew that if she married a freed slave, her children would be free too. Dr. Norcom also knew this, so he would not allow it. When Harriet confronted Dr. Norcom and told him that she loved the boy, Dr. Norcom hit her. He said, "Do you know I have a right to do as I like with you—that I could kill you, if I please?"

Harriet responded, "You have the right to kill me and I wish you had; but you do not have the right to do as you like with me."

Dr. Norcom said he would kill the boy if he saw him. He was indignant that she would prefer the proposals from a colored man over those of a white man. The situation was futile, because even if she had been able to marry the boy she loved, Dr. Norcom wouldn't have allowed him to buy Harriet. So her lover could never have had the ability to protect her from Dr. Norcom. The depths of hypocrisy were dark. If a slave woman had a white man's baby, then the baby was reared for the market with no sense of shame. However, if a white woman had a black man's baby, then the baby was either sent away and never seen again, or it was a victim of infanticide.

The Choice

Thus the intolerable decaying of the human spirit continued. Dr. Norcom repeated his incessant appeals for Harriet to acquiesce to his sexual whims. He offered to build a house for the two of them. He continually tried to pollute her mind, undermining the moral upbringing she had received from her grandmother. One day Mr. John Sawyer—a white, upper-class, educated gentleman in the neighborhood—became attracted to Harriet. He started wooing her with kind words and his acknowledgment of the unfairness of her situation. Harriet was flattered that this man would care for her. She was smitten by the idea that to "be an object of interest to a man who was not married, and who is not her master, is agreeable to the pride and feelings of a slave."

Remaining in the stifling environment of Dr. Norcom's house awakened Harriet's determination to never have children with Dr. Norcom. Harriet, still a young girl, became seduced by the romance of loving a man who didn't control her: "There is something akin to freedom in having a lover who has no control over you, except that which he gains by kindness and attachment." Harriet rationalized that if she had children with one of Dr. Norcom's slaves, her children would always be slaves, and if she succumbed to Dr. Norcom, bearing his children, then they also would always be slaves and forever be at the mercy of his tyrannical ways. But if she had children with this white gentleman, Mr. Sawyer, a man for whom she had a fondness of heart, respect, and appreciation, then her children would be out of the cyclical forces of her immediate prison. Her children would be well supported and most likely freed. Harriet's burning desire was that her children be free.

It is prudent here to note a situation that's taken for granted by most modern women. Pregnancy was unequivocally unavoidable until modern times. Harriet was being pressured from all sides. She was not allowed to marry the man she loved, a freed slave. If she had married one of Dr. Norcom's slaves, then her children would always be slaves, and Harriet would continue to be the sexual object and "right" of Dr. Norcom. Harriet's subsequent children with Dr. Norcom would always be slaves. Harriet was going to have children— it was unavoidable. So she chose the man—the strong, respectable white man—who could best protect their inevitable children. He would also, if he truly loved her, love their children, treat them with dignity, and eventually buy them and free them. Harriet must have also surmised that Dr. Norcom might diminish his advances when he discovered her lover was a white man. Out of these inordinate pressures and meager options, Harriet chose Mr. Sawyer. She made a headlong plunge when she was fifteen years old to becoming a mother of a white man's children and, consequently, a single mother for life.

Harriet, of course, became pregnant. Her grandmother was furious, screaming at Harriet that she was shameful and indolent. She kicked Harriet out of the house, and Harriet was absolutely demoralized by her grandmother's wrath. Her grandmother had never admonished her in such a way. Shortly, Aunt Martha came and sat beside her. Harriet wept unabashedly and told her about the horrific situation she had been enduring. Her grandmother wrapped her arms around her and rocked her, saying, "Poor child. Poor child." Aunt Martha confronted John and asked him "why he could not have left her one ewe lamb." He promised to take care of Harriet's child and that he would buy her when the conditions allowed it.

Meanwhile, back at the Norcom household, Dr. Norcom told Harriet that the house he had built for the two of them was finished. He ordered Harriet to move into it, but she said she couldn't because she was pregnant by another man. Dr. Norcom was overwrought with anger. Harriet replied, "I have sinned against God and myself, but I have not sinned against you." She told him she "was unwilling to have a child with a man who had cursed it and me also." So he declared he would never sell her. "Hope died away in my heart as he closed the door after him. I had calculated that in his rage he would sell me to a slave trader; and I knew the father of my child was on the watch to buy me." Harriet was kicked out of Dr. Norcom's house by Mrs. Norcom, because she believed the child to be his, and even if it were not, Harriet was of untrustworthy character.

Harriet's baby was born with great difficulty, and afterward Harriet was "a mere wreck of my former self." The baby's father came to visit him and bestowed kindness upon him. He also offered his name to the baby. Mr. Sawyer, however, had no legal claim to it because she was "the property" of Dr. Norcom, who would have considered it a crime. The babies could have Mr. Sawyer's name but not as long as Harriet's master lived.

Dr. Norcom visited the house and continued to seduce Harriet. When she refused, he would threaten to sell her children. Then Harriet became pregnant with her second child. Dr. Norcom, upon hearing the news, visited Harriet at her grandmother's house, cut her hair close to her head, hit her, and threw her down the stairs.

Harriet bore a baby girl, and when she heard that it was a girl, her heart was heavy, for "slavery is terrible for men; but it is more terrible for women." After the birth of her baby girl, Norcom visited the house and made her stand while holding the baby. He recognized the resemblance of the baby to her father, and he hurled insults upon her. Harriet fainted and Dr. Norcom shook her violently. Harriet was sick for some time after this incident, but she would not call the "doctor" to help her.

Mr. Sawyer tried to purchase Harriet and the children through various guises. To these attempts, Dr. Norcom would reply, "She is my daughter's property, and I have no right to sell her. I mistrust you come from her paramour. If so, you may tell him that he cannot buy her for any money; neither can he buy her children." Dr. Norcom continued to come to the house. He would barge in unexpectantly and search the house for Harriet's lover. He visited one day, and as he was getting ready to attack Harriet, her little boy, Benjamin, ran and put his protective little arm around his mother. Dr. Norcom threw the little one across the room.

One day he was about to hit her when Harriet's grandmother walked into the room, and she spewed her wrath at him. She commanded,

> Get out of my house! Go home, and take care of your wife and children, and you will have enough to do, without watching my family . . . You ain't got many more years to live, and you'd better be saying your prayers. It will take 'em all and more, too, to wash the dirt off your soul.

Aunt Martha's devotion and love were ever present, but Harriet felt as if her grandmother looked "weary of incessant life." Harriet worried it would diminish the love she had for her. Yet Aunt Martha was "always kind, always ready to sympathize with my troubles. There might have been peace and contentment in that home if it had not been for the demon slavery."

As the years advanced, Dr. Norcom's passions did not diminish. He continued to offer Harriet his cottage in the country, yet she always refused. One day he gave her an ultimatum. He offered her the house he had built for the two of them, or she had to go work on the plantation with her children by her side. She chose the plantation, which was not that far from her grandmother's house. Aunt Martha was overcome with fear for Harriet's health and safety. However, Harriet was determined not to be swayed by Dr. Norcom's sexual overtures; she didn't want to bear his children.

Harriet left her boy, Benjamin, behind because he was sick and took her toddler daughter, Ellen, with her to her new destination. When they arrived at the new house, baby Ellen was separated from her mother, so she sobbed incessantly. At night Harriet would escape with Ellen and visit her grandmother and Benjamin. He once awakened upon her arrival and said, "O, Mother, you ain't dead, are you? They didn't cut off your head at the plantation, did they?" As she gazed upon the angelic faces of her children, Harriet was haunted by the sordid future that was potentially awaiting to destroy their sweet spirits. She wrote,

> When I lay down beside my child, I felt how much easier it would be to see her die than to see her master beat her about, as I daily saw him beat other little ones. The spirit of the mother was so crushed by the lash that they stood by without courage to remonstrate. How much more must I suffer before I should be "broke in" to that degree?

HARRIET'S PLAN
Harriet ventured into the night and visited her parents' graves,

recalling her grandmother's words, "There the wicked cease from troubling and there the weary be at rest." She felt determination rising in her soul as she reckoned with her fears. Her lover, Mr. Sawyer, had not yet been able to buy her children and secure their freedom.

Harriet, drawing upon conclusions in her heart, "knew that doom awaited my fair baby in slavery, and I determined to save her from it, or perish in the attempt." She knelt down to kiss her parents' graves and "poured forth a prayer to God for guidance and support in the perilous step I was about to take." She echoed within her heart Patrick Henry's motto, "Give me liberty or give me death."

Harriet's plan was to hide herself at a house of a friend, hoping that after a time Dr. Norcom would lose interest in the children and sell them. Harriet knew that when this opportunity arose the children's father would buy them and free them. Ellen had been sent home from the plantation because she had grown ill. The new bride was arriving at the plantation, and Harriet learned that after conspiring with Dr. Norcom's wife, the new bride was going to make Harriet's young children physically work at the plantation.

That very night Harriet, sneaking into her grandmother's house, prayed beside her children. She then decided that this was the time. It was now or never. She leapt into the great abyss of the unknown. She didn't know what would happen to her or if she would be killed. She didn't know if she would ever see her children again, but she did know that she was attempting to gain freedom for them. She flew out the door before she could change her mind. The emotional pain of leaving her children must have been excruciating. She groped in the dark, searching for her friend's house.

The next morning the discovery was made that Harriet was missing, and like hound dogs on a fox Dr. Norcom's search party was relentless in their hunt for Harriet. They pounded on Aunt Martha's door and furiously searched every nook and cranny of her property. Dr. Norcom told Aunt Martha he would take Harriet's children unless she became responsible for them; so, of course, Aunt Martha said she would. Rewards were posted: "$300 reward, runaway slave, intelligent, bright, mulatto girl, 21 years of age."

Harriet decided she was putting her friend at great risk, so she escaped into the bushes in the inky night. She felt something on her leg and quietly tried to remove it. A snake was coiled around her leg and bit her. Eventually, Aunt Martha became privy to Harriet's hiding place. A local woman, who loved Aunt Martha and sympathized with the slaves, asked Aunt Martha to get word to Harriet that she should would provide a refuge for Harriet in her home. Harriet hobbled on an immensely swollen leg to her new shelter. Her lovely benefactress put her into her spacious attic with a window. Her benefactress said that she would be fed in the morning when the children were busy with breakfast and also in the evening. She was locked in the attic with a key.

Harriet hoped that Dr. Norcom would eventually become exasperated and put her children up for sale. Unfortunately, he did no such thing. Instead, he took Harriet's brother and aunt, who had served his family for twenty years, and her two children, Benjamin and Ellen, and thrust them into jail. Harriet was overwhelmed with despair, but the mistress comforted her by telling her that the children would be in the safety of their uncle and her aunt.

Dr. Norcom eventually let Harriet's aunt out of jail, because Mrs. Norcom couldn't carry on without her. They also took Ellen because she had recently had the measles, and they were affecting her eyes. Ellen cried miserably, screaming that she wanted to go back to the jail. Harriet recalled, "I always considered it one of God's special providences that Ellen screamed till she was carried back to the jail."

When someone approached the house who was considered dangerous, Betty, one of the slaves of the household, would hide Harriet under some planks in the floor. Betty would walk over the planks and act as if she were talking to herself. In the process, she would inform Harriet about what was happening in the house. Ironically, Dr. Norcom visited this house where Harriet was being sheltered to borrow five hundred dollars from the mistress. Harriet could hear this interaction, hiding above Dr. Norcom as he borrowed the money. He was planning to travel to New York City to search for Harriet.

Free at Last!

Dr. Norcom eventually returned from New York, having had no success after sixty days of searching and allowing Benjamin and Ellen to sit in jail with their Uncle William. So Mr. Sawyer thought it might be the right time to try and buy the children. This was the moment Harriet had prayed would come to fruition. This was the reason she had chosen Mr. Sawyer as a lover and why she had executed her escape. This was the pivotal opportunity. She had planted the seeds and now they were sprouting, by the goodness of God. She had planned all of these events, but at that time, Harriet didn't know they were transpiring. She was secluded in a musty attic.

In respect to the children, Mr. Sawyer was honoring his word. He sent an anonymous buyer to Dr. Norcom and offered $1,900 for William, Benjamin, and Ellen. Dr. Norcom, who was in monetary straits, agreed during a moment of weakness. Later, having second thoughts, Norcom returned to the buyer, demanding that they had to be sold out of state. He was told that he was too late, because "our bargain is closed." The buyer knew he had bought them for their father, but he didn't reveal it.

Aunt Martha was privy to the event but was told to pretend they were really leaving. She arrived at the jail with food and clothes. Little Benjamin showed her how he had made notches in the wood marking his sixty days in prison. When she saw her grandson, William, in chains, Aunt Martha fainted and had to be taken home. The three of them were escorted out of town in a wagon. Harriet recalls, "Slaves were driven away like cattle, husbands torn from wives, parents from children, never to look upon each other again this side of the grave."

Once they were out of town they were set free, and they returned to Aunt Martha's house where there was great jubilation among the family, including their father. They were all free, free at last and in their father's hands. They were free of the wicked Dr. Norcom. Harriet had received a premonition in her attic hideaway. When she heard the news and her instincts were confirmed, she said,

I had my season of joy and thanksgiving. It was the first time since my childhood that I had experienced any real happiness . . . Whatever slavery might do to me, it could not shackle my children. If I fell a sacrifice, my little ones were saved. It was well for me that my simple heart believed all that had been promised for all their welfare. It is always better to trust than to doubt.

Harriet had fulfilled her dream to break the cycle and break the chains of bondage from her family. She held her head high and succeeded. They were free . . . but Harriet was not.

DOUBLE JEOPARDY

Still in her benefactress's attic, Harriet was in jeopardy of being caught and killed at any time. One day, a curious slave, Jenny, came to the attic with the secret keys and tried to open the attic door. The mistress of the house, Harriet, and Betty all knew they were in danger. So a plan was devised. The mistress took Jenny away for a day trip. Meanwhile, Harriet dressed as a sailor and walked toward her grandmother's house. Her face was blackened with charcoal. Ironically, she walked right past Mr. Sawyer, who didn't recognize her. She hid in the bushes until dark and then ran to her grandmother's house.

There was a small shed above the house—a pent roof covered with shingles. The garret was "only nine feet long and seven feet wide . . . the highest part was three feet high and sloped abruptly to the loose board floor . . . There was no admission for either light or air." Her uncle had built a trap door that opened into the storeroom so they could communicate. The storeroom opened into a piazza. Harriet climbed up into the attic in the darkness. This attic was not large and airy like the one she had experienced at the benefactor's house. Harriet recalls, "The air was stifling, the darkness total." She could sleep on one side but not the other because she would roll down. Rats and mice romped over her night and day. This despicable place became Harriet's new home for the next seven years, the place she preferred over slavery.

Why did Harriet enter this self-imprisonment? Why didn't she just run away? Why did she stay there for so long? First, while she couldn't be with her children, she knew they were free. She could hear their voices, and she didn't want to leave that precious sound. Also, it's hard for us to comprehend the degree of degradation that existed during the times of slavery and the sordid manipulations done to a slave's mind. They had witnessed beating after merciless beating and cruel, heartless killings without any refuge of justice. Fear permeated the inner core of Harriet and her family.

There was great anxiety that Harriet would be discovered. The consequences she would have to face if discovered were indescribable. The environment was permeated with distrust, and the air was filled with the smell of fear, lashings, chains, rape, and death. It was in this society, beyond our modern comprehension, that Harriet lay defenseless and immobilized. It's a wonder she had the ability to withstand the psychological abuse of Dr. Norcom, but her mental toughness was extraordinary. She had found the courage to do what no one else in her family had been able to do by breaking the cycle of servitude with amazing self-sacrifice.

Aunt Martha was incapable of coping with the possibility that Harriet would get caught. She was blinded by the visions of disaster that would be awaiting Harriet and her children. The entire family was in danger because they were hiding Harriet and deceiving Dr. Norcom. Harriet had committed a great crime by running away, and the repercussions would be fierce. It was in this milieu that Harriet and her family were rendered mute and paralyzed without options. There was no means of escape. Even if she could escape, Harriet wouldn't leave her children.

Harriet yearned for air more than light in her dungeon; but more than that she longed to see her children's faces and to tell them that she was alive and living above them. "How I longed to speak to them! I was eager to look on their faces, but there was no hole, no crack, through which I could peep." She couldn't speak, however, because her presence endangered the children's lives. The irony of her situation was cruel. In Harriet's words, "It seemed horrible to sit or lie in a cramped position day after day without one gleam of light. Yet I would have chosen this, rather than my lot as a slave."

Harriet's mother had a twin sister named Aunt Nancy. It was with Aunt Nancy that Harriet had slept at Dr. Norcom's house. Aunt Nancy nurtured her niece like a daughter. While Aunt Martha was overwhelmed with fear, Aunt Nancy had encouraged Harriet to escape her cruel master when others encouraged her to yield. It was her mother's sister who kindled Harriet's flame. She fostered Harriet's dream that she might be able to gain freedom for her children, and even if she perished doing it, her children would not be subjected to the same persecutions. When Harriet was a hostage in her dungeon, Aunt Nancy's words echoed in Harriet's ears, "I am old and have not long to live, and I could die happy if I could only see you and the children free. You must pray to God . . . , as I do for you, that he will lead you out of this darkness." Harriet recalled that "the whole family depended on her judgment and were guided by her guidance."

Random searches of Aunt Martha's house didn't cease. Harriet, in her secret space, would try to read and sew by the light filtering in through the wooden slats above her head. Her grandmother would bring her food in a clandestine code. She had four different places where she would knock and each position meant something different. It was impossible for her to stand or move in an erect position; so she crawled around for exercise. One day, while crawling about, Harriet came upon a gimlet—a small tool for boring holes—accidentally left by her uncle in the attic. She used it to bore three holes. One was for air and the other two provided a view of the street. The first person she saw through her newly bored hole was, paradoxically, Dr. Norcom. In time, the heat and cold extremities of weather became unbearable. One winter she was so cold and numb from lack of exercise that she was rendered unconscious for sixteen hours and became delirious.

As the years progressed Benjamin and Ellen developed into little children, and Mr. Sawyer became a Whig candidate for Congress. He won. As he prepared to move to Washington, Harriet became anxious. He had not emancipated their children, and if he were to die, the children could become enslaved at the whim of his heirs. Overcome with fear for her children's welfare, she decided something had to be done. Mr. Sawyer couldn't leave without making their freedom secure. She decided she had to risk everything and emerge from her attic prison.

As Mr. Sawyer was visiting the children, bidding them good-bye, Harriet climbed down into the storeroom and awaited his departure in a hiding place. As he exited she said, "Stop one moment, and let me speak for my children."

He paused momentarily, not sure of what he had heard, then he walked away. Harriet was numbed and stricken with helplessness. Did he not care for her at all? Was she mistaken to have believed in him? Suddenly Mr. Sawyer returned, finding Harriet hidden in the storeroom. He was amazed. He didn't even know she was in town.

He exclaimed, "Why do you come here? Why do you risk yourself in this house? They are mad to allow it. I shall expect to hear that you are all ruined."

Harriet begged him to emancipate their children. He promised to do it. He also promised to help her.

Harriet returned to her hiding place. She became so weary of it that she wished to die, but for the sake of the children she was willing to "bear on." Aunt Nancy would visit her and bring her the news with her cheerful countenance. Harriet, in her hibernation, schemed to protect her illusionary escape. She wrote letters and had someone mail them from New York so that Dr. Norcom would believe she was in New York City.

In time, Mr. Sawyer returned from Washington with a bride at his side. She passed Benjamin in the street and commented, "What a pretty little Negro!" Mr. Sawyer told his new bride the tale about his children, including the fabrication that the children were motherless. They were not motherless! Harriet was disappointed and saddened that he had represented her as dead.

Mr. Sawyer took Benjamin and Ellen into his home. After a while, his wife's sister, Mrs. Hobbs, wanted to take Ellen back East with her, but Mr. Sawyer's wife wanted to keep Benjamin. Harriet was alarmed and distraught. Were her children to be freed or treated as slaves? They were *still* not emancipated. She was realizing "how lightly slaveholders take their parental relations." Harriet now had a new mission. "I had no trust in thee, O' Slavery. Never should I know peace till my children were emancipated with all due formalities of law." After all of Harriet's sufferings and heroic actions, her children were once again being sucked back into the evil intricacies of slavery. How incredibly horrified and forsaken Harriet must have felt. She sent her beloved and ever-devoted grandmother to Mr. Sawyer's home to relay the message that she was not dead, she felt very unsure of his plans, and she wanted him, once again, to emancipate the children.

Mr. Sawyer responded by saying that he never intended to claim them as slaves and that they were better off up north, because Dr. Norcom was lamenting that they really still belonged to him, claiming they had been sold illegally, because they were really his daughter's property. Mr. Sawyer negotiated for Ellen to move to the East with Mrs. Hobbs, contending that she would be safer there and would also receive an education. Aunt Martha negotiated the details. Mr. Sawyer was to take her to Washington with him, and from there she would travel to Brooklyn.

Harriet's heart was breaking. She lamented, "Oh, how it tried my heart to send her away, so young, alone, among strangers! Without a mother's love to shelter her from the storms of life; almost without memory of a mother!" She begged her grandmother to let her have one night with her daughter in the open chambers and see her face once again before she left. She wanted her daughter to know that she still had a mother. She and Ellen had not seen each other for five years. Details were arranged and Harriet emerged from the trap door. She walked up to her daughter, looked into her incredulous eyes, and said, "Ellen, my dear child, I am your mother." Ellen was initially frightened, but "then sweetly laid her cheek against mine, and I folded her to the heart that had been so long desolated." Harriet told her she was a slave and that is why she must never tell anyone where she was hiding. She advised her daughter "to say her prayers, and remember to always pray for her poor mother, and that God would permit us to meet again. Ellen wept. But I did not check her tears. Perhaps she would never again have a chance to pour her tears into a mother's bosom." Harriet then nestled her sweet daughter in her arms. They wept, and through her tears Ellen whispered, "Mother, I will never tell," and she never did reveal her mother's secret.

After just a few short hours with her precious, darling daughter, Ellen was on her way to Washington. The tide was changing. Harriet's comfort, within the confines of her attic, was only tolerable if she had her children near her to rally her strength. After five years, Dr. Norcom's fury was ebbing. Harriet could now occasionally slip down and stretch her legs. She was very nervous about Ellen's journey and anxious to know that she had made it safely to Brooklyn. She finally received a letter. Within the letter, Ellen, who could not write, was quoted as saying, "I will try to do as you told me to and I pray for you every night and morning." Mrs. Hobbs wrote that Mr. Sawyer had "given" Ellen to her to be "her little waiting maid." She also said that she was going to send Ellen to school and that, hopefully soon, she could write Harriet with her own hand. Harriet was appalled by the letter's words "little waiting maid." Was Ellen to stay at the house until she could support herself, or was she given away as a piece of property? Harriet, overcome by conflicting thoughts, reasoned, "Surely there must be 'some' justice in a man; then I remembered how slavery perverted all the natural feelings of the human heart."

Harriet described her years in the dungeon,

Season after season, year after year, I peeped at my children's faces and heard their sweet voices, with a heart yearning all the while to say, "Your mother is here." Sometimes it appeared to me as if ages had rolled away since I entered upon that gloomy, monotonous existence. At times I was stupefied and listless; at other times I became very impatient to know when these dark years would end, and I should again be allowed to feel the sunshine, and breathe the pure air.

Two years after Ellen's departure, Mr. Sawyer arranged for Benjamin's move to the North, as soon as his Uncle Benjamin could escort him there. Harriet was feeling very restless. If her children were leaving, then she was ready to risk her life. She wanted to accompany them to the North. Her heart was heavy and she didn't have an inner peace that her children's best interests were being served. Mr. Sawyer was doing an obligatory job, but it was not up to Harriet's standards. Nothing would suffice until they had certain and definitive freedom. She became increasingly restless and said,

I had lived too long in bodily pain and anguish of spirit. Always I was in dread that by some accident, or some contrivance, slavery would succeed in snatching my children from me. This thought drove me nearly frantic and I determined to steer for the North Star at all hazards.

Harriet's Escape

God provided for Harriet. Word came from a friend that there was a timely chance for her to escape. She hesitated because she would be leaving Benjamin behind, but she knew he was free and was soon coming to New York with her uncle. This might be her only chance, and she wasn't going to be left behind.

Aunt Martha was beside herself with grief about Harriet's departing. Harriet ventured down to console her and someone knocked on the door. Aunt Martha said, "Come in," before she thought. Into the house walked the same Jenny who had tried to discover Harriet seven years earlier. Harriet hid behind the furniture, but there was a chance Jenny had seen her, which reinforced Harriet's decision. Her departure was a certainty now.

Harriet knew she must see Benjamin before she departed. It had been seven years since he had seen his mother. So Harriet greeted Benjamin in the storeroom. He wept when he saw her, saying he had known for the past two years she was up there, because he thought he had heard her cough one day before Ellen left. Benjamin had also overheard Aunt Martha advising Ellen to never tell that she had seen her mother. He hadn't spoken about it. Harriet recalled that during the past two years, when she watched Benjamin through her peephole, she had noticed that he would be protective of Harriet's side of the house. She wasn't surprised about his keen instincts, "but slaves, being surrounded by mysteries, deceptions, and dangers, early learn to be suspicious and watchful, and prematurely cautious and cunning."

As she left, Harriet told Benjamin she would send for him soon. Her grandmother gave her a bag filled with her hard-earned money. She said, "You may be sick among strangers and they would send you to the poor house to die." Harriet was overcome with sadness. She was leaving everything she had ever known, for better or worse. She would never see her beloved grandmother again, the woman who had nurtured her soul with all of her tenderness and steadfast love. Her grandmother gathered Harriet and Benjamin for a prayer. Harriet recalls, "On no other occasion has it ever been my lot to listen to so fervent a supplication for mercy and protection. It thrilled my heart and inspired me with trust in God." As Harriet departed, "The light of hope had risen in my soul." Harriet was hiding in the bushes when her son snuck in beside her and said, "I've been peeping into the doctor's window, and he's at home. Good-bye, Mother. Don't cry; I'll come."

Harriet was finally on her way to fulfilling her destiny, her vision. She had garnered the nerve to defy a hateful, abusive master. She had risked her life to break the bonds of slavery that bound her family. She had found the courage to leave the ironic sanctuary of her dungeon in the attic and the familiarity of her grandmother's motherwit. She reflected on her life as the winds of freedom were brushing against her cheek. God's grace had never left her. Even if she could have escaped her dungeon years earlier, she would not have done it. She was not going to leave her children.

God never gives us more than we can handle. When the time was right, God orchestrated it all so Harriet and her children were leaving simultaneously. Aunt Martha was also ready. She could reconcile herself with the risks and accept the dangers. Harriet was finally

HOLDING HER HEAD HIGH

doing it after waiting seven years. She heard God's calling; so she reached for the stars and God gave her the ladder.

Ten days after leaving North Carolina, Harriet arrived in Philadelphia. She was introduced to a colored Reverend Jeremiah Durham. He and his wife invited Harriet into their home for dinner and rest. He inquired about Harriet's husband. She proceeded to tell him her amazing story, to which he replied, "Don't answer everybody so openly. It might give some heartless people a pretext for treating you with contempt." These words stung and pierced Harriet's heart like a knife. She had sacrificed everything for her children's freedom, endured the wrath of a vengeful master, and lived in an attic where she could not even stand up for seven years. Now this man deigned to judge her. This was Harriet's first day as a free woman, and instead of joy, she felt as if she had been slapped. "The word 'contempt' burned me like coals of fire. God alone knows how I have suffered; and He, I trust, will forgive me. If I am permitted to have my children, I intend to be a good mother, and to love in such a manner that people cannot treat me with contempt." Single mothers from all races, countries, and origins have felt these emotions and judgments throughout the centuries. Life is always full of challenges. Challenges do not dissipate; they just restructure. It is our flexibility in dealing with these challenges that reveals our true strength of character.

Harriet set out promptly to find her daughter. The Anti-Slavery Society had offered to pay her way north, but she declined because she had her grandmother's money. She wanted other less-fortunate slaves to profit from their generosity. When the reverend returned with her ticket, she was surprised that it was in the back of the train. She offered the reverend more money, and he replied, "They could not be had for any money. They don't allow colored people to go to first-class cars." Harriet was stunned. Freedom evidently had many definitions.

Harriet arrived at Mrs. Hobbs's home to visit with her daughter. She hadn't seen Ellen in two years. Immediately visible to Harriet's motherly discerning eyes were the signs of her nine-year-old daughter's neglect. Upon meeting Harriet, Mrs. Hobbs looked at her and said, "I suppose you know that my cousin, Mr. Sawyer, has 'given' her to my eldest daughter. She will make a nice waiting maid for her when she grows up." Harriet quietly endured the indignity of her comment, but she was inwardly tormented. "How could she, who knew by experience the strength of a mother's love, and who was perfectly aware of the relation John bore to my children, how could she look me in the face, while she thrust such a dagger in my heart?" Like the grumbling of a bear awakening from hibernation, Harriet stumbled upon the realization that her lover, Mr. Sawyer, had no intention of emancipating her children. Ellen looked at her mother and said, "Mother, when will you take me to live with you?"

Harriet was helpless. She had no source of income and no home for her daughter. So she had to leave her with Mrs. Hobbs and visit as she could until she could provide for her daughter. Harriet promptly found a job with a woman named Mrs. Bruce. Harriet describes her fortune of meeting Mrs. Bruce: "The heavenly Father had been most merciful to me in leading me to this place. Mrs. Bruce was a kind and gentile lady and proved to be a true and sympathizing friend."

Harriet saved her money when she could. It was difficult because she also provided for Ellen's welfare. Complications arose when Mrs. Hobbs expected Harriet to do things, such as purchase Ellen a much-needed pair of shoes, yet wouldn't allow Harriet to take Ellen to the eye doctor. "Situated as I was, it was not polite to insist upon it, I made no complaint, but I longed to be entirely free to act a mother's part towards my children."

Harriet was in the North but she was not free from the dangers of being discovered. Dr. Norcom, still vengeful after seven years, received a tip about Harriet's location. He made another trip, one of his many, to New York City in search of her. Harriet was warned and had to leave quickly, escaping to Boston. While she was in Boston, another miracle happened. She and Benjamin were reunited. He had been sent to New York and then proceeded to Boston to see his mother. He rushed in to greet her, shouting, "O mother! Here I am! I run all the way; and I come all alone. How d'you do?" Harriet was finally reunited with her son and daughter. She could see their faces and hold them in her arms!

She was no longer a captive in an attic, merely overhearing their voices and capturing obscure optic glances through a peephole. Battles had been won, but Harriet's war was not yet over.

Free but Fearful

Dr. Norcom left New York City, having searched for Harriet in vain. She then returned to New York City and, not yet having a home of her own, left Benjamin in Boston under the care of her brother, his Uncle William. The environment in the North was, perhaps, more liberal for slaves, whether freed or runaway, but the streets were ominously filled with spies ready to capture runaway slaves and return them to the South. Harriet always felt she must hide her face and was constantly ultra-sensitive about what was potentially lurking in the shadows. Discovery meant doom.

Harriet continued to visit Ellen, and though her daughter was stoic and never complained, Harriet could perceive Ellen's unhappiness. When pressed, it was revealed that Mr. Hobbs and Mrs. Hobbs's brother, Mr. Thomas, drank excessively, exposing Ellen to vile language and tawdry behavior. Harriet was desperate to remove Ellen from that environment. She had saved a hundred dollars, which was remarkable but not enough for a home of her own.

One day Harriet arrived and discovered a distraught Ellen. She had overheard one of Mr. Thomas's conversations and gathered that he was going to betray Harriet. Mr. Thomas had ripped up a letter outside, and Ellen pieced the fragments together, which confirmed her suspicions. Mr. Thomas had offered to help Dr. Norcom capture Harriet. Will it never end? Dr. Norcom was on his way to New York City again, exhibiting a maniacal obsession regarding Harriet, making yet another trip to New York City in search of her.

Harriet explained the situation to Mrs. Bruce, who kindly offered to take her to a friend's house in the country. Harriet was determined to take Ellen with her. Harriet's safety and freedom had been irreversibly compromised by Mrs. Hobbs's brother, consequently endangering Ellen's safety too. Thus Harriet marched up to Mrs. Hobbs's house and reclaimed her daughter and took her to Mrs. Bruce's house.

As they were leaving, Ellen was shivering due to her lack of appropriate clothing. Harriet took off her skirt and put it on her daughter. Mrs. Bruce ran into the house and retrieved a shawl and hood for Ellen. Harriet recalled, "Truly, of such souls as hers are the kingdom of heaven."

Heaven on Earth

Harriet and her daughter traveled to Boston:

> The day after my arrival was one of the happiest of my life. I felt as if I was beyond the reach of the bloodhounds; and for the first time during many years, I had both my children together with me. They greatly enjoyed their reunion. And laughed and chatted merrily. I watched them with a swelling heart. Their every motion delighted me.

Harriet shared a home and expenses with a friend. She provided for the family with her sewing, as her children sat by her side learning to read and write. She lived in this God-given heaven on earth for two years.

Harriet's brother, William, offered to send Ellen to a boarding school. Harriet was overwhelmed with this decision. How could she part with her sweet, precious daughter whose companionship she treasured? She believed her daughter deserved this opportunity, though, so she agreed. Ellen responded, "Mother, it is very hard to leave you alone. I am almost sorry I am going, though I do want to improve myself. But you will write me often, won't you, mother?" Harriet felt as if they should discuss Ellen's father before she started boarding school. She started to share her story and explain the circumstances regarding her father when Ellen stopped her and said,

> O, don't mother! Please don't tell me any more. I know all about it, mother. I am nothing to my father, and he is nothing to me. All my love is for you. I was with him five months in Washington, and he never cared for me. He never spoke to me

HOLDING HER HEAD HIGH

as he did to his little Fanny. I knew all the time he was my father, for Fanny's nurse told me so; but she said I must never tell anybody, and I never did. I used to wish he would take me in his arms and kiss me, as he did Fanny; or that he would sometimes smile at me, as he did at her. I thought if he was my own father, he ought to love me. I was a little girl then and didn't know any better. But now I never think anything about my father, all my love is for you.

With tender tears of inseverable unity, Ellen moved to New York to attend school. William asked Harriet to move to Rochester with him and open the Anti-Slavery Reading Room. She spent a year there with Isaac and Amy Post. Afterward William wanted to move to California, and he wanted to take Benjamin with him. Harriet once again faced the excruciating pain of parting with her gentle, brave son. It seemed so recently that she had just been united with him. The years they had shared physically together as a family had been indescribably sweet. Still, she allowed him to go, making one of those decisions that selfless mothers make. So Benjamin moved to California, and Harriet returned to work for Mrs. Bruce's son, because Mrs. Bruce had died. Soon after, she was once again faced with a threat from the vengeful Dr. Norcom. His wrath was truly insatiable! If this scenario had been written in a screenplay, it would certainly have been deemed implausible.

THE FUGITIVE

The Fugitive Slave Act had been passed in 1850, making the atmosphere even more tenuous in New York City. Dr. Norcom was on his way to New York City, so Harriet once again had to leave her employment and home. Mr. and Mrs. Bruce were so accommodating that Mrs. Bruce, trusting Harriet implicitly, even let her take her baby with her. The Fugitive Slave Act stated that the penalty for harboring a slave was imprisonment and one thousand dollars. Mrs. Bruce, mirroring her former mother-in-law's heart, stated, "I will go to the state's prison, rather than have any poor victim torn from my house, to be carried back to slavery." Harriet was sent to New

England and sheltered by the wife of a senator. This senator had not voted for the Fugitive Slave Act—which stipulated that all slaves who had escaped to the North, if caught, had to be returned to their owner. After Dr. Norcom left New York City, Harriet returned to Mrs. Bruce. And although Dr. Norcom was back home in North Carolina, his essence prevailed. Harriet wrote, "I could never go out and breathe God's free air without trepidation at my heart."

Harriet finally received news that Dr. Norcom had died. Amazingly, his dying words were that Harriet should never be free as long as a child of his survived.

Thus Harriet's new enemy was Mr. Dodge, the husband of Dr. Norcom's daughter, Emily. He sent word to an acquaintance of Harriet's that he might possibly permit Harriet to buy her freedom. To this statement, Harriet's friend replied,

> I don't think it would be of any use, sir. I have heard her say she would go to the ends of the earth rather than pay any man or woman for her freedom, because she thinks she has a right to it. Besides, she couldn't do it, if she could, for she has spent her earnings to educate her children.

Mr. Dodge then threatened to take not only Harriet but also her children. He used Dr. Norcom's rationale that they had been sold illegally, because they were really Emily's property, and she had not been of age. Harriet later reflected,

> This it was. More than anything else, that roused such a tempest in my soul. Benjamin was with his uncle in California, but my innocent daughter had come to spend a vacation with me. I thought of what I had suffered in slavery at her age, and my heart was like a tiger's when a hunter tries to seize her young.

Mission Accomplished

Harriet was so weary of running. Yet once again, she was running to safety in New England with her daughter, Ellen. Mrs. Bruce took things into her own hands, hiring a man to negotiate with Mr. Dodge. She proposed three hundred dollars for him to relinquish all claims on Harriet and her children forever. Mr. Dodge grumbled at the low offer, but obviously desperate, he accepted. It was done! Harriet and her children were officially free. She had finally accomplished the mission she had envisioned as a fifteen-year-old girl in North Carolina. Mrs. Bruce wrote, "I am rejoiced to tell you that the money for your freedom has been paid to Mr. Dodge. Come home tomorrow. I long to see you and my sweet babe."

Harriet was mesmerized by the event. Someone validated it by saying, "It is true, I have seen the bill of sale!" Harriet reeled at the words "bill of sale." "Those words struck me like a blow. So I was 'sold' at last! A human being 'sold' in the free city of NY! The bill of sale is on record, and future generations will learn from it that women were articles of traffic in New York, late in the nineteenth century of the Christian religion."

Nevertheless, Harriet was most grateful to her generous friend who had taken it upon herself to free Harriet legally. Mrs. Bruce had been a generous ally in Harriet's battle to free her family from the bonds of slavery. God had obviously led Harriet to Mrs. Bruce's home, for He knew the compassion of the Bruce family and what the outcome would be. "I felt as if a heavy load had been lifted from my weary shoulders. When I rode home in the car I was no longer afraid to unveil my face and look at people as they passed."

God's grace also continued to carry Harriet's grandmother, Aunt Martha. She lived to rejoice in Harriet's freedom. She had lost her children to slavery, but her granddaughter and great-grandchildren were free. Feeling as though her life had reached completion, she died and journeyed to "where the wicked cease from troubling, and the weary are at rest." Harriet's Uncle Philip died shortly thereafter, and an unusually insightful obituary reflected on the black man's fate: "Now that death has laid him low, they call him a good man and a useful citizen; but what are eulogies to the black man, when the world has faded from his vision? It does not require man's praise to obtain rest in God's kingdom."

Harriet remained with Mrs. Bruce. She yearned for a place of her own for her children but as she wrote, "But God so orders circumstances as to keep me with my friend Mrs. Bruce. Love, duty, gratitude, also bind me to her side. It is a privilege to serve her who pities my oppressed people, and who has bestowed the inestimable boon of freedom on me and my children." In summarizing her own account Harriet reflected upon her life and her arduous journey. She wrote,

It has been painful for me, in many ways, to recall the dreary years I passed in bondage. I would gladly forget them if I could. Yet the retrospection is not altogether without solace; for with those gloomy recollections come tender memories of my good old grandmother, like light, fleecy clouds floating over a dark and troubled sea.

As Harriet reflected upon the extensive turmoils and volatile emotions of her life, she made a pronounced reference to her grandmother. There are many heroines in this story—heroines who held their heads high. Motherwit prevailed. Harriet obviously felt an intense love and boundless sense of gratitude for her grandmother, whose strength, faith, and constancy gave Harriet the springboard from which to leap beyond her limitations. It was because she knew she could rely on her grandmother's selflessness and devotion that she could take the risks she did. If there had been no one to care for her children, Harriet could not have run away and hidden in an attic for seven years.

Aunt Martha was a single mother, single grandmother, and single great-grandmother. Not only did she raise her surviving children after her daughter died, she raised Harriet and then Harriet's children. Aunt Martha gallantly accepted the continual challenges she inherited with an unshakable faith in God. She was the rock foundation for the whole family. Upon her rock, the dreams of Harriet were born. Upon her boundless generosity, Harriet's visions soared. Their freedom was born, their cycle of slavery broken, due to the dependability of Aunt Martha and the bold defiance of Harriet. Each attribute contributed to the other in accomplishing this magnificent feat.

Aunt Nancy was also a heroine in that she continued to nurture Harriet's hope. Aunt Nancy believed in what Harriet was doing, though Aunt Martha was more tentative in her approach. Aunt Nancy shared Harriet's vision and helped her continue to see beyond the horizon when the view was bleak and miserable in her cramped, airless attic. Harriet's benefactress, who sheltered her in her home when she first escaped, was a woman of compassion and conviction. In her home Harriet sat in the attic, listening as Dr. Norcom came to borrow five hundred dollars so he could travel to New York and look for her.

Mrs. Bruce and her daughter-in-law, also Mrs. Bruce, were heroines too. They were willing to bear the price of prison and a thousand-dollar fine to aid Harriet during her times of trouble. They helped her escape and find shelter. The second Mrs. Bruce even allowed Harriet to take her baby with her as a decoy. And it was this same Mrs. Bruce who finally completed the mission, bringing the horror to an end, by purchasing Harriet's freedom.

All of these women, these sisters, these heroines worked together for the benefit of mankind. They united their attributes, visions, and passions to accomplish the forbidden—freedom for the black woman from the vile and pernicious bonds of slavery. Yet the greatest of these heroines is Harriet—the ultimate self-sacrificing, single mother who schemed, even before her children were conceived, about how her children could be free. Her children's lives were going to be different. Resonating deep within her soul was a calling. Many people hear a call but don't have the fortitude or will to heed that beckoning. It's easy to cheer someone's far-reaching dreams; it's quite another to actually be the one to achieve them.

Harriet, praying to God over her parents' graves, wept from the fear that echoed in her chest. She knew she must burst through the impenetrable barrier of injustice, and she showed the character and the determination to do it. She kissed her angels' sleeping faces and then ran into the vast unknown of blind faith. She had only God as her shield and guide, literally, as she groped through the darkness, not only for that night but for years to come. She hid in her bleak, airless, lightless attic, willing only to hear the sweet sound of her children's voices rather than leave their presence. She suffered the severities of cold, intensity of heat, illness, and delirium for seven years in order not to risk the lives of the ones she so dearly loved.

A deep sense of never-ceasing determination carried Harriet through one battle after another, including the unwillingness of the lover she had chosen to strive beyond half measures for the freedom of their children. Harriet was not a woman of half measures. She was a woman who was not going to cease until the troublin' ceased. Half measures availed her nothing. Her unyielding, undying, lioness persistence led her to knock on locked doors until they swung open for her.

Harriet was born a victim, but she died a victor. With God as her guiding force, with the belief that He spoke to her and was not going to forsake her, she jumped into the deep rivers of faith. God led Harriet to higher ground because He knew she would follow and that Harriet's spirit would serve as an example to all who are bound in similarly dire circumstances. She would elicit hope. She would define bravery. She would conquer injustice. She would hold her head high.

Life Lesson: Don't Give Up Before the Miracle

The gravity of Harriet's situation would have defeated a weaker woman. She was a hostage in the sordid world of Dr. Norcom, who abused her physically, emotionally, and mentally. She must have wondered if those times would ever end. *Where was the miracle?* God whispered courage in her ear.

She was a prisoner in an insufferable holding cell for seven years. She surely was competing with the devil for her sanity and her health. *Where was the miracle?* God gave her the ability to endure.

She could not be with her children for seven years. *Where was the miracle?* He let her be near and hear their voices.

She lived as a hostage of fear in New York City, where she was destined to be betrayed at any moment. She most certainly felt trapped in the mire of anxieties. *Where was the miracle?* God put people in her life to protect and assist her.

During any of these events in her life Harriet could have thrown in the towel and resolved to accept her fate. But she did not. She grasped the coattails of God's timing and held firm. She did not give up before the miracle. Through long, tedious, and sometimes overwhelming challenges, Harriet persisted one day at a time and didn't relent until she overcame them. God placed upon her heart the calling to reach for higher ground, and He was not going to drop her before it was accomplished. At times Harriet must have felt that He was abandoning her, but He did not. God was guiding her, God was walking with her, because God saw eternity in perspective. And He eventually did solidify Harriet's freedom and the freedom of her children!

Harriet's job was to not give up before the miracle. In the process, she held her head high. She resolved that her children would never have to be victims of the salaciousness of slavery. She risked everything, including her life and well-being, so they would not have to endure what she had endured, what her ancestors had endured. She accomplished these feats as an unwed single mother. Her lover was never really there to help her or her children. So Harriet was a beacon of enlightenment on many levels—an awakening for a society that was ignorant to the horrors of slavery; encouragement for women who were still caught in the misery of slavery; hope for unwed single mothers; and a shining example for her children.

So, whatever you're going through in life, whatever you're suffering, have faith and show up. You don't want to miss it. You don't want your children to miss it. Hold your head high, and don't give up before the miracle!

Argument provokes argument, reason is met by sophistry,
but narratives of slaves go right to the heart of men.

—One northern editor

CHAPTER FOURTEEN

Pioneer Single Mothers— Setting the Stage

1800s

The gaunt and sad-faced woman sitting on the front seat of the wagon, following her lord where he might lead her, her face hidden in the same ragged sunbonnet which had crossed the Appalachians and Missouri long before. That was America, my brethren! There was the seed of America's wealth. There was the great romance of America—the woman in the sunbonnet; and not, after all, the hero with the rifle across the saddle horn.[1]

—EMERSON HOUGH

Pioneers. Wild West and women's suffrage. The heartbeat of America. Trails of trials and trails of tears. Bravery bequeaths adventure. Wagons and sunbonnets. Parades and speeches. Society on the move. Women weather extremities. Women resist injustice. Who will be their voice?

The pioneer single mother. At this point in the book, I just want to break out into the words of Helen Reddy's song, "I Am Woman; Hear Me Roar!" The pioneer woman was the "seed of

America's wealth." She packed up, usually at the beckoning of her husband, and left her extended family, friends, and way of life behind, never to see them. The dangers were unforeseen, the outcome unpredictable.

The pioneer single mother embarked on these adventures either as a woman who lost her husband on the way, who left in pursuit of her husband who had run off, or who just packed up the kids to head west. She faced dangers uniquely her own with a gusto born in the wild grasses of the plains and the blazing sunsets of the western sky. Once again the American woman was called to make a pilgrimage. Like her foremothers who had braved the seas, these women endured endless roads of rock and desert. Men may have broken the ground, but it was often the women who planted the seeds—seeds created from their blood, sweat, and tears, their joys and passions that knew no boundaries.

WESTWARD, HO!

Pioneer single mothers trekked with their children for a six-month, two-thousand-mile wagon trip. They sometimes rode, but many times they walked, encountering intense heat, freezing cold, floods, and drought—sometimes all in one trip. They suffered from starvation, thirst, and illnesses such as cholera, fevers, dysentery, smallpox, and scurvy. Children were often lost or kidnapped.

These women endured accidents as well as deaths of family members and friends. One woman lost her husband on the trip when high winds toppled a tree, and it fell and killed her husband and her son. She had to continue on the trip with her three small children. They were spotted walking beside the wagon carrying loads bigger than themselves.

Elisha Brooks's son remembers traveling with his mother and five siblings. They were approached by a band of Indians as all of her children were coming down with the measles. The Indians fell in beside them for a week. He recalls they were "colorful, well dressed, well provisioned, and peaceful."[2] Elisha also remembers how they were "all lying in a row on the ground of the tent with the measles, while six inches of snow covered the ground and the trees were brilliant with icicles."[3]

A pioneer slave single mother and her three daughters walked the entire way, herding the cattle, from Mississippi to California. When her owner wanted to cross the plains again to Texas, she sued for freedom to stay in California. She won.

Mollie Kelley's husband, in 1863, had "heid him away to that Rebel Paradise, Montana."[4] She waited and waited for his return. After he didn't return, she decided to go from Kansas to Virginia City without him. She hitched the mules to the wagon and headed west with her two daughters, ages eight and three. She drove the team of mules herself as her girls played in the wagon bed.

Mary Wells Yates was a widow with thirteen children. Her first journey was traveling sixteen hundred miles on horseback from Virginia to Missouri. She took her three boys across the plains with her six cows pulling her wagon. She sold the cows, made a profit, and then went back and got some more of her children. During the next trip by mule-drawn wagon, her daughter bore a child, and Mary became a grandmother. She crossed the plains from Missouri to Montana thirteen times on her own and became known as the legendary Granny Yates.

THE PLIGHT OF CHILDREN

Children were often the most remarkable ones—they left their homes and grandparents, aunts and uncles behind, and sometimes their beloved pets. One boy remembered having to leave his cat behind and was haunted by the image of the cat following them to the gate and watching them leave. One boy's pet ox was pulling the family's wagon. When the ox's partner collapsed, the boy's ox fell down beside his partner and refused to budge. The family had to move on, but the boy went back with some hay and sat by his ox through a snowstorm until the oxen, once rested, decided to get up again.

Some children perceived the two-thousand-mile trip as an adventure and remember it as the best time of their lives. Others were not so fortunate, losing their parents or siblings along the way. These children were in the wagons as they rolled back and forth over the graves to prevent predators from getting to the bodies. They then had to leave their mom or dad, brother or sister in a tiny, unmarked spot in a vast area, never to be found again.

The children often walked beside or behind the wagons barefoot. Benjamin Bonney recalled, "We children were barefooted and I can remember yet how we limped across the desert, for we cut the soles of our feet. . . ."[5] One thirteen-year-old girl walked the whole way from Missouri to Willamette Valley in Oregon. She was in charge of watching the horses so they didn't stray. She walked in the dust of hundreds of animals and wagons. At the end of the day, she would arrive at the camp covered from head to toe with dust in her hair, ears, and mouth, with no hopes for a bath.

The boys would hunt and keep watch at night. The girls would sew, cook, and clean but also ride ponies and drive wagons. Some girls complained that they would help the boys with their jobs, but the boys would never help with the sewing or cooking and cleaning. The kids would run and play while they were camped, sometimes discovering things like braids from a dead girl or bleached skulls with verses written in them from previous children.

From Dawn to Dusk

If the modern single mother feels she has no time for her children, she should peek into the life of the pioneer single mother. She sawed logs, dug cellars, plowed fields, dug canals, and erected fences. She would harness the horses, harrow the fields, thresh the hay, and brand the cows. She would capture, kill, and skin her food, milk the cows, churn the butter, dress the chickens, and cook the meals. She would clean up after the meals, make candles, spin wool, sew the clothes, make soap, and wash the clothes in hot springs. One pioneer woman said she felt "worse than a stewed witch"[6] after spending a day over the washtub. Another woman reported, "I was merely an overworked mother of four trying to make ends meet under conditions that were none too easy" and yet she was considered "not gainfully employed."[7] These single mothers were so busy that it was hard to always watch the myriad of children running around the prairie who sometimes fell victim to wells, rivers, snakes, or wild, running horses.

Pioneers were often vulnerable to Indian attacks. When one pioneer woman's cabin was attacked, her husband and two of her older sons were killed. The mother, who was wounded, insisted that her eleven-year-old son go on without her and take the baby. The boy ran, carrying his baby brother out of the burning house and for fifty miles to safety. The mother somehow survived and was later reunited with her son and baby. Another mother went into labor alone in her cabin with her two baby girls. She was unable to call for help in the middle of the prairie, so she resorted to tossing apples across the room to keep her little girls occupied while she gave birth.

Pioneer children were put to work on the prairie at a young age. Nine-year-olds were asked to reclaim stray horses. Children, like their mothers, fetched water with horse and buggy from the nearest well. They milked the cows before school and after school, rounded up the cattle, gathered eggs, tended to the chickens, and churned the butter. They emptied the slop jars and chopped wood. The girls also helped the boys set traps and catch animals for the evening meal. Children were sent out to kill antelope, geese, deer, and prairie chickens. Pioneer children attended school in tents, mud houses, boxcars, or converted chicken houses. They arrived on foot or on horseback, carrying tablets and pails of food. And they all drank water from a common dipper. Many children were needed for the harvest and, thus, they were not allowed to attend school until after harvest was completed.

Many children lost both parents or were being raised by destitute parents. In 1853 the Children's Aid Society moved 150,000 homeless children to the rural towns and ranches of the West. They arrived on orphan trains. Then they were displayed on platforms so people could pick and choose which children they wanted. One could tell if a child had been recently orphaned by the fact that his/her head had been shaved for lice. Some children, as may be expected, loved their new surroundings and families. One child, who had to return to his real family, said, "For three short years I had love."[8] Other children were not so lucky and ended up in abusive situations.

Slow Progress

Pioneer women who journeyed with their families would some-times end up in the middle of the prairie with an alcoholic or abu-sive husband. The mother's and children's lives were compromised. Children were still considered entities and the property of the father. If a woman left, the husband would still get to keep the chil-dren. Many, for the sake of the children, remained in miserable and dangerous situations. These tragedies continued until the end of the century when Belva Lockwood's bill, The Married Women's Property Act, passed in 1896. One of the many benefits of this bill was that women were finally given the automatic right to their chil-dren. Western states such as Indiana, South Dakota, and Nevada were slowly becoming more liberal in granting divorces.

The pioneer single mother, whether her husband was killed on the wagon trail or killed once established on the prairie, whether she gath-ered up her children, hitched the wagon, and journeyed two thousand miles in search of a missing husband or was already a widow, was an example of the enduring American spirit. She embodied stamina, strength, faith, and the adventurous spirit of a rebel. She blessed the frontier and her children with hope, love, and grace—grace exhibited under inordinate pressures. These pioneer mothers often look miser-able in those old tin-type photographs, but somewhere there must have been a smile in their hearts because, well, they were still alive. They were with their children, posing for the photographer, and that was an amazing feat. Their stalwart characteristics were evident in their children, who were posing with a glimmer in their eyes, an emergence of the Wild-West persona. The heartbeat of America!

The stories of the youngsters on the emigrant trails
are a remarkable testimony to the resiliency of the human spirit.[9]

—EMMY WERNER

Adventuresome Single Mother

1876–1933

SNAPSHOT	Elinore, Jerrine, and Mrs. Louderer dashing full speed through the snow to deliver the "twelve disciples"
MOTHER MOMENT	Galloping through the prairies of Wyoming with baby Jerrine sharing her saddle
CHALLENGE	Orphaned single mother struggles to overcome adversity and provide for her child
STEWARDSHIP	Met all challenges with humor and kindness
SCRIPTURE	A cheerful look brings joy to the heart, and good news gives health to the bones. (Proverbs 15:30 NIV)

CHapter FIFTeen

Heal with Humor

Jerrine was always such a dear little pal.

—Elinore Pruitt Stewart

Late 1800s. Oklahoma and Wyoming. Beautiful and spacious. Pastures and mountain vistas. Clean, bubbling brooks and a menagerie of wild animals. Coyotes howl and horses run knee-deep in flowers. Churning butter and killing dinner. Solitude and independence. Beautiful, dangerous, exciting. Take a deep breath and smell the sage. Feast your eyes on the beauty of the western plains. Listen to the stories that define America.

Researching Elinore Pruit Stewart was like experiencing a breath of fresh air. She is the comedic relief in a Shakespearian tragedy. Her perspective on life was one that greeted her challenges with a sense of adventure. She exuded humor and friendliness. Elinore is like a piece of Wrigley's Spearment gum after garlic pasta or an ice-cold snow cone on a hot summer day. She puts a smile on my face.

Elinore's life was not easy. She was raised in the Indian territory of Oklahoma and was the oldest of nine children. Her family was very poor. Her father died, then her mother, then her stepfather when she was a young girl. She assumed the responsibilities of her eight orphaned brothers and sisters. She was self-educated, so finding employment was difficult. Most of her jobs included hard labor.

Elinore finally married, but something went awry, and she ended up giving birth without her husband. Afterward, she was on her own as a single mother. Elinore simply adored her baby daughter, Jerrine. Elinore yearned for fresh air and wide-open spaces. She wanted to be one of the first female homesteaders. So she packed up her daughter and headed west. She documented her life's adventures in letters to her former employer in Colorado. Her letters represent her spunk, vigor, and keen sense of humor. They are simply delightful. She takes us on a journey through the wild West. We get to glimpse, through her bright and gregarious eyes, the escapades of a single mother in pioneer America.

Timeless Scenario: Girl is born poor in Indian territory. Girl is orphaned. Girl is a hard worker. Girl meets boy. Girl and boy marry. Girl and boy are separated. Girl is single mother. Girl loves her baby girl. Girl encounters hardship in city. Girl and baby pioneer in the Wild West.

THE YOUNG ELINORE

Elinore was the firstborn of Josephine Elizabeth Courtney Pruitt's nine children. She was born in the region called White Bead Hill in the Chickasaw Nation Indian Territory (Oklahoma) on June 3, 1876. Elinore's father was in the military and was killed on the Mexican border. Elinore's mother remarried and subsequently bore her remaining eight children with her new husband. Elinore's family was poor, dirt poor. She had no shoes until she was six years old. She attended school for a short while, but the school was abruptly shut down because her teacher was hung from a sycamore tree outside the schoolhouse for stealing a horse. Elinore's inquisitive, insatiable mind looked for knowledge where she could find it. She read from scraps of paper and depended upon the mercies of the local folk to help her with her words.

On January 10, 1893, Elinore's mother, thirty-five years old, died from repercussions of birthing her ninth child. The following year,

Elinore's stepdad was killed in a work-related accident. Elinore, eighteen years old and the eldest, was now responsible for her five brothers and sisters. The other siblings had married at quite young ages.

Random relatives tried to break up the family and divide the children, but as Elinore wrote, "We refused to be raised in halves and so we arranged to stay at Grandmother's and keep together." Their grandmother was poor and blind, thus the children had to manage the farm. "Consequently," Elinore wrote, "I learned to do many things which girls more fortunately situated don't even know have to be done." Things didn't work out with Elinore's grandmother, so the children were forced to go out into the world and provide for themselves. Most of them found employment with the railroad.

Becoming a Single Mother

Elinore worried that her hands had become so rough that a boy would never woo her. So when a man started to woo her, rough hands and all, she jumped at the chance to marry. In 1902 at age twenty-six Elinore married Harry Cramer Rupert, eighteen years her senior. Something happened within Elinore's marriage; exactly what is a mystery, but she was no longer living with Rupert by 1906. She left him when she was pregnant, and a woman wouldn't do that, especially in the 1800s, unless there were serious problems.

After she left Rupert, Elinore most likely lived with her sisters Josephine and Susie in Oklahoma City. She worked as a domestic servant at 322 West 12th Street, which provided room and board.

Elinore gave birth to Mary Jerrine at St. Anthony's Hospital in Oklahoma City. She appears to have been a single mother from that moment on. There are conflicting stories about what happened to Rupert. One rendition says they were divorced; another says Rupert was killed when a bridge he was inspecting on the Canadian River collapsed. Divorce may be the more reliable version. Records produce a patent that Harry C. Rupert filed in Oklahoma in 1908. In 1915 he appears to have married a woman named Bertha. Regardless of which version is true, Elinore was alone.

Working odd jobs to provide for Jerrine, Elinore cooked, cleaned, scrubbed floors, and was responsible for stoking the coal furnaces. She worked in the hospital in Oklahoma and she, who had never completed her schooling, wrote short articles and submitted them to the local newspapers. Some were published in the *Kansas City Star*.

When Jerrine was nine months old, Elinore was allegedly warned by a police matron that Rupert's relatives from Ohio wanted Jerrine and that official proceedings to take Jerrine away from Elinore had begun. Fearing for her daughter's safety, she took Jerrine and her two sisters and boarded a train bound for Colorado. Elinore became very ill with erysipelas and could not finish the journey. After she recovered, they once again proceeded, eventually arriving in Denver.

Elinore sought employment and eventually found a job with a lovely, widowed schoolteacher from Boston, Juliet Coney. Elinore worked seven days a week as a nurse and housekeeper for two dollars a week. As a single mother, Elinore sometimes needed help. She reached out to the Sunshine Rescue Mission that was founded by James Goodheart. The mission offered a helping hand to men, women, and children as they also provided for their spiritual needs. The Reverend Father Corrigan, a Catholic priest, offered to help Elinore study for the civil service test, a type of schooling certificate.

One day as Elinore was working and had to "tote the coal over, and then drag it across to the hungry furnace," she felt a pain in her side, which was a precursor to the grippe. She had an appointment with the reverend to study . . .

> so I went over to let him see how little I knew. I was in pain and was so blue that I could hardly speak without weeping, so I told Reverend father how tired I was of the rattle and bang, of the glare and the soot, the smells and the hurry. I told him what I longed for was the sweet, free open, and that I would like to homestead.

ELINORE'S VISION
A nurse had enlightened Elinore to the wonders of Wyoming. Visions of the West became Elinore's only solace during her sick-

ness: "I was so discouraged because of the grippe that nothing but the mountains, the pines, and the fresh clean air seemed worth while." In the depths of the physical, mental, and emotional fatigue that illness causes, Elinore started to fantasize about homesteading in Wyoming. Her sense of adventure and desire for a better life for her daughter led her to embrace the unpredictable, unreliable unknown. What hardship could the West offer that surpassed the rigors of dragging coals to a "hungry furnace"?

With waning strength, Elinore announced to the reverend that she wanted to homestead in Wyoming; as a single woman she had that right. He advised her that a good plan would be to get a job as a housekeeper for a rancher, who could teach her about the land and essentials of survival. She could make a living as she perused the land for homesteading. He suggested to Elinore that she take an ad out in the paper. Elinore writes, "I did so, and because I wanted as much rest and quiet as possible, I took Jerrine and went uptown and got a nice quiet room."

There are two conflicting versions about who placed the ad in the newspaper first, Elinore or the Scottish widower Clyde Stewart. They may have both issued ads simultaneously. Clyde's ad was in the *Denver Post* on March 7, 1909, and stated, "Wanted—young or middle-aged lady as companion and to assist with housework on Wyoming ranch; a good permanent home for right party. Box 3, W117-Post."[1]

One way or another, Elinore met Clyde Stewart. She wanted the safety of the mission and for her friends to "size him up," so they met at the Sunshine Mission. Elinore was a conscientious person and a pragmatic one. She wanted to make sure that she and her baby would be safe alone with this man in the wilds of Wyoming. She requested the assistance of Father Corrigan to interview him as well. Father Corrigan suggested that Elinore meet Mr. Stewart's mother and, thus, she visited with his mother for a week in her home.

Approvals were met and Elinore was hired as a housekeeper and hired hand. In April 1909, Elinore and her two-year-old Jerrine embarked on the journey from Colorado to the sage-covered fields of Wyoming. They were accompanied by Elinore's new employer, the Scottish Mr. Stewart. They rode on the train for twenty-four hours and then encountered another grueling two days of travel by horse-drawn stagecoach.

Elinore's Letters

Elinore wrote of her journey to her former employer, Mrs. Coney, exhibiting a rare and invaluable quality of seeing humor in all situations.

Burnt Fork, Wyoming
April 18, 1909
Dear Mrs. Coney,

Are you thinking I am lost, like the Babes in the Wood? Well, I am not and I'm sure the robins would have the time of their lives getting leaves to cover me out here. I am 'way up close to the Forest Reserve of Utah, within half a mile of the line, sixty miles from the railroad. I was twenty-four hours on the train and two days on the stage, and oh, those two days! The snow was just beginning to melt and the mud was about the worst I ever heard of.

The first stage we tackled was just about as rickety as it could very well be and I had to sit with the driver, who was Mormon and so handsome that I was not a bit offended when he insisted on making love all the way, especially after he told me that he was a widower Mormon. But, of course, as I had no chaperone I looked very fierce (not that that was very difficult with the wind and mud as allies) and told him my actual opinion of Mormons in general and particular.

Meanwhile my new employer, Mr. Stewart, sat upon a stack of baggage and was dreadfully concerned about something he calls his "tookie," but I am unable to tell you what that is. The road, being so muddy, was full of ruts and the stage acted as if it had the hiccoughs and made us all talk as though we were affected in the same way. Once Mr. Stewart asked me if I did not think it a "gey duir trip." I told him he could call it gay if he wanted to, but it didn't seem very hilarious to me. Every time the stage struck a rock or a rut, Mr. Stewart would "hoot," until I began to wish we would come to a hollow tree or hole in the ground so he could go in with the rest of the owls.

At last we "arriv" and everything is just lovely for me. I have a very, very comfortable situation and Mr. Stewart is absolutely no trouble, for as soon as he has his meals he retires to his room and plays on his bagpipe, only he calls it his "bugpeep." It is "The Campbells are Coming," without variations, at intervals all day long and from seven till eleven at night. Sometimes I wish they would make haste and get here.

There is a saddle horse especially for me and a little shot gun with which I am to kill sage chickens. We are between two trout streams, so you can think of me as being happy when the snow is through melting and the water gets clear. We have the finest flock of Plymouth Rocks and get so many nice eggs. It sure seems fine to have all the cream I want after my town experiences. Jerrine is making good use of all the good things we are having. She rides the pony to water every day.

I have not filed on my land yet because the snow is fifteen feet deep on it, and I think I would rather see what I am getting, so will wait until summer. They have just three seasons here, winter and July and August. We are to plant our garden the last of May. When it is so I can get around I will see about land and find out all I can and tell you.

I think this letter is about to reach thirty-secondly, so I will send you my sincerest love and quit tiring you. Please write me when you have time.

Sincerely yours,
Elinore Rupert

With her new saddle horse and a shotgun, Elinore was to venture forth and not only kill dinner but also clean and cook the dinner. She also would work as the "hired hand." She helped with the ranch chores, such as branding, farming, irrigating, haying, and doctoring of the cattle. Elinore wrote about her chores to Mrs. Coney,

> I am adding feathers to my cap in a surprising way. When you see me again you will think I am wearing a feather duster, but it is only that I have been said to have almost as much sense as a "mon" and that is an honor I never aspired to, even in my wildest dreams. . . . I have done most of the cooking at night, have milked seven cows every day, and have done all the hay cutting, so you see I have been working. But I have found time to put up thirty pints of jelly. . . .

WIDE, OPEN SPACES

When Elinore wanted to go exploring the land, heeding the call of the wild, she would simply hop on her horse, pull Jerrine up behind her in the saddle, and gallop through the fields. "I saddled the pony, took a few things I needed, and Jerrine and I fared forth. Baby can ride behind quite well. We got away by sunup and a glorious day we had."

Elinore and Jerrine rode through the streams breathing the "tang of sage and pine in the air." She guided their horse through prairies that tickled the horse's back with rabbit brush covered in flowers. "The blue distance promised many alluring adventures, so we went along singing and simply gulping in summer." Running beside them were sage chickens, jackrabbits, and antelope.

Elinore made camp and as Jerrine chased after grasshoppers to use as bait for fishing, Elinore made the fishing rod from a birch tree. They fished and Elinore skinned the catch of the day and proceeded to cook it over the campfire she built. They rested with the grasses of the plains as their bed. Bliss.

On the ride home, "We would come over the top of a hill into the glory of a beautiful sunset with its gorgeous colors, then down into the little valley already purpling with mysterious twilight. So on, until just at dark, we rode into our corral and a mighty tired, sleepy little girl was powerfully glad to get home."

The Homestead

Elinore's mission was to be a woman homesteader, and she wasted no time acquiring her land. She was originally going to homestead in the mountainous reserves, land that was miles away from her current residence with Mr. Stewart. Deciding that she didn't want to wait for the snow to melt in order to access it both visually and physically, she opted to homestead the land next to Mr. Stewart's. She had to travel to the homesteader's office in order to become an official homesteader. She saddled her horse, placing Jerrine with her in the saddle, and set forth on a journey that would take a week. They camped out and Elinore had "more fun to the square inch than Mark Twain or Samantha Allen 'ever' provoked." She commented that Jerrine would be so stimulated and enthralled that she ate "like a man."

Appraising the beauty that surrounded her was a joy for Elinore.

It was too beautiful a night to sleep, so I put my head out to look and to think. I saw the moon come up as if it were discouraged with the prospect, and the big white stars flirted shamelessly with the hills. I saw a coyote come trotting along and I felt sorry for him having to hunt food along so barren a place, but when presently I heard the whirr of wings I felt sorry for the sage chickens he had disturbed. At length a cloud came up and I went to sleep, and next morning was covered with several inches of snow.

When Elinore arrived she was greeted with disdain that was common for women of the day; however, Elinore dealt with it with her usual flair.

When I went up to the office where I was to file, the door was open and the most taciturn old man sat before a desk. I hesitated at the door but he never let on. I coughed, yet no sign but a deeper scowl. I stepped in and modestly kicked over a chair. He whirled around like I had shot him. "Well?" he interrogated.

I said, "I am powerful glad of it. I was afraid you were sick, you looked in such pain." He looked at me a minute, then grinned and said he thought I was a book agent.

Elinore concluded to Mrs. Coney that her mission had been completed, and she was officially a woman homesteader:

Well, I filed on my land and am now a bloated landowner. I have a grove of twelve pines on my place, and I am going to build my house there. I thought it would be romantic to live on the peaks amid the whispering pines, but I reckon it would be powerfully uncomfortable also, and I guess my twelve can whisper enough for me; and a dandy thing is, I have all the nice snow water I want. . . ."

Elinore, as a single mother, had envisioned a better life for herself and her daughter. She was bringing her dreams to fruition. She had found a job, traveled across the country and made her mark, set her stakes, and was now a woman who owned land—land that her daughter would inherit. Jerrine was inheriting more than land, though; she was inheriting spunk, a sense of adventure, and the indelible print of her mother's fresh, unbridled perspective through her delectable stories.

In the tiny cabin on the wild plains of Wyoming, Jerrine learned to amuse herself and be as inventive as a modern-day Montessori schoolchild. Elinore wrote Mrs. Coney,

Baby has the rabbit you gave her last Easter a year ago. In Denver I was afraid my baby would grow up devoid of imagination. Like all kindergartners, she depended upon others to amuse her. I was very sorry about it, for my castles in Spain have been real homes to me. But there is not fear. She has a block of wood found in the blacksmith shop, which she calls her "dear baby." A spoke out of a wagon wheel is " Little Margaret," and a barrel-stave is "bad little Johnny."

When she wanted an adventure, and when she had a respite in her chores, Elinore would scoop up Jerrine and off they would go to chase the horizon. She commented that "Jerrine was always such a dear little pal." Single mother and child, they ventured out together to explore the world. One such adventure Elinore described as a "camping out expedition." They merely hopped on Elinore's horse and rode in no certain direction with no comprehensive idea of their location, no maps, no compass, just the sun and the stars. (I am living vicariously through Elinore!)

They galloped into the glory of sage and butte-lined vistas for seven hours, eventually finding a beautiful site and dismounting. Elinore shot a rabbit and set up camp along a "sheer wall of rock" and built a roaring fire. "Then I put some potatoes into the embers, for Baby and I are both fond of roasted potatoes. Jerrine and I sat on the ground and ate. Everything smelled and tasted so good!" They watered and re-staked Jeems the horse and rolled some logs onto the fire. They fell asleep hearing the wails of the coyote chorus that echoed though the hills. "When the howls ceased for a moment we could hear the subdued roar of the creek and the crooning of the wind in the pines." Elinore awakened to a pebble striking her check. Something on the bluff prowling above them had knocked it loose. Unabashedly—after they feasted on breakfast—they remounted and galloped away through the snowy peaks.

Friend in the Snow

The second night they slept on pine needles by a roaring fire. Elinore awakened, rather alarmed, to the quiet of a blanket of snow. They were still pretty toasty, as the fire had not diminished. Elinore exclaimed that it was "such a snowstorm I never saw." She realized they were in the middle of nowhere. She didn't have a clue where they were because the snow had obliterated all trails and confused her senses. Elinore estimated they were thirty to forty miles from home "in the mountains where no one goes in the winter and where I knew the snow got to be ten or fifteen feet deep." Alone with her toddler she was in a bit of a bind, "but I could never see the good in moping, so I got up and got breakfast while baby put her shoes on."

They ate their breakfast by the campfire, then Elinore and Jerrine mounted Jeems and held on for dear life as he stumbled down the mountain, following the billowing of chimney smoke Elinore had spotted in the distance. Eventually they came to a clearing, and with great relief saw a house. Elinore wrote,

> I knew by the chimney and the hounds that it was the home of a Southerner. A little old man came bustling out, chewing his tobacco so fast, and almost frantic about his suspenders, which it seemed he couldn't get adjusted. As I rode up, he said, "Whither, friend?" I said, "Hither." Then he asked, "Air you spying around for one of them dinged game wardens arter that deer I killed yisteddy?" I told him I had never even seen a game warden and that I didn't know he had killed a deer. "Wall," he said, "air you spying around arter that gold mine I diskivered over on the west side of Baldy?" But after a while I convinced him that I was no more nor less than a foolish woman lost in the snow. Then he said, "Light, stranger, and look at your saddle." So I 'lit and looked, and then I asked him what part of the South he was from. He answered, "Yell County, by gum! The best place in the United States, or in the world, either."

This spry old man was Zebulon Pike Parker. Elinore, to paraphrase Will Rogers, "never met a man she didn't like." In true Elinore fashion she, who made the best of any situation and saw the best in any person, exhibited a depth of compassion for her daughter. She became enchanted with the lonely old man who talked a blue streak.

> Only two "Johnny Rebs" could have enjoyed each other's company as Zebulon Pike and myself did. He was so small and so old, but cheerful and so sprightly, and a real Southerner! He had a big, open fireplace with backlogs and andirons. How I enjoyed it all! How we feasted on some of the deer kelled

"yisteddy," and real corn-pone baked in a skillet down on the hearth. He was so full of happy recollections and had a few that were not so happy! He is, in some way, a kinsman of Pike of Oike's Peak fame, and he came west "jist arter the wah" on some expedition and "jist stayed." He told me about his home life back in Yell County, and I feel that I know all the "young uns."

They spent the night at his house, and old man Zebulon put "a buffalo robe and two bearskins before the fire for Jerrine and me," and then he played the fiddle until almost one o'clock in the morning. Like all people that Elinore met, they became dear friends forever. He had not seen his family in years, because he had no one to look after his sheep, which Zebulon had fondly named and nurtured. Elinore took it upon herself to find someone to tend to his "critters," so he could go back and visit his long-lost beloved family. Elinore was a steward of goodwill with a heart of gold.

THE MATCHMAKER

Elinore had many talents, and matchmaker proved to be one of them. She had befriended a mother and her twin daughters—one frail, thin, and haughty; the other round, healthy, and jolly. The girls were fighting over a future husband. The haughty sister was certain that he would love her. Elinore helped the man unite with his true love—the round, healthy, and jolly twin. Wedding plans ensued and Elinore planned the wedding, hosted it, decorated their cabin, and cooked and baked all the food.

Mr. Stewart was in charge of getting the fabric for the wedding gown while he was in town. He got Scottish plaid. After the bride said her devotionals in her Scottish plaid wedding gown, they adjourned for the dance hall.

We went in sleds and sleighs, the snow was so deep, but it was all so jolly. Zebbie [Zebulon], Mr. Stewart, Jerrine, and I went in the bobsled. We jogged along at a comfortable pace lest the "beastie" should suffer, and every now and then a merry party would fly past us scattering snow in our faces and yelling like Comanches. We had a lovely moon then and the snow was so beautiful!

A Special Christmas

Elinore radiated empathy and exemplified charity. Sitting around the fire one night, she heard the story of an old German widow who lived in a cabin in the adjacent county. Her son had left her to go and fight in a war. He had survived the battlefields, and as he was walking back home, he got lost in the snow. He knew there would be no one to rescue him in the wilderness and that he was going to die. So he left a note on his body to please tell his mother that he had died in battle. He knew she would be haunted if she knew of his ironic death. The community named the day he died "Benny's Day." It was Christmas and Elinore decided she and Jerrine must visit the woman.

I was so sorry for the poor mother that I resolved to visit the first opportunity I had. I am at liberty to go where I please when there is no one to cook for. So, when the men left a few days later, I took Jerrine and rode over to the Louderer ranch. I had never seen Mrs. Louderer and it happened to be "Benny's Day" that I blundered in upon. I found her to be a dear old German woman living all alone, the people who do the ranch living in another house two miles away. She had been weeping for hours when I got there, but in accordance with her custom on many anniversaries, she had a real feast prepared, although no one had been bidden. She says that God always sends her guests, but that was the first time she had had a little girl. She had a little daughter once herself, little Gretchen, but all was left was a sweet memory and a pitifully small mound on the ranch, quite near the house, where Benny and Gretchen are at rest beside "der fader, Herr Louderer." She is such a dear old lady! She made us so welcome and she is so entertaining. All the remainder of the day we listened to stories of her children, looked at her pictures, and Jerrine had a lovely time with a wonderful wooden doll that they had brought with them from Germany.

The old lady inquired about their Christmas plans, and Elinore responded that they would probably be homesick. Mrs. Louderer suggested that they spend Christmas together: "She said it was one of their special days and that the only happiness left her was in making someone else happy." Mrs. Louderer planned that they would cook and bake and then take it to the lonely sheepherders. Elinore heartily responded that she would love to assist her Christmas spirit. As they spent the night cooking and cleaning, Elinore commented, "I never worked so hard in my life or had a pleasanter time." A man arrived to feed and get the horses ready, and Elinore, Jerrine, and Mrs. Lauderer prepared to disperse their goodies to the lonely sheepherders.

The man had four horses harnessed and hitched to the sled, on which was placed a wagon-box filled with straw, hot rocks, and blankets. Our twelve apostles—that is what we called our twelve boxes—were lifted in and tied firmly into place. Then we clambered in and away we went. Mrs. Louderer drove, and Tam O'Shanter and Paul Revere were snails compared to us. We didn't follow any road either, but went sweeping along cross-country. No one else in the world would have done it unless they were drunk. We went careening along hillsides without even slacking the trot. Occasionally we struck a particular stubborn bunch of sagebrush and even the sled-runners would jump up into the air. We didn't stop to light, but hit the earth several feet in advance of where we left it. Luck was with us, though. I hardly expected to get through with my head unbroken, but not even a glass was cracked.

Mrs. Louderer was lonely and sad, yet she had made it a Christmas tradition to not wallow in her misery but to reach out and help others who were lonely and sad. In the process she and Elinore had a lot of fun and spread a lot of love. Elinore's actions exemplified an intrinsic sense of humanity. Love is the healer of all wounds.

ELINORE'S PASSION

Elinore's passion was homesteading. Federal regulations stated that homesteaders had to build and occupy a residence on their claim. She built a house that adjoined Mr. Stewart's house. She did this so she could "hold down my land and my job at the same time." Her boundary line ran within two feet of Mr. Stewart's land. She exhorted her enthusiasm to Mrs. Coney in the letters she wrote. Her desire was to broaden her horizons and shape her own future, yet she also yearned to encourage other women to follow her lead and find a better life. She wrote,

> I am very enthusiastic about women homesteading. It really requires less strength and labor to raise plenty to satisfy a large family than it does to go out to wash, with the added satisfaction of knowing that their job will not be lost to them if they care to keep it. Even if improving the place does go slowly, it is that much done to stay done. Whatever is raised is the homesteader's own, and there is no house-rent to pay.

She continued in another letter,

> To me, homesteading is the solution of all poverty's problems, but I realize that temperament has much to do with success in any undertaking, and persons afraid of coyotes and work and loneliness had better let ranching alone. At the same time, any woman who can stand her own company, can see the beauty of a sunset, loves growing things, and is willing to put in as much time at careful labor as she does over the washtub, will certainly succeed; will have independence, plenty to eat all the time, and a home of her own in the end. I would not, for anything, allow Mr. Stewart to do anything toward improving my place, for I want to be able to speak from experience when I tell others what

they can do. Theories are very beautiful, but facts are what must be had, and what I intend to give some time. . . . But I am only thinking of the troops of tired worried women, sometimes even cold and hungry, scared to death of losing their places to work, who could have plenty to eat, who could have good fires by gathering the wood, and comfortable homes of their own, if they but had the courage and determination to get them.

ELINORE'S EXAMPLE

Elinore was a steward of her wounds, and she did it with her head held high. She had experienced the rigors of working in the city and personally knew the hardships many women faced. She had daringly grabbed the tiger by its tail and gambled on the great frontier. She wanted to encourage more women to follow her example. She wanted them to be able to enjoy the fruits of nature and the rewards of owning land and a home. She knew it was not for every woman, but for those who dared to live life to the fullest, she encouraged them to explore the vast amount of opportunities awaiting them in the West. She had a gift for not only exploration but also for writing amusing, charming, informative stories. She consequently instilled hope, laughter, and direction into the lives of many women and was a brave example for many single mothers and other women who dreamed of a better life.

In spite of Elinore's sunny disposition, she confronted poverty, illness, insecurities, and deaths. She always found a way to put a positive spin on her hardships. She wrote about the ways in which she reconciled her self-doubts:

December 28, 1909
Mrs. Coney,

If you only knew how short I fall of my own hopes you would know that I would "never" boast. Why, it keeps me busy making over mistakes just like some one using old clothes. I get myself all ready to enjoy a success and find that I have to fit a failure. But one consolation is that I generally have plenty of material to cut generously, and many of my failures have proved to be real blessings.

I do hope this New Year may bring to you the desire of your heart and all that those who love you best most wish for you.

With lots and lots of love from baby and myself,

Your ex-washlady,

Elinore Stewart

Mrs. Coney was so impressed with Elinore's letters that she took them to her friend Ellery Sedgwick, the editor of the *Atlantic Monthly*. He concurred and published the letters in a series from October 1913 through April 1914. Ellery Sedgwick also put to words his impression of Elinore's character:

Elinore Rupert was a young woman, vigorous in body and mind, but Destiny seemed determined to test her out before showing and she was left with a two-year-old daughter. She determined to turn homesteader and stake out a claim of her own in the world. . . . it really mattered very little what life Elinore Rupert had been born into. She could have made a go of anything. She might have become the perfect servant; as mistress of a great household she would have kept everybody happy, and if the dance of her genes had revolved in high circles, she would have made a very respectable Duchess.[2]

"She could have made a go of anything." Words aptly written, a perfect description of Elinore. At last, Elinore decided to marry Mr. Stewart, perhaps because true affection was born out of the arrangement. She died in 1933, due to a blood clot that went to her brain after gallbladder surgery. Previous to the gallbladder surgery she hadn't felt well for years, reportedly never recovering from an accident while baling hay in 1926. She was fifty-seven years old. She left behind three beautiful children she bore with Mr. Stewart, as well as her beloved Jerrine.

Nevertheless, Elinore and Jerrine had survived many hardships together, and Elinore, as a single mother, had instilled the virtues of courage and adventure, borne from both will and willingness. She and Jerrine established a bond that would last a lifetime. Jerrine maintained a fierce commitment to her mother, a commitment that has manifested coincidentally in all of the children in this book. These commitments were mutual; the children mirrored their mothers. It's not by chance that these children feel this way about their mothers. Children observe, and the mothers' devotion is not oblique to their senses. They know the loyalty. They feel the love. They recognize the sacrifice. Elinore exemplified all of these attributes.

Elinore was also a trailblazer and a subsequent role model for women. She was resolute in her endeavors and delved into a world where few single mothers dared to go. She was one of the first female homesteaders of the West, and she shared her experience, strength, and hope through entertaining letters to Mrs. Coney. Elinore, a self-taught reader from random pieces of paper after her teacher was hung from a sycamore tree, became a respected writer whose letters were published in the *Atlantic Monthly*. An inquisitive mind, an eager soul, a nurturing single mother, she was an active participant in the game of life. She overcame hardships with a full measure of compassion, a twinkle in her eye, and laughter in her heart. Elinore's snapshots of life left her children a legacy, perspectives that burned brighter, and futures that beamed with hope.

LIFE LESSON: HEAL WITH HUMOR

Life has its ups and downs regardless of the century. There is an ebb and flow to nature. Every sentiment has its season. Thus we might as well hang on for the ride, have fun, and see the humor in all situations. Laughter truly is the best medicine, and a cheerful disposition reaps cheerful companionship.

Elinore saw the jewel in everyone's crown. She appraised a situation and spun it to success, and she did it with a sense of humor. Who would we rather be around—a sourpuss or someone who makes us chuckle? Isn't the laughter of a child the richest blessing in the world? Blessed are the children who hear their mothers' laughter.

Heal with humor. Find the light within everyone you encounter. Look around you, observe the absurdities of life, and find the magic. Don't choose pessimism, choose optimism. Hold your head high, find the sparkle in spontaneity, and make 'em laugh.

But when you get among such grandeur you get to feel how little you are and how foolish is human endeavor, except that which unites us with the mighty force called God. I was plumb uncomfortable, because all my efforts have always been just to make the best of everything and to take things as they come.

—Elinore Pruitt Stewart

AUNT CLARA BROWN

Persevering Single Mother

c1800–1885

SNAPSHOT	Clapping her hands and praising her Lord as she's working in her front yard
MOTHER MOMENT	Cleaning Eliza Jane's pink pinafore as she stood on the auction block
CHALLENGE	Family and daughter are kidnapped by auctioneers
STEWARDSHIP	Became the mother to many new daughters and families
SCRIPTURE	You need to persevere so that when you have done the will of God, you will receive what he has promised. (Hebrews 10:36 NIV)

CHAPTER SIXTEEN

Persevere with Praise

We will put "Aunt Clara" against the world, white or black
for industry, perseverance, energy and filial love.'

—WILLIAM BYERS

Nineteenth century. The country is new. Slavery is old. It's Virginia. It's Kentucky. It's Bleeding Kansas and Colorado. Americans are on the move crisscrossing the landscape looking for fortune. Lush fields and flowering trees. Wagon trains and roadside cemeteries. Wandering freed slaves. A nation redefining itself.

Aunt Clara Brown's spirit defined hope, perseverance, and the Good Samaritan. She endured many hardships, including living with the unrequited desire planted in her heart to be reunited with her daughter, for more than forty years.

The remarkable aspect of Aunt Clara is the way she chose to live her life while waiting for God to answer her singular, persistent prayer. She rode the waves of trials and tribulations with an unsinkable soul. She didn't rest on her laurels while she waited for her Father in heaven to answer her most ardent plea. Instead, she exuded love for her God and reached out as His angel to disciple those in need.

Aunt Clara Brown was born a slave, but she never had a pessimistic attitude. As a slave, she pioneered the wilderness trail; as a free woman, she walked beside the wagon trains for over six hundred miles. Aunt Clara started her own laundry business, making fifty cents a shirt. She became a pillar of the Methodist church and one of the richest women of the West. She witnessed to the weary and prayed over the downtrodden. She fed the hungry and rocked the dying.

Most importantly, Aunt Clara never relinquished her hope of being reunited with her long-lost daughter. She asked every person. She searched many states. She blazed a trail back and forth across the country in search of her daughter for almost half a century. Though her prayers seemed to fall on deaf ears, she continued to praise God for her blessings, dropping to her knees when she felt compelled to pray, and clapping her hands in the air, singing praises to her Lord. Aunt Clara Brown was unique and special, known as "Angel of the Rockies."

Timeless Scenario: Girl meets boy. Girl and boy fall in love. Girl and boy marry. Girl is ruthlessly separated from her husband, her children. Girl yearns for her "kidnapped" daughter. Girl searches the country. Girl never gives up hope. Girl becomes mother to many lost children.

On the Wilderness Road

Aunt Clara Brown was born in Spotsylvania County, Virginia. The actual date of her birth is unknown because birth certificates were not issued for slaves. She estimated that she was born around 1800. Three years after her birth, Aunt Clara experienced the first of two harrowing experiences on the auction block. She stood beside her mother as they were bid on like cattle and sold to Ambrose Smith, a farmer who lived in Fredericksburg, Virginia.

In 1809 Mr. Smith decided to move to the virgin territory of Kentucky. Ambrose, Mary, their three children, and their slaves, including Aunt Clara and her mother, waved good-bye to Virginia as they rode off on the Wilderness Road. The wilderness trail was aptly titled, as it was a wild and treacherous road. It had been hand-chopped by Daniel Boone and his men in 1775. On the journey they had to cross boulders, narrow rock passageways, mountains, and dangerous rivers. Horses struggled and wagons broke. To assist the horses up the steep inclines, ropes were tied around trees to ease the burden. Many horses broke their legs on this treacherous route.

At the young age of approximately nine, Aunt Clara watched people die and horses be shot. There was an unceasing fear of Indians on the trip by everyone, except Aunt Clara and her mother. They were part Cherokee. Aunt Clara's grandmother had been a full-blood Cherokee. "You see, I'm part Indian myself, honey, and even if I wasn't, why I'd never have been afraid of them."[2] Aunt Clara was brave from the very beginning.

When they finally arrived in Kentucky, the reward was a paradise. There was infinite raw land dotted with emerald hills. There was a rushing creek called Big Muddy that raced through the property, nourishing flowering trees. Mr. and Mrs. Smith were very kind. She recognized Aunt Clara's intelligence and eagerness to please; so she taught her to read and write. Mrs. Smith educated Aunt Clara, disregarding the widespread belief that an educated slave might result in a runaway slave. Defiantly, Mrs. Smith risked the potential punishment of jail and proceeded to teach Aunt Clara.

The Smiths also insisted on taking Aunt Clara and her mother with them on Sundays to the Methodist Chapel. Most slaves were left behind to congregate on their own. In 1810 a huge Christian revival took place on the Muddy River. The Smiths once again took Aunt Clara and her mother. It was at this revival that Aunt Clara had her "awakening." The Lord visited her and promised to be with her always. From that day forward, Aunt Clara never wavered in her faith and the belief that God was her guiding force. Aunt Clara recalls, "Lordy me, darlin', I was nothing but a child when God came to me and took me to Jesus."[3] It was through this experience that Aunt Clara constantly believed that her Lord would "bear her up" when times were scary, unpredictable, and dark.

Married with Children

Aunt Clara spent her childhood running though the lush Kentucky fields and wading through the wild Big Muddy creek. In

1818, when she was eighteen years old, she fell in love and married a fellow slave named Richard. Mr. and Mrs. Smith presented them with a lovely wedding feast. Aunt Clara and Richard lived with the rest of Aunt Clara's family in the same log cabin nestled among the fresh and beautiful Kentucky pastureland.

Aunt Clara worked beside her mother baking pies, cooking the meals, and making candles. Though they were slaves, they knew they were blessed to be living among the kind and nurturing Smiths. Aunt Clara had her first child in 1820 and proceeded to birth many more babies. By the year 1826 she had a total of four children. She had her son, Richard Jr., a daughter, Margaret, and twin girls, Eliza Jane and Paulina Anne.

In 1834 Aunt Clara's mother died. This tragedy was followed by another one—Aunt Clara heard deafening screams echoing throughout the pasturelands. They all ran to the river where Eliza Jane and Paulina Anne had been playing. Paulina had gotten caught on something at the bottom of the river and could not get free. She drowned. Aunt Clara was devastated, and Eliza Jane was inconsolable. Aunt Clara could only rock herself by the fire in the mental, emotional, and physical darkness that encompassed her life.

Eventually, without knowing what else to do, Aunt Clara fell to her knees and wailed to her God, then she begged Him to help her. He did. He gave her the will to keep on living. This would be the first of many times Aunt Clara would drop to her knees whenever she felt His spirit calling her or when she felt a need to call on Him. Many people were moved by her reverent aspirations and were drawn to the spirit of the Lord by her example. This was the first of many times Aunt Clara would have to call upon her inexhaustible, ever-present God.

Eliza Jane did not prove to be as resilient as Aunt Clara. She was distraught, weeping incessantly and enduring horrific nightmares. Her body was racked with jitters and shaking. Aunt Clara had to endure the proclamations that Eliza Jane had lost her mind. As her mother, she knew that Eliza Jane simply needed her love, nurturing, and the healing of time.

In 1836 the kind and respected Mr. Smith died. The family didn't manage well, and they fell on tough times financially. Thus the dreaded inevitability happened—Aunt Clara, her husband, her son, and her two daughters were to be put on the auction block again. The fear and helplessness must have been unbearable for Aunt Clara. She knew she might be separated from her lover, her husband, and her precious children. She was most worried about her delicate and sensitive Eliza Jane. How could she ever survive? Aunt Clara was haunted by the thought of it.

The day arrived and they all were taken to the market filled with the calls of farmers selling their cattle, the craftsmen selling their goods, and the auctioneer selling Aunt Clara's family. Her husband was first. A master walked up to Richard and arrogantly appraised him. Aunt Clara had a bad premonition about this man. He bought her husband and her firstborn, Richard Jr. They were taken away from her without another kiss or a touch or a hug. Gone forever.

Next was her elder daughter, Margaret. Aunt Clara had desperately hoped she would be sold together with her two girls, as she had been sold with her mother years before. She was not. The same fate awaited her Margaret. They took her away without a moment's consideration of the sadness the family was feeling.

Next was Eliza Jane. Not her Eliza Jane! Aunt Clara prayed fervently that God would give Eliza Jane courage to "bear up." Eliza Jane walked onto the auction block in her pink pinafore, shaking with tremulous fear. As the men perused her, she threw up all over her fresh, new dress. She stood there immobilized. Aunt Clara did the forbidden—she rushed to help her daughter. She was halted. Her Eliza Jane stood alone in her humiliation.

Finally, Aunt Clara was allowed to go up on the auction block and clean the vomit off of her daughter. Oh, how she must have wanted to grab her and run. But she would have been killed if she had tried to escape. With legs of lead and her heart anchored in sorrow, she managed to step back down to witness the fruition of her nightmares. Eliza Jane was sold and carried away. She was led through the crowded market, looking over her shoulder, her eyes pleading with her mother. There was nothing Aunt Clara could do. Her whole family had, in a matter of moments, been physically stripped from her. Her world went black.

Aunt Clara remembered nothing of what was to follow. God graced her with a respite from reality. She remembered nothing of her own experience on the auction block, her sale, or her new owner. When her mind was reawakened, and she could once again grasp reality, she gathered her wits and promptly hit her knees. She prayed to her Lord to give her the courage to continue with the life He had given her. Of particular note was the lack of cynicism or resentment in Aunt Clara. She resumed her life with a lack of defiance. She found a willingness to accept her life coupled with the knowledge that God was giving her the strength to bear up.

The Search Begins

Aunt Clara was now in the home of Mr. Brown. She realized that she was in an environment very different than her previous home. Mr. Brown was a hat maker and had a shop in town. She was given a stylish black uniform with a starched white apron and a white cap. In this house she would drop to her knees and pray when she felt the calling or the need. Her body may have been captive but her soul was not. She would pray ardently and sing praises to her Lord.

Aunt Clara became absolutely adored by the Browns and she found her environment pleasing. Through Mr. Brown she discovered the whereabouts of her daughters. He couldn't find her husband and son, and her instincts told her they were not going to survive their new master. Eliza Jane and Margaret were still in Kentucky. She was not able to visit them, however, because the distance was too great. They couldn't write letters due to their illiteracy. She discovered later that Margaret had died of an illness as a teenager.

All resources that led to Eliza Jane's whereabouts were lost in 1852, and Aunt Clara no longer had the comfort of knowing where she was living. Through the years, Aunt Clara continuously prayed for Eliza Jane, her sweet, delicate child. She was obsessed by the vision of her standing on the auction block shaking and trembling. She yearned to see her again and wrap her arms around her one more time. She asked her Lord to wrap His arms around her until she was able to do it herself.

In 1856 Aunt Clara's master, George Brown, died. His will contained a momentous surprise. He had bequeathed to Aunt Clara $300 and his intention to give Aunt Clara her God-given freedom. In order to be effective in Kentucky, the law required that Aunt Clara would have to be put, for the third time in her life, on the auction block and sold to the highest bidder. Then, if Aunt Clara could pay one-quarter of the price of her sale, she could be set free. That was Mr. Brown's reason for giving Aunt Clara $300.

Mr. Brown's daughters were present at the auction and intended to outbid anyone who bid on Aunt Clara. If anyone outbid the Brown girls to the point that Aunt Clara could not purchase her freedom with $300, then she would remain a slave and become beholden to a new owner. The bidding escalated but finally stopped at $475. Aunt Clara paid her $188 and she was free. She was free at the age of fifty-six! In the state of Kentucky a freed slave couldn't remain in the state for more than one year. Aunt Clara continued to work for the Brown sisters as she saved her money. She began to plan how to bring her dreams to a reality. Now that she was free, how could she find her baby Eliza Jane?

In 1857 Aunt Clara decided to go to St. Louis, Missouri. The population was booming there, and she believed that maybe Eliza Jane was living there. The Brown sisters wrote a letter of recommendation for Aunt Clara that represented her talents and remarkable sense of honor. With this letter and her freedom papers tied neatly in a sack, Aunt Clara Brown, taking Mr. Brown's name, stepped upon a tobacco flatboat and ventured into her new life.

Aunt Clara could now direct her own course from morning until night. So she directed her energies into finding Eliza Jane. She didn't even know Eliza Jane's last name. No one was allowed to own slaves north of the Mason-Dixon Line. Aunt Clara could have gone there and found a safer haven. Missouri had been a slave state since the Missouri Compromise was passed in Congress in 1821. There were dangers lurking in every corner for a freed slave in slave states. A freed slave could be potentially kidnapped at any time. But Aunt Clara was going to look for her daughter, wherever she was, and she wasn't going to be afraid. Fear was not going to be her new master.

The first thing Aunt Clara had to do was find employment. She found the home of a German friend of the Brown sisters. Upon reading the radiant letter of recommendation, Aunt Clara was hired on the spot. She cooked, cleaned, and sewed for her new employers. She worked six days a week. On her day off she would travel down the docks and ask anyone who would listen if they had seen her daughter. Eliza Jane would be approximately thirty years old at this time. No one had seen her; however, Aunt Clara believed she would see her some day. She believed her God would provide this miracle, and she was never going to relent. One person at the dock might tell another person. Word of mouth was the only tool she had at her disposal— no phones, no telegraphs, no radio, no television, no photographs, no Amber alerts.

Aunt Clara discovered that freedom bore many new characteristics, such as loneliness. She had always lived with other slaves, but now she was without their companionship. She sought comfort from a neighboring German Methodist church. Though she had to sit in the colored section, Aunt Clara didn't let this hamper her enthusiasm for worshiping her Lord or making friends with His children. Aunt Clara always exuded a spirit that wasn't daunted by the whims of negativity whispered by a defeatist voice.

On the Prairie

With the Panic of 1857 times became hard, and Aunt Clara's employer wanted to move to Kansas. Aunt Clara had not been able to find her daughter in Missouri; so she decided to accompany them on their travels and look for Eliza Jane in Kansas.

Fort Leavenworth, Kansas, was a vivid place. It was called a "lick skillet" because the town consisted of freed slaves, Missouri slave kidnappers, U.S. soldiers, and immigrants from Germany, Ireland, and Holland. They settled in Goosetown, and Aunt Clara's first steps were toward a church. She joined the First Missionary Baptist Church, and for the first time in her life Aunt Clara didn't have to sit in a special section in the church of her Lord. First Missionary Baptist was an all-black congregation.

It was at this church that Aunt Clara met a woman who would change her life. Her name was Becky Johnson. In 1854 the census of Leavenworth listed "ninety-nine men and one negro woman who took in washing."[4] That woman was Becky Johnson. Becky was a freed slave from Kentucky too. She proved to be Aunt Clara's mentor and encouraged her to start her own washing business.

Kansas proved to be too fierce for Aunt Clara's employers. It had been given the nickname "Bleeding Kansas." Kansas couldn't be an official free state for slaves until it was officially a state. Thus it was a den of rebels and gunfire between the two factions—one that wanted it to be a free slave state and one that didn't. Aunt Clara's employers decided to leave this place of contempt and escape to California. Aunt Clara didn't believe Eliza Jane would be in California, so she bid them good-bye and remained in Kansas. Before they left, Aunt Clara used their stove, tubs, and kettle to start her own business. Becky taught her the ways of business and how to save money. Aunt Clara soon had enough money to buy her own laundry business essentials. With every shirt she laundered, she spread the word that she was looking for her long-lost Eliza Jane. She never stopped asking; never stopped seeking; never stopped believing.

Times were tough in the mid-1800s. Following the Panic of 1857, there were outbreaks of tuberculosis. The rumblings of a civil war were becoming prevalent. A ray of hope in the depression was a new gold rush. This one was the Rocky Mountain Gold Rush. Aunt Clara didn't find her daughter in Kansas; she hadn't found her daughter in Missouri; so she decided to head west and move with the exodus of people who were heading west to get rich quick. The only richness Aunt Clara wanted was the incomparable beauty of her daughter's big smile connecting her high Cherokee cheekbones.

How does a freed slave get to Colorado? Aunt Clara approached a man by the name of Colonel Wadsworth. He was familiar with the trails and had successfully endured the journey. With her characteristic bravery, she approached a group of men and asked them if she and her laundry equipment could join the wagon train. The reply was that he had no desire to have an aging slave in their convoy. Nothing ventured; nothing gained. Aunt Clara boldly replied that she was a freed slave and that she would do all of the cooking and laundry in return for being allowed to accompany them. Colonel Wadsworth agreed. Aunt Clara was to join sixty people consisting of five families and twenty-six single men. The trip would take two months and had to be accomplished in this amount of time or they would run out of supplies.

Aunt Clara walked the entire two months beside the wagons. She had survived the wilderness trail as a child, and she told herself she could survive this. She was approximately fifty-eight to sixty years old. At noon, when the wagons stopped, she cooked and cleaned for the twenty-six single men. She had never cooked for so many people, and she prayed to her Lord for the stamina to survive. At night she would cook and clean again. Aunt Clara would also catch fish and hunt and bake bread for the whole week. She would then milk the cows and make butter. At night there was a raucous debate as to where Aunt Clara would sleep. Should a colored woman sleep inside the wagon with the other women? Most nights Aunt Clara stoically wrapped herself in blankets and slept under the wagon.

The Christians demanded a Sabbath and, thus, on Sundays they rested. Under the skies of heaven, with a tree or a cactus as a cross, they worshiped as they read from the Bible and prayed together. As they continued, the terrain and weather were a source of constant adjustment. They started the trip surrounded by greenery and lush lands. Soon they encountered dry grasslands. At one juncture, they gazed at the hills dotted with trees and knew they sheltered Indians. As expected, the Indians stampeded across the flatlands and approached the wagon train. As the Kiowa Indians rode silently beside the wagons, Aunt Clara walked with them, tall and steadfast. She did not fear the Indian people, because she was one of them. Colonel Wadsworth sat with them, passed the peace pipe, and traded goods. All's well that ends well.

As they continued along the trail, they encountered storms, muddy trails, snow, and then the "Smokey Hell," a dusty part of the trail. They endured temperature fluctuations that ranged from mild to freezing to ninety degrees. Throughout the whole ordeal, Aunt Clara walked beside the wagons, motivated by the hope of seeing the smile of her Eliza Jane. At night she would doctor her feet and mend her shoes and socks. The *Rocky Mountain News* called the trail the "route for the foolhardy and insane."[5]

Approximately forty thousand couldn't bear the difficulties of the journey or became discouraged, turned around, and traveled back to their homes. Aunt Clara, however, was not a quitter and continued onward through the vacillating climate and circumstances. They searched desperately for a source of water. It was recorded in some of the travelers' diaries that some people didn't have water for forty-eight hours. They traversed over graves and broken wagons, peering into the wanton faces of the pioneers returning home. Finally, they spotted the Republican River. The worst had been endured.

On June 8 the wagon train pulled into an area between Denver City and Auraria. In true Aunt Clara fashion, she dropped to her knees and praised her Lord that she had survived the ordeal. She had walked beside the wagon for two months. Would she find her Eliza Jane here? As she perused her surroundings she realized she was the only woman of color in the midst of a mass of men. She must have been discouraged. If she were the only woman, what were the odds of finding Eliza Jane? But she didn't despair. She quickly sought fellow Christians, discovering a small Methodist group that congregated when possible in tents, saloons, and sometimes simply under the trees. They were all men. Two Methodist preachers were on the way, Jacob Adriance and John Milton Chivington. Aunt Clara found solace in reaching out and helping others. She was determined to do all she could to help the Methodist church succeed.

Aunt Clara bought a cabin for twenty-five dollars. Many cabins had been abandoned and could be purchased inexpensively. It was here that she established her laundry business and her prayer meetings. Cherry Creek was rowdy and filled with loud, gun-slinging, uproarious men. The editor of the *New York Tribune*, Horace Greeley, described the infamous town in his newspaper article. He wrote that there were "more brawls, more fights, more pistol shots with criminal intent in this log city of 150 dwellings than in any community of equal number on earth."[6]

One thing was good, though—Aunt Clara would have the opportunity to wash many shirts and clothes. She asked every single customer if they had seen or heard of Eliza Jane. Maybe Eliza Jane would show up, because five hundred new settlers arrived every week. Denver City and Auraria were becoming boomtowns. The Methodist minister finally arrived and, recognizing his loneliness, Aunt Clara would frequent his cabin and take him homemade soups, pies, and bread. They had prayer meetings in his cabin, and Aunt Clara unceasingly prayed and asked others to pray for her Eliza Jane. She didn't wallow in her misery. When the tired or sick knocked on the minister's door, she arrived with nourishment for everyone. During the first Christmas season, Aunt Clara instigated gathering gifts for the children. She made turkey dinner and celebrated with a small gathering of friends in Reverend Jacob's cabin.

Reverend Jacob decided to build his church not in Denver City or Auraria but in the snow-capped mountains where the miners were working and living, Mountain City, later renamed Central City. Aunt Clara decided to follow her minister to Central City, and in 1860 they all traveled to this new location by stagecoach, except Aunt Clara. It was against the law to allow a non-white to travel by stagecoach. Again she didn't succumb to pity. Instead she simply paid a man to let her accompany him. She dressed in disguise as his slave. The trail was forty miles with a four-thousand-foot incline. Aunt Clara, at the age of approximately sixty, endured yet another grueling trip as a pioneer. When she arrived she perused the town. Supposed to be a wonder, it was really a muddy mess with temporary buildings. Yet Aunt Clara loved the fresh air and beautiful mountains. She found a two-room cabin on Lawrence Street and started her laundry business again. She continued to charge fifty cents per shirt.

Aunt Clara didn't have her family, but she quickly adopted a new family. She had her friends over for meals and continued to pray with those who were in need. She was the person people sought when they needed food or simply a place to lay their heads. As she worked in her laundry or walked through the streets, she would impulsively drop to her knees and pray, or break into song praising her Savior. One day, as she was clapping her hands and joyously singing to her Lord, an attorney walked by and was awestruck by her happiness. He wanted that unbridled enthusiasm in his life. He inquired how she obtained her elation, and she told him it was from her Lord. This attorney became one of the first members of the Mountain (Central) City Methodist Church.

Everyone in Central City considered Aunt Clara a blessing and a ray of God's golden light, the only gold that really mattered. The people called her an "angel" because she would miraculously appear just at the right moment. They never knew the burden Aunt Clara carried in her heart. Through all the sorrows and hardships she had encountered, she never wavered in her faith. She knew with an all-consuming certainty that God never left her side. She exuded His grace because she sought Him as her solace and she held her head high.

Aunt Clara laundered many, many shirts. She saved her money, yet she was also generous with her money. She consistently provided food for the ones who were hungry, and she also allowed exhausted miners to live in her place until they rested enough to go back to work. In return for her generosity, many of these miners gave Aunt Clara a share of their future profits in the gold mines. With gratitude, they actually drew up papers, which Aunt Clara marked with an *x*. She invested wisely. She bought houses and land as she continued to save her money for her search for Eliza Jane. She soon owned land in Central City, Georgetown, Denver, Idaho Springs, and Boulder. In ten years she earned ten thousand dollars.

Aunt Clara, a woman who had been the victim of the auction block three times in her life and had been a slave for fifty-six years was now one of the richest women of the West. She was not seeking the monetary fortune; she was seeking the fortune of family, friends, and God's love.

Aunt Clara wanted to go on an extended search for Eliza Jane, but the Civil War was imminent, and the atmosphere was tumultuous. So she was advised to wait. In Central City, even a woman as revered as Aunt Clara was the victim of foul behavior. The *City Miners Register* wrote an article documenting the incidents:

> We are in receipt of a communication from Old Aunt Clara, than whom there is not a more respectable upright colored woman in the territory, in which she complains of some very indecent, disgraceful, and insulting language addressed to her on one of our streets by some low-lived fellow who considers himself far her superior. We have only to say that it is never honorable for a big boy to pick on a little boy, or one who claims to be superior to insult his inferior. No gentleman will do it. Whenever we hear of an attempt on the part of rowdies to maliciously injure anyone, whether black or white, no matter how low down on the scale of society, we put down the rowdies as lower than those they attempt to injure. In the days of slavery in the South he who would so injure a slave was sure at once to be made to feel the penalties of the law. We mention these things because we have heard of several like instances of late, and they are certainly disgraceful to any community.[7]

After the war ended in 1865, as Aunt Clara mourned Abraham Lincoln's death, Denver experienced a terrible flood. All of Aunt Clara's land claims in Denver were washed away. She found solace in the fact that her Methodist church had a congregation of 225 members. Aunt Clara had donated more money for the building of the new church than any other member.

The Search Is Resumed

The country was united but slavery was still legal in some parts until the Thirteenth Amendment passed. Aunt Clara decided the time had come for her to resume her search for her daughter, Eliza Jane. This time she would not have to walk beside a wagon train cooking and cleaning for two months, nor pretend to be a slave. This time she purchased tickets for a twelve-day journey by stagecoach bound for Kentucky. In October 1865, after six years of searching in three states, Aunt Clara temporarily closed her laundry business and departed with tireless faith and determination. When she reached Kentucky she visited with her former employers, the Brown sisters. They assisted their beloved friend by writing the letters that she was not capable of writing. Aunt Clara did not find Eliza Jane in Kentucky. Due to the ratification of the Thirteenth Amendment, Aunt Clara thought, perhaps Eliza Jane had traveled to Tennessee. So Aunt Clara left Kentucky and went to Gallatin, Tennessee.

In Tennessee, Aunt Clara witnessed the masses of slaves wandering around in a state of shock. They were unsure of their futures and uncertain about how to proceed with their new lives. She felt compassion for them. She searched the masses for her daughter. She asked all of them if they had seen or heard of Eliza Jane. She inquired in tents and along the roads. But her efforts were to no avail.

Aunt Clara dropped despondently to her knees. She was sixty-five years old, and Eliza Jane would now be in her forties. They had been separated for more than thirty years. Why did she still feel such a longing to see her daughter? Why did she still feel within her heart that she was alive? Why did she believe if she persevered she would find her fragile, little Eliza Jane in the pink pinafore dress? She asked God these questions and begged Him for guidance.

God responded to Aunt Clara's beseeching by putting an idea into her heart. He told her to build a new family. There were so many people in need, so many people who had no family, no destination, no hope. So God told her to find a new family and take them back with her to her home in Central City. She couldn't nurture her own family, her Eliza Jane, but now she was going to have a new family to nurture. How would she discover this new family? She stumbled, by divine intervention, onto the path of a man named Jackson Smith. They both believed that they were, perhaps, related. He may have been her nephew. She decided to take Jackson back to Central City with her, and together they gathered nineteen other men and women as Aunt Clara's new family. She didn't have her Eliza Jane, but she held her head high. If she couldn't find her own daughter, her family, then she would help others who couldn't find their families either. They would heal one another.

Aunt Clara provided for her new family with the money she had earned as a laundress. She purchased a wagon train to transport them all back to Colorado. No one was going to walk beside the wagons on this trip! They all rode in the wagons. The trails were less foreboding now because rest stops were prevalent, and they were able to access food, water, and supplies.

Sweet, loving Aunt Clara had not fulfilled her deepest, most ardent desire, finding her daughter, yet she rode into Denver clapping her hands and singing praises to the Lord. She was arriving with her new family. The newspaper recorded their arrival by stating, "They arrived . . . happy and triumphant."[8] From Denver City she took them to her home in Central City. The *Rocky Mountain News* recounted Aunt Clara's journey with her new family in an article entitled "A Woman in a Thousand." In the article it explained how Aunt Clara had "traveled through the length and breadth of Kentucky and Tennessee, gathering together her flock."[9]

For the next ten years, with thoughts of Eliza never waning, Aunt Clara provided for her new family. She gave them her lands and houses in which to live, and she eventually found employment for all of them. Her finances were dwindling, but she still was a landowner; the only black woman to own land. Eventually, Aunt Clara decided to put out a one-thousand-dollar reward for knowledge of Eliza Jane's whereabouts. She spread the word through her church and had letters circulated throughout other churches in the country.

At the age of seventy-eight, Aunt Clara, after getting her new family settled and at peace, found no peace within her heart. She was not ready to give up her search for her daughter. She heard about the "exodusters," thousands of former southern slaves who were moving to Wyandotte, Kansas. They were setting up camp in Mississippi Town, and they were poor, confused, and dying from lack of food and sickness. Aunt Clara thought that perhaps her beloved Eliza Jane would be there. Thus, at seventy-eight she decided to travel to Kansas again. She took a stagecoach to Denver and then a train to Kansas. Aunt Clara had lived to see and benefit from the vast changes in the transportation industry. She was born in 1800 and now it was approximately 1878. This time she could make the trip in two days.

Aunt Clara had garnered a certain amount of fame by the time she was seventy-eight years old. She was famous for her search of Eliza Jane and for her charitable acts. When she arrived in Kansas, she was greeted by Governor St. John. She presented to him donations for the exodusters. The donations had been collected from Henry Reitze and from several churches in Denver, Central City, and concerned citizens. Aunt Clara arrived in Wyandotte, and like an ancient Mother Teresa, immediately started to help the starving and the dying. She fed the sick and prayed over the dying as they met their demise in her arms. She remained for a year, asking every person she met if they had seen Eliza Jane. Not one person had seen her. Despondently, Aunt Clara returned to Central City at the age of seventy-nine.

Upon her return, the local paper wrote an article about her journey to Mississippi Town:

> Aunt Clara Brown, whom everybody in Central knows, returned from a visit to Kansas some few days since, whither she went to look into the condition of the colored refugees, and in the interest of the sufferers generally. There are about 5,000 all told, and they are getting on as fast as could be expected. The greater portion have found employment, and the balance will, doubtless, in the course of time. Aunt Clara says they are an industrious and sober class of people, who only ask an opportunity to make an honest living. Their saying is work, work, and that is being given to them as fast as possible. She was kindly received by Gov. St.

John and the people generally. She thinks that in another year these people will be well to do and self-supporting.[10]

The stamina Aunt Clara had exhibited throughout the years was remarkable, a feat of human endurance. At the age of seventy-nine she was still serving others. Upon her return, she was starting to feel the effects of her old age. Perhaps the hope within her heart was ebbing, as the mind always influences the body. The *Central City Register-Call* described Aunt Clara's health in an article written on September 23, 1879:

> Unfortunately, the long trip had taken its toll on Clara's health. She was nearly eighty, and she couldn't tramp around the country the way she had in her younger days. She had dropsy, which swelled up her feet and her hands, making it difficult to get around by the end of the day. Even worse, she had heart trouble. Whatever herb she had self-prescribed for her heart and her breathing wasn't working. She couldn't trudge up the steep streets delivering freshly ironed laundry anymore. She simply didn't have the breath to do it.[11]

Aunt Clara was going to have to move from her beloved cabin in Central City, a home that had been lit by the light of God's grace, where she had healed and sheltered innumerable people. No longer would the residents of Central City see the "Angel of the Rockies." No longer would they witness Aunt Clara walking down the street, clapping her hands and praising God. No longer would the church members see her loving presence. No longer would the community receive her blessings of charity. Yes, Aunt Clara Brown would be sorely missed.

Aunt Clara had no money. She had given it all to her new family. Now it was time for her generosity to be reciprocated, and someone did. An anonymous person donated a house for Aunt Clara to occupy until her death. Friends surrounded her bedside and brought her food and provided her with companionship. When Aunt Clara was eighty years old, she received a letter that officially proclaimed her as a member of the Colorado Pioneer Society. This was a prestigious honor, and she was the first woman of color to be named an Official Pioneer. This honor included a monthly pension that she would receive for the rest of her life. As she sat in her home, always a very active person, it must have been very hard for her to reconcile why the God she had worshiped and adored had not answered her most passionate prayer. Why had she not been able to see her special baby girl's face again? Why did she still long for her so desperately? Why did Eliza Jane's image on the auction block in her stained, pink pinafore dress haunt her so relentlessly?

Answered Prayer

On February 14, 1882, Aunt Clara received a letter. It was from a woman who had once lived in Denver but was now living in Iowa. She had been in the post office picking up her mail when she heard the woman standing next to her request to pick up her tickets for *Uncle Tom's Cabin* with the name of Mrs. Brewer. The clerk asked if her name was Eliza Jane Brewer. Eliza Jane? She replied that yes, she was Eliza Jane Brewer.

The woman from Denver almost dropped her mail. She asked Eliza Jane if she had once lived in Kentucky. She said she had but she had been sold as a small girl. The woman asked her if her mother's name was Clara. Eliza said she didn't know; she had always called her mother Mammy. Eliza had assumed that her mother had died years ago. The woman asked if she had had a twin sister that drowned. This was the turning point. Eliza burst into tears. Yes, she'd had a twin sister who had drowned in the Big Muddy River. Eliza Jane had been found! The *Denver Republican* wrote,

> When told her mother was living in Denver she almost became frantic to see her . . . And the letter was written in order to fully verify whether the relationship was true beyond the shadow of a doubt. Aunt Clara was unable to take the matter philosophically, and ever since the letter, has been crying for joy and thanking God for his goodness in restoring her child to her.[12]

Aunt Clara's spirit had been revived, and consequently her body. She prayed to God that she would not die until she had seen her daughter once again. She had waited forty-six years for this day! She was determined to see her baby Eliza Jane. Sadly, Eliza Jane didn't have the money to travel the six hundred miles from Iowa to Denver, and Aunt Clara didn't have the money to travel to Iowa. The *Denver Republican* wrote a story on February 18 detailing Aunt Clara's plight:

> The Old auntie has no funds to pay . . . her passage, and she is waiting until her friends secure a pass or raise enough money to pay her fare. The old lady has had a half-fare ticket for several years, and if a full pass cannot be secured, her friends will contribute enough to buy a railroad ticket. The old lady's face beams with delight as she anticipates meeting her daughter again, and says if her friends will buy a ticket for her she "can cook up enough to eat and take it along in a basket." The case is one of *The Most Remarkable* . . . of the many sad stories that have been handed down from the days of slavery, and transportation should be provided for the old mother so that she can leave for Council Bluffs as soon as possible. It is a case worthy the consideration of the charitable people of Denver. If a pass cannot be secured, a contribution should be taken up, so that Aunt Clara may be able to go on her way rejoicing.[13]

The goodwill of the people resulted in a rousing response. They came to her door laden with clothes, money, and food. The Union Pacific Railroad covered the remainder of her round-trip ticket to Council Bluffs. Aunt Clara, with resounding enthusiasm, wrote a letter to Eliza Jane that she was coming to find her. She was going to see her at last! Eliza Jane Brewer responded by telegram that she would meet her at the Eighth Street Trolley Stop in Council Bluffs, Iowa, on Saturday afternoon, March 4.

Aunt Clara Brown, eighty-two years old, was bound on yet another trip. This was the best trip of her life. She had traveled from Kentucky to Missouri to Kansas to Denver City, Colorado, to Central City, Colorado, to Kentucky to Tennessee to Central City, Colorado, to Kansas in search of her daughter. She was now traveling to Council Bluffs, Iowa, on her last journey. The haunting that she could not console and hug her baby girl for over forty-six years was almost alleviated. Eliza Jane was now in her late fifties, but to Aunt Clara she would always be her little girl. Now she understood why she had never been able to release Eliza Jane from her heart. She was still alive! Her gracious God was not going to let her die without once again touching her daughter's face.

On March 3, 1882, Aunt Clara boarded the Union Pacific Train in Denver. She was traveling all alone. With diminishing sight and aging, limited body, she was going to have to call upon her inner fortitude to find her way through train changes and trolley cars in the midst of strange states. During her lifetime she had endured much worse. God would give her the courage to bear up.

Aunt Clara slept on the train, arriving in Omaha, Nebraska. Standing in solitude, she waited for hours, but eventually she caught the horse-drawn trolley car. As the horses trotted across the Missouri River to Council Bluffs, Iowa, Aunt Clara's heart was pounding with unmitigated joy. She watched as rain darkened the skies, but it couldn't put out her ray of light.

When she arrived at the Eighth Street trolley stop and looked left and right, she peered through the drenching rain. She did not see her Eliza Jane. She waited. She had waited for over forty-six years. She could wait a few more moments. Suddenly, she heard footsteps. She looked down the lane and a woman was approaching. As she got closer the woman whispered, "Mammy?" Aunt Clara looked into the eyes of her baby Eliza Jane. She watched her smile exuding her daddy's big grin, and she reached up to touch her high Cherokee cheekbones. This was her Eliza Jane, at last. She reached out and drew her daughter into her arms. She gave her that long-awaited, much-desired, everseeking hug. She was reunited physically with her daughter, who had never left her in spirit. They hugged each other so intensely that they both fell into a puddle on the street. They didn't care; perhaps they didn't even notice. All they saw, all they felt, was each other. The bonds of slavery had not severed this beautiful bond of love.

Eliza Jane returned to Denver with her mother in March 1882. She had remembered being carried away by strangers and ruthlessly separated from her mother. She had lived with the Covington family and eventually married a man named Jeb. She bore nine children and lived with the Covingtons for twenty years. Jeb had died and all of her children were grown and on their own. It's not known how she ended up in Iowa. Aunt Clara was honored at a banquet at the Colorado Pioneer Society on September 24. She proudly sat in her wheelchair with her daughter on one side and her granddaughter on the other. They listened to the praises bestowed on Aunt Clara. She had been a persevering pioneer and a shining beacon of God. She had devoted herself to the well-being of others with an unshakable spirit representing the enduring nature of God's grace.

In June of 1885, a reporter described Aunt Clara Brown at the age of eighty-five: "She is a tall woman, very aged, yet she does not show the advance of years, save she is toothless. She has a remarkable face, with high cheekbones, a long pointed nose, and very black eyes. Her cast of features is strong and almost classical, and the hair which curls above her temples is as white as the snow."[14] When asked about her childhood and her ever-present faith, Aunt Clara responded, "When I was a girl, I relied on His mercy, and He fetched me through."[15] On October 26, 1885, at the age of eighty-five, Aunt Clara departed from her sweet Eliza Jane into the hands of her ever-loving Lord. Before she departed she spoke a final word. She reached out to Eliza Jane and cried out, "Mammy!"

Aunt Clara truly epitomized the pioneer spirit, and her life is a compelling composition. She was simply astonishing and profoundly symbolized God's guiding force. And to her great credit she pursued life with an amazingly generous and non-judgmental attitude. She harbored no resentment or ill will. She did it with her ceaseless, unrelenting faith in God. She leaned on Him for her every need and desire. She dropped to her knees at will and called on her God to give her the strength to bear up. And He did. Because she chose to listen to God's voice, she was able to bring happiness and healing to others as she simultaneously endured her pain. She never bowed to bitterness or defeat. As she helped to heal them, she healed herself as well. That's the phenomenon of Jesus' message.

Why did God take so long to answer Aunt Clara's prayers? Perhaps, if her wound had been healed, she would not have been motivated to reach out to the countless people who needed her, the people at Mississippi Town and her new family, for example. The eternal, residual effects of her charity were, perhaps, not entirely revealed to her, but they were surely known by God. He needed her in those places.

Life Lesson: Persevere with Praise

Aunt Clara personified perseverance. She proceeded through her maze of trials with a never-ending respect and reverence for God. The one consistent aspect of her life that never ceased was her worship and adoration of God, even when she didn't understand His motives. This is very hard to do. It's one thing to praise God when things are going our way; it's quite another to praise Him when times are tough. Usually when times are tough, we *plead* with God, we don't *praise* Him. Aunt Clara always had a good disposition and a smile on her face. With her great big smile and sparkling eyes, she symbolized God's kind and gentle nature. Her nature and actions imitated Jesus' love and compassion. "Come to me, all you who are weary and burdened, and I will give you rest"(Matthew 11:28 NIV).

My pastor, Dr. John McKellar, preached a fabulous sermon one Sunday about what is being reflected from our faces. Essentially, when someone looks into my face, they should see the reflection of God, the face of God. I reflect on his message frequently. I ask myself, *How is my face reflecting God's love today?* I think of it when I drive through a restaurant, when I'm waiting in line for a plane, when I'm working, and most importantly, in regard to my daughter. Does she see the grace, the loveliness of God in my face?

Many times children's image of God is a mirror of the parent, an authority figure. We represent God to them. If a parent is unforgiving and judgmental, then the children will perceive God as unforgiving and judgmental. Thus our countenance tells stories about our lives. Many times this is easily accomplished simply with a gracious smile. Aunt Clara Brown smiled. She smiled and sang songs, clapping her hands in the air. She praised God as she persevered. She praised God when times were good. She praised God when her heart was breaking, and He rewarded her devotion. Aunt Clara suffered hardships throughout her lifetime, yet she also received many blessings. The best blessing of all was seeing the smile of God reflected on her precious Eliza Jane's face. Surely that was God saying, "Job well done."

When times are tough, hold your head high and persevere with praise. Praise God!

Oh, child, just stop and think how our Blessed Lord was crucified. Think how He suffered. My little sufferings was nothing, honey, and the Lord, He gave me strength to bear up under them. I can't complain.[16]

—AUNT CLARA BROWN

BELVA LOCKWOOD

Renegade Single Mother

1830–1917

SNAPSHOT   Passionately lecturing for women's
                  rights, dramatically pacing the stage
                  wearing her flowing black gown
                  with white ruffles and a flower
                  adorning her hair

MOTHER MOMENT   Belva and Lura sitting side by side
                  as they read by the fireplace

CHALLENGE   Limitations placed upon her
                  achievements as a woman

STEWARDSHIP   Relentlessly opened new doors
                  for women

SCRIPTURE   They will soar on wings like eagles;
                  they will run and not grow weary,
                  they will walk and not be faint.
                  (Isaiah 40:31 NIV)

CHAPTER SEVENTEEN

Soar on Eagle's Wings!

I began to realize that it was a crime to be a woman;
but it was too late to be put in denial, and I
at once pleaded guilty to the charge of the court.[1]

—BELVA LOCKWOOD

New York and Washington, D.C. America's East Coast. Women. Collective consciousness. Gowns versus bloomers. Chauvinism versus women's suffrage. Peace versus war. Slavery versus freedom. Temperance versus tempers. A roller coaster of social issues. Movers and shakers create momentum. Women define themselves.

Belva Lockwood was a woman of great intelligence and stamina. A relentless instigator for justice. She broke all social mores and defied chauvinism. She pursued an education as a single mother when it was considered improper. She attended law school when it was unfathomable; became a lawyer during a time when women didn't even have the right to vote; fought endlessly and succeeded in being the first woman admitted to the bar of the United States Supreme Court; and she, not Hillary Clinton, was the first woman to officially be on the ballot for president of the United States.

None of these events was a natural occurrence, and none of them was without sacrifice. Belva bolted through social barriers, raising her daughter as a single mother for over fifteen years. This resulted in a mutually devoted bond between mother and daughter that lasted throughout their lifetimes. Belva was a trailblazer, a renegade, a revolutionary thinker. She set the stage upon which we, as women, walk today. She was student, teacher, lawyer, politician, avid supporter of women's suffrage, humanitarian, mother, and single mother. Belva was determined to prove that her God-given talents were not a mockery, but a gift to pursue. She chose to seize the day, and in the process she chose destiny.

Timeless Scenario: Girl is smart. Girl loves to learn. Girl meets boy. Girl falls in love. Girl and boy marry. Girl and boy have a baby girl. Boy dies. Girl needs job. Girl thinks it unfair not to be paid what boys are paid. Girl gets education. Girl fights injustice. Girl and daughter succeed.

PUSHING THE LIMITS

Belva Lockwood was born on October 24, 1830, as Belva A. Burnett. Her mother, Hannah, gave birth to her in a log cabin in Royalton, New York. She had married Belva's father, Lewis, when she was fifteen and he was twenty. Belva was the second-eldest daughter, and she had three younger brothers and sisters. Lewis was a farmer, and Belva grew up in the company of cows, chickens, and fruit trees. Her father harvested fruit for a living as Belva rambunctiously ran through the fields. Her fearless spirit was matched by an intellectual curiosity. She read the Bible from cover to cover by the age of ten. From the Bible she gleaned that with faith anything was possible.

Belva attended the local school in her rural neighborhood, which was restricted from girls after the eighth grade. The theories of that day were that girls should be home helping their mothers and that educated girls became old maids. Belva's eagerness and tireless pursuit of what she wanted was evident even as a young girl, and she was determined to continue her education. Why should she be limited? She had the mind and the willingness. Belva's father balked at the notion of higher education for his daughter; it just wasn't done and had never been done. Belva's mother understood her daughter's quest and lovingly interceded on her behalf. Eventually, Lewis acquiesced and agreed Belva could go to school if she could pay for it, because they could not.

Emboldened, Belva marched into town and held a meeting with five trustees of the village of Royalton. They were looking for a summer teacher, and Belva knew she was the answer to their inquiry. She convinced the men that she could teach school as a fourteen-year-old girl and that she could manage the boys. Blessed with an inner sense of confidence, she was not willing to be stopped by, in her own words, "the prejudices of the centuries past, that have had no foundation in reason, in nature or in nature's laws."[2] She believed that obstacles could always be overcome. She won the job and began teaching with a salary of five dollars a week. She was prudent with her money and had saved enough by the end of the summer to be able to attend the Girl's Academy of Royalton.

Belva began her education at the Academy in 1846. She was sixteen and worked as a housekeeper during the school year to pay for her meals and her room. She cherished her education. She continued her summer teaching job for two more years, making an extra dollar per week each year, so she could continue her education at the Academy. Much to her father's relief, Belva's educated mind didn't make all the boys wary. One such boy was Uriah McNall. He courted Belva and they fell in love. He was wise enough not to propose until Belva had graduated from the Academy. After Belva's thrilling achievement of graduating, Uriah proposed marriage and she accepted. At the tender age of eighteen, Belva, a blushing bride, married Uriah on November 8, 1848, in Royalton, New York.

Belva moved to Gasport with Uriah, commencing her new life. Uriah worked in a sawmill and Belva worked beside her beloved new husband. She commented that she had "measured up many thousand feet of lumber."[3] She became pregnant almost immediately, and true to the American revolutionary female tradition, she managed many jobs. She grew the vegetables, did the cooking and the sewing, and sold the livestock and produce. Belva, still eighteen years old, gave birth to a daughter, Lura McNall, on July 31, 1849. She and

Uriah were proud parents, and Belva bestowed upon Lura the same radiant enthusiasm that was indicative of her own nature. Among many other occupations, Belva wrote articles for a local newspaper and literary magazines. In the *Lockport Daily Journal* she wrote a poem in honor of a mother who had lost her child. It was published on November 12, 1851:

> *Weep not, Mother, for the love done*
> *That so soon has passed away*
> *Has left a world of sorrow*
> *For a bright and glorious day.*

Belva would have to call on these words in relation to Uriah. When Lura was two years old, Uriah had an accident at the sawmill. He caught his foot in the machinery, and falling logs crushed his body. He was carried to their house, where he lay unconscious for two days. Belva, twenty-one years old, was consumed with grief. She sobbed by his side. After regaining her composure, she called on her faith and resiliency and began to take charge. She managed the farm and the sawmill, tended to Lura, and took care of Uriah, who never fully recovered from the accident. It appeared to have robbed him of his spirit, and that was, perhaps, coupled with tuberculosis. He died at the age of twenty-eight in 1853. Belva and Uriah had been married for only four short years.

FINDING WINGS TO FLY

Belva's life was drastically altered. She was a twenty-two-year-old widow left alone in the world with her three-year-old Lura. She attended the funeral alone, but her brother and sister came to live with her, as they had decided to attend Gasport Academy. Belva was now the sole provider for Lura. She decided that she could return to her former employment, teaching.

Belva visited with Royalton Academy and inquired about a regular position as a teacher. They enthusiastically offered Belva the full-time job at seven dollars a week. Belva was shocked. Her final salary had been seven dollars for the summer teaching position. They were offering her the same amount for the yearly teaching position. Belva inquired about the salary men were paid for the same job. They responded that they were paid ten to fifteen dollars because they had a family to support. Belva responded with the blatant fact that she, too, had a family to support. They would not budge. Astonished by the injustice, Belva, who desperately needed the job, turned it down. The whole event "raised her dander," and the winds of change swept Belva into motion. The emotional turmoil of losing her husband and the indignation of her former employers stiffened Belva's resolve. She decided that she would not simply accept this defeatist mentality. She had wings and she was going to fly.

Belva had observed that the great achievers and thinkers of the world had been highly educated. She ascertained that the way to garner respect and better pay was to follow in their footsteps and obtain a higher education. So she attended Gasport Academy with her brother and sister, using the money that they were paying her for room and board as tuition. After a year at Gasport, she made a decision that was remarkably brave as a single mother and a woman, especially in the mid-1800s. She possessed an uncanny ability to visualize the future. She realized that by making herself a better woman she, as a mother, would be a better nurturer, provider, and role model. So she determined to leave her daughter in the care of her mother as she sought a higher education. Belva was going to be one of the rare women of her day to attend college. She decided to attend Genesee Wesleyan Seminary in Lima, New York.

In order to pay for her continuing education, Belva's father-in-law assisted her in selling the property in Gasport, encountering the disapproval of many. The prevailing attitude was that a woman's place was not in college; a young mother's devotion should be to her child. College was for men only, not for women. Belva wrote about that time in her life, saying, "I was isolated from my family and friends, all of whom had strenuously objected to my taking college courses believing, as many did in that day, that college courses were for boys and young men, but not for women."[4]

How many of the people who recited these tired comments were single mothers? How many were solely responsible for the welfare of their children? Only Belva could walk in Belva's shoes. Only Belva heard her higher calling. Only Belva knew that she was doing this for the benefit of her daughter. She alone had the courage to reach for the unattainable, make the sacrifice, and take the risk. To quote the old, wise adage, "To avoid criticism, do nothing, say nothing, be nothing." So with her head held high and her focus on her path to the future, Belva bid a tearful good-bye to Lura and departed for Genesee Wesleyan Seminary.

In September of 1854, Belva Lockwood walked across the threshold of Genesee Wesleyan, a college for women. But after a few months, Belva considered the college too easy, and she walked with determination to see President Cummings of Genesee College, a boys' school with only a few girls. She informed him that she wanted to transfer to Genesee College. He replied that many of the girls had not been able to keep up with the curriculum. She boldly asserted that she would not struggle and that she would succeed. Overcome, surely, by her intensity and ambition, he agreed to allow her transfer.

Belva's days were grueling. She started at seven in the morning with four hours of recitation that included the study of such courses as the Constitution of the United States, mathematics, magnetism, and political economy. Students were required to study all afternoon and in the evenings. Their only free time was a walk after the evening meal.

Belva anxiously awaited her opportunity to visit Lura. After her first year of college, she returned to Royalton to visit her family. Mother and daughter were joyously united. But the joy soon dissipated when her mother and father informed her they were moving to Illinois. Belva was devastated. Lura would no longer be relatively near; she would be living much farther away, and Lura would not have the funds to visit her. It was more emotionally challenging than Belva expected it to be. Torn, but never swaying from her belief that she was building a better future for Lura, Belva once again returned to college as Lura moved with her grandparents to Illinois.

Rebel Causes

Belva discovered that she could finish her college in two more years instead of three. She seized the opportunity, because she would be able to see Lura sooner. On her off days she would attend lectures and study the ways of the orators. One renowned orator was Susan B. Anthony. Belva was inspired by this rebellious woman and her revolutionary message, which echoed Belva's sentiments. This experience flamed Belva's passion for justice for women and ignited her heart. She studied intensely, and in 1857 she graduated with honors. She received a Bachelor of Science degree. She had accomplished her mission, and in only three years. Additionally, she shined as one of the top students in her coeducational class.

Belva's first action after completing school was to immediately go and retrieve her daughter. As she was about to begin her trip to Illinois, she was offered the prestigious position as principal of the Union School District in Lockport, New York. As a twenty-six-year-old, Belva would be in charge of all the teachers and students from six merging schools. She was offered four hundred dollars. The men were earning six hundred for teaching positions only, but Belva considered this to be a raise in salary from seven dollars a week and a wonderful opportunity. Though still torn by her desire to see Lura, she was finally persuaded to accept the job because of the scholastic opportunity Lura would receive. She would attend school at Lockport, be a recipient of its fabulous education, and be near her mother. Belva accepted the job. She didn't have enough money for a round-trip ticket to Illinois, so she had to wait until she had received some of her salary and reunite with Lura at Christmas.

Happy was the day when Belva was finally reunited with Lura. She hadn't seen her for two years. She was afraid that Lura wouldn't remember her mother's face, but Lura ran to embrace her. Mother and daughter were reunited. Though her family had not been able to share the graduation ceremony with her, she was with them now. Belva had sacrificed three years of her daughter's life to obtain the education that would now yield a wider and greater field of opportunities. They would both reap the benefits.

Belva was twenty-seven years old and Lura was eight. They would never be separated again.

Belva and Lura moved to Lockport as Belva resumed her job as teacher and principal, and Lura began her fine education beside her mother. Belva immediately put her mark on the school by initiating some radical new thoughts. She, to the horror of many fathers, created a class for the girls on the subject of public speaking, which wasn't considered proper for women. The girls enjoyed it, however, and many of them thrived.

Her next renegade action was incorporating, perish the thought, physical education for the girls. She was walking by the boys' gym class and was intrigued by what they were doing. She inquired about it and insisted that the girls have their own version of gymnastics. The coach was dumbfounded. She also gathered her girls for nature walks. Belva left her indelible mark on the Lockport, New York, Union School District.

On Her Own

After four years, Belva decided it was time to spread her wings. She was employed once again as a principal. She accepted the job at the Female Seminary in Gainesville, New York. Always ready for an adventure, Belva and Lura packed up and moved to Gainesville. Belva shocked all of her superiors when she suggested that ice-skating should be added to the curriculum.

After a year, Belva was frustrated with the school administrator's lack of inventiveness. So she accepted a job at another all-girls' school, a ladies' seminary in Hornellsville. In 1863 Belva was annoyed by her inability to carve a new perspective and opportunities for the girls at these schools. Thus in 1863, in true Belva fashion, she simply purchased her own school. She had always acted wisely in regard to her financial earnings, and now she was reaping the benefits. She was able in her own school to dictate her own visions for American girls—public speaking, higher intellectual pursuits, and physical education. Belva was a widow, and not being married enabled her to purchase land, homes, buildings, and schools. If Belva had been a married woman she would not have had the right to buy property.

By the age of thirty-three, Belva had paid for all of her education at the Girl's Academy, Gasport Academy, Genesee College, and had purchased her own school. She had graduated with honors and more than doubled her salary. She was working in an environment that benefited her daughter. Lura reaped great rewards from her mother's persistence and intellectual stimulation. They traveled together, studied together, and read together by the firelight in the evenings. Belva was an exemplary single mother and a visionary with a renaissance style. She was blazing new trails. She was a renegade in the mid-1800s.

At her new school in Owego, New York, Belva was able to nurture her girls and provide them with greater insights. Her curriculum included an education in the classics that exceeded the limitations placed on girls in other schools. She peppered the academic studies with the burning issues of the time: abolition, prohibition, suffrage, and peace. She believed in freedom for all individuals, and she abhorred slavery. She believed in prohibition because she witnessed the damages alcohol could reap. Many women were left in poverty and were abused by their husbands due to alcohol. Suffrage was a hot button for Belva too. It was beyond her realm of reality to comprehend why women were denied a voice, a vote, equal pay, and equal rights.

Belva was always kind-hearted and willing to serve anyone who needed her assistance. In November 1864 she received a visitor, Mrs. Skott. It was a woman seeking employment at her school. As they talked it became apparent that she was applying for a job as a janitor because she was penniless. She hadn't been receiving her widow's pension. Belva was incensed. She promptly took the woman's cause under her wing and wrote letters on her behalf. Leaving no stone unturned, she wrote to the War Office, to her congressman, to the treasurer of the War Relief Fund, and to the president of the United States. Not surprisingly, Mrs. Skott immediately started to receive her widow's pension. Belva was a peace activist as well. She disagreed with war as a solution, yet when the Civil War erupted, Belva encouraged her girls to contribute. She wrote, "The burden of war is for all to bear."[5]

Belva was educating and producing a new breed of woman. She took great pride in this accomplishment, but she felt an inner calling to extend her horizons. She believed that Washington, D.C., was a "great political centre—this seething pot."[6] She decided that she and Lura would move to Washington, D.C., where she could "learn something of the practical workings of the machinery of government, and see what the great men and women of the country felt and thought."[7] Always the businesswoman, she sold her school in Owego, doubling her money on her investment. In 1866, with enthusiasm in her soul and a little money in her pocket, she and Lura moved to Washington, D.C. Belva was thirty-five years old and Lura was sixteen. Together, with gusto, they sought new beginnings. They had a three-month supply of money.

Belva was enthralled with Washington. She was inspired by the radiance and greatness that surrounded her. She wanted to completely absorb this new world, so she would sit for hours, presumably with Lura by her side, and observe sessions of Congress and the Supreme Court. She and Lura also attended lectures on the topics of suffrage, peace, and temperance. She accepted a job as a teacher at Harrover's Boarding School as a way to provide for Lura, which also included her school tuition.

In 1877 Belva made another wise financial investment. She invested in a large hall called Union League Hall on Ninth Street. She and Lura lived in one section of Union Hall, and she rented the large halls to organizations that wanted to hold lectures and seminars. These rentals provided income for Belva and Lura and also provided a lively, inspiring atmosphere. Belva also opened her own school in this hall, McNall's Academy. It was an all-girls' school that opened its doors to boys in 1877. This investment provided Lura opportunities for employment. She taught French and Latin. The school became both respected and successful.

As women in the South were recuperating from the ravages of war, and the pioneer women were trying to survive the wildness of the West, the women in the East were on the warpath for equal rights. They were led by a select group of courageously defiant women such as Susan B. Anthony, Elizabeth Cody Stanton, and yes, Belva Lockwood. Many women were representing their defiance by their wardrobe. They were dressing as "bloomer girls," a trend started by Julia Holmes. The bloomers were long, flowing pants that bunched at the knees. Belva, however, didn't believe that a woman had to abandon her femininity. Women were women. They were not men in physique. They were unique in that respect. Their minds and abilities were comparable and of equal stature, and that's where Belva put her emphasis. She did not change her dress. She would engage in her speaking engagements wearing long, beautiful dresses, adorning her hair with a flower. She was a feminine, elegant rebel.

Belva was appointed vice president of the Universal Franchise Association. This organization was dedicated to bringing the vote to everyone, regardless of race or gender. When Belva lectured, whether at a meeting for the Universal Franchise Association or women's suffrage, they were raucous events. The people would throw vegetables and loudly bang pans to the point that the speaker could not be heard. They were attempting to end the meetings by discouraging the speakers. They didn't know with whom they were competing. Belva would not relent; her message would be heard. These meetings would conclude with singing. One such song was reflecting upon women's place in a hundred years. They sang,

> One hundred years hence what a change will be made
> In politics, morals, religion and trade.
> In statesmen who wrangle or ride on the fence
> These things will be altered a hundred years hence.
>
> Then woman, man's partner, man's equal will stand
> While beauty and harmony govern the land.
> To think for oneself will be no offence,
> The world will be thinking a hundred years hence![8]

Wedding Bells

At one of these meetings a tall, lanky man stood up to defend Belva and quieted the crowd. This man was a Washington, D.C., dentist and a Baptist preacher. His name was Dr. Ezekial Lockwood, and he was famous for being the first dentist to use nitrous gas during dental work. He had also served as chaplain during the Civil War. His chivalry was aptly noted. Dr. Lockwood was captivated by Belva and was not intimidated by her brilliance and motivating nature. Belva was intrigued and refreshed by Dr. Lockwood's gentle heart and the twinkle in his eye. Lura was eighteen years old when Dr. Lockwood and Belva met.

Belva had raised Lura as a single mother for fifteen years! With no money and nothing but talent and will, she had educated herself. She had paid for her own education during a time when jobs were few for women and the pay meager. After her education, she found reputable, respectable employment at higher wages, providing a prestigious education for her daughter during a time when girls were rarely given that opportunity. They had journeyed to many places and experienced many adventures together. Belva had been completely and solely devoted to her daughter.

Lura was now a lovely and obviously intelligent young woman. She had witnessed her mother's tenacity, gusto, and complete dedication to fairness in humanities. Belva was good, kind, and persevering. Lura's admiration for her mother elicited a boundless devotion to her until the day she died. Lura was now moving into a new chapter in her life. She was dating a young scientist named DeForest Ormes, who she had met at one of her mother's lectures.

Thus, with God's good timing and unerring wisdom, Ezekiel Lockwood presented himself to Belva at just the right moment. They began to date, fell in love, and were married at Union League Hall on March 11, 1868. Belva was a thirty-seven-year-old bride and Ezekiel a sixty-five-year-old groom. Ezekiel moved in with Belva at the hall. Lura moved to a neighboring boarding house and continued her teaching position at McNall's Academy. Lura followed in her mother's footsteps and married DeForest the same year.

Though Belva is married and Lura is grown at this juncture, we continue with Belva's life story because she became a single grandmother later in her life. I also elaborate because Belva's accomplishments during this phase of her life were stellar, steadfastly stoic, and worthy of notation. Her life, however, was not without tragedy.

Babies and Battles

On January 28, 1869, Belva had another baby at the age of thirty-eight. They named her Jessie Belva. Delighted with her baby, Belva found it difficult to leave her side, and she didn't do so for many months. Eventually, she continued to heed the call of righteousness with her rallies. She opened a Washington, D.C., chapter of the Equal Rights Association. This was an organization representing women's rights that included fierce advocates such as Susan B. Anthony.

Still, in 1869, almost one hundred years after the Revolution, women were denied the right to vote. They also continued to be subjected to the injustices of former centuries. Married women couldn't own property or even inherit it. Husbands controlled all of the property, even property the women had brought into the marriage. Women, who were victims to abusive and alcoholic husbands, were left with no resources. Higher education was still rare, and avenues for women were closed. Women were paid much less than men for the same jobs, and last but not least, women still had no rights over their children's welfare. If a woman and a man were divorced, the man, by law, retained all rights to the children. This left many women bound in relationships that were unhealthy for the mother and the child, because they couldn't bear to part with their children, or perhaps because they didn't want the child left unprotected in their father's hands.

These injustices were unfathomable, and Belva was determined to do something about it. She believed that if women had a voice, only then could they be represented. Belva's influence in this area began when she initiated public speaking courses for her female students. The ultimate goal was for women to have the right to vote. The Equal Rights Association was dedicated to these reformations.

Later, the group split and Belva joined Susan B. Anthony's new group, the National Woman Suffrage Association. Belva spoke at lectures, lobbied in Congress, and wrote and distributed petitions.

Belva felt that limitations barred her progress. She, once again, silently observed who had the most influence: lawyers. So Belva decided that law was to be her new vocation. But how did a woman in the 1800s get an education in law when most law schools were closed to women? She followed the adage, "If at first you don't succeed, try, try again!"

In 1869 Columbian College started a new law class. They invited Belva and Ezekiel to attend the first lecture. Belva was enthralled. She immediately seized the opportunity and rushed to sign up for the class. They, however, refused her money because she was a woman. She would have to send in an application to be assessed. She sent in her application and, in return, received a letter regarding her application:

Columbian College
October 7, 1869

Mrs. Belva A. Lockwood:
  Madam-The faculty of Columbian College have considered your request to be admitted to the Law Department of this institution, and, after due consultation, have considered that such admission would not be expedient, as it would be likely to distract the attention of the young men.

                    Respectfully,
                    Geo. W. Samson, President[9]

A distraction to the men! This would not do. Belva was not to be subdued or have her destiny barred. She was going to find a better school.

In 1870 Belva noted that her rambunctious toddler, who was bright and very active, was unusually tired and languid. She immediately called for the doctor. Jessie proceeded to run a high fever. Typhoid fever. Belva was frantic. She did everything she could to revive her daughter, but it proved unsuccessful. Her baby Jessie died when she was eighteen months old. Belva was inconsolable. This was the saddest time of Belva's life to date. The family grieved together. Belva did not know if she would ever resume her enthusiasm for life.

The Thrill of Victory

Belva did eventually regain her capacity for life, and women today benefit immensely from her resiliency. As Belva continued her battle to get into law school, her knowledge was solicited in regard to an injustice within the federal government. If a woman were employed by the government, her salary was limited to seventy-five dollars a month. Even if she held a job that was higher than a man's job or of equal rank, the woman could only make seventy-five dollars. Incensed at the injustice, Belva wrote a bill that would require the federal government to pay its female employees the same amount as men. After she wrote the bill, she circulated it through Congress. Congressman Arnell of Tennessee introduced the bill and it passed. Success! Now, women working for the federal government would have equal pay for equal work and adequate pay according to the job.

Eventually, a university opened its doors to women who wanted to study law. It was National University in Washington, D.C. The chancellor decided to conduct the law classes for women. Belva enthusiastically registered for the class with fourteen other women. They studied the same curriculum as the men, attended the same lectures, but had to recite their lectures separately from the men. The men were indignant and complained about the presence of the women at their lectures. Thus, during Belva's last quarter, the women were restricted from attending the lectures. The chancellor provided the lectures for the women in private quarters.

Throughout the program, thirteen women, considering it too difficult, had dropped out, and only Belva and Lydia S. Hall remained. As Belva studied she maintained her fervor for women's suffrage. In 1871 she and her comrades marched down the streets of Washington and tried to register to vote. They were denied. They then tried to actually vote and were denied again. They subsequently sued, declaring that as American citizens they had the right to vote.

In 1872 Belva passed all of her final exams at law school. This entitled her to a law degree and a diploma certifying her accomplishment. Belva's feat was monumental and a task that only a handful of women had ever achieved. The celebrations were abruptly halted when it was made evident that she and Lydia would not be allowed to accompany the men on the stage for the graduation ceremonies. The insults continued. They were also told that they were not going to receive diplomas. The diploma was essential. It was the proof that a person had successfully completed law school. By denying them diplomas, the college deliberately constrained Belva and Lydia's right to practice law.

In 1871 the District Supreme Court of Washington, D.C., (not the U.S. Supreme Court) had removed the word "male" from its admission rules. In February 1872 a black woman named Charlotte E. Ray had graduated from Washington's Howard University. She had received a diploma and was the first black woman to be admitted to the bar of the District Supreme Court. One could be accepted into the bar if a member of the bar introduced that person, they had a diploma, and they passed the examination.

In July 1872 Belva was introduced to the bar of the District Supreme Court. She heard nothing, however, regarding her subsequent examination. Motivated by the lack of propriety, Belva marched back to the court and demanded a hearing. She was given her examination and questioned for three arduous days. Belva responded magnificently. She waited for a report announcing the court's decision. It didn't come. So she marched back down to the court again and inquired about the neglect to the court's Justice David K. Carter. He appointed yet another committee, and they again questioned Belva unceasingly for three days. Once again, they refused to recognize her. The lack of a diploma was most assuredly the excuse they utilized.

Belva was disappointed and distressed. She had earned a diploma; she was just denied the physical evidence of it. She had succeeded in being able to practice in some places, but she was absolutely determined to practice law everywhere. So she decided to go back to law school. Georgetown University would not allow women into their law school, but Howard University did. It was the same university that had given Charlotte E. Ray her diploma. In 1873 Belva started attending classes at Howard University. As she sat in the classes, studying for the second time what she had already learned, she became incensed at the utter lack of justice she was receiving. She decided she was not going to law school twice; she was going to demand her diploma. Belva did not tolerate injustices well, whether they were against her, other women, or any human being. Her forthright tenacity was honorable. This was the key to her success, as it is any person who succeeds. She was unwilling to accept defeat when others would have found the battle too tedious. In her own words, she "grew a little bolder and to a certain extent desperate."[10]

As she was planning her next strategic move regarding her diploma, she did practice limited law. In one case they were so astounded that a woman was practicing law that it was telegraphed all over the country. In the fall of 1873 Belva decided that she would go straight to the top. She would write to the president of the United States. Ironically, President Ulysses S. Grant was also ex-officio president of the National University Law School, Belva's alma mater. She wrote,

No. 432 Ninth Street, N.W.
Washington, D.C., September 3, 1873

To His Excellency U. S. Grant, President, U.S.A.

Sir: You are, or you are not, President of the National University Law School. If you are its President, I desire to say to you that I have passed through the curriculum of study in this school, and am entitled to, and demand, my diploma. If you are not its President, then I ask that you take your name from its papers, and not hold out to the world to be what you are not.

Very respectfully,
Belva A. Lockwood[11]

Amazingly, Belva received her diploma the very next week. It was signed by "Chancellor and President Ulysses S. Grant." Belva had waited one year and four months after graduation for her diploma. Within days she was admitted to the District bar, and shortly thereafter, she was admitted to the District Supreme Court. This was the court that had questioned her for six grueling days without the courtesy of comment.

Belva, at the age of forty-three, was finally embarking on her new career. She was now a legitimate practicing lawyer. When she was admitted to the bar of the District Supreme Court, the clerk commented, "You went through today, Mrs. Lockwood, like a knife. You see the world moves in our day." Justice Carter was less appreciative and caustically commented, "Madam, if you come into this court, we shall treat you like a man." Justice McArthur told her, "Bring on as many women lawyers as you choose. I do not believe they will be a success."[12] The justices' taunting words could not overshadow Belva's sweet success. She celebrated with Lura. Another victory, another feat accomplished.

On a Woman's Terms

Though Belva was operating in a man's sphere, she was not a man. She embraced the dichotomy by dressing her five-foot-six-inch frame in black-velvet dresses with white ruffles that highlighted her face and her gesticulating hands. She wore kid gloves, beads, pens, and a blue coat that enhanced her waist. How wonderful to be a woman with an intellect that matched a man's.

Belva's first case was *Folker v. Folker*. Mary Ann Folker was a mother with two children. Her husband was a drunkard who beat her and neglected the children by not providing money for food. She

HOLDING HER HEAD HIGH

wanted a divorce, but if she obtained a divorce, she did not want her husband to retain the children. She wanted custody of the children. This was almost an impossibility in the mid-1800s. Who did she hire? Belva Lockwood. On September 29, 1873, Belva filed the papers. When the time to appear in court arrived, Belva took command of the court and began to speak,

> There has been testimony to contradict that this poor woman has been treated worse than a slave. Yet her master does not even provide her with food and shelter. You call women the weaker sex, but you do not give them protection in this world where they are barred from earning a living. Do you not feel shame that men have brought women to such a sorry state of degradation?[13]

Belva and her client won, and Mary Ann Folker received custody of her children. The judge ordered that Mr. Folker pay all attorney fees and alimony support. Belva knew he would never pay, and he didn't. So she filed again against Mr. Folker for debt collection. The court demanded that he pay his debts to his wife. He still refused. Belva would not relent until he was sent to prison for indebtedness. After Mr. Folker was released from prison, he decided, perhaps, it was wise to pay the allotted alimony to his former wife. Don't mess with Belva Lockwood!

Belva was besieged with clients. Lura worked closely with her mother, managing her office and cases. Belva sold McNall's Academy because, with all of her new law clients, she and Lura were quite busy. Lura and DeForest also started having children, and Belva was a proud grandmother. Lura followed in her mother's footsteps, wearing many hats as a mother, manager, activist, and journalist. She was heavily invested in women's rights and was also a journalist for the *Lockport Daily Journal* under her maiden name, Lura McNall.

THE AGONY OF DEFEAT
Belva had been accepted to the bar of the Supreme Court of the

District of Columbia, but she could not yet practice in any federal courts, such as the United States Court of Claims or the United States Supreme Court. She was hired by a client to represent him regarding a case against the government. It had to be argued in front of the United States Court of Claims. To be accepted to the bar of the United States Court of Claims, one first had to be nominated. She was nominated by a member of the bar, A. A. Hosmer.

As was the routine, Belva was summoned before the court. When she rose and stood before one of the judges, Justice Drake, he looked at her in astonishment and said, "Mistress Lockwood, you are a woman." Flabbergasted, Belva would later recall, "I began to realize that it was a crime to be a woman; but it was too late to be put in denial, and I at once pleaded guilty to the charge of the court."

The chief justice, unable to reconcile his thoughts, adjourned to resume the following week. Then she was summoned by the court again. This time she arrived with her husband, Ezekiel. She rose and stood in front of the chief justice. He stared at Belva with consternation and said, "Mistress Lockwood, you are a *married* woman!"

Annoyed, yet resolute, she acknowledged her husband and said, "Yes, may it please the court, but I am here with the consent of my husband." Outrageous! Ezekiel stood up and took a bow before the court. The chief justice adjourned again due to his inability to rationalize this situation in his mind. He was utterly baffled with the nuance of a woman presenting herself to practice law in the United States federal courts. After consideration, they refused Belva's request to be admitted to the bar with no explanation. She was forced to hand her case over to a man. He lost.[14]

Belva was faced with defeat yet another time in her life. A person of less conviction would have tossed in the towel, but not, of course, Belva. She marched to the United States Supreme Court and requested to read the admission rules. They stated that "any attorney," not man or male citizen, who was in good standing before the highest court of any state or territory for three years shall be admitted when presented by a member of the bar.

By October 1876 Belva had been practicing law for three years before the highest court in her territory, the District Supreme Court. Thus she marched back to the Supreme Court, daring them to find an excuse. The rules simply stated "any attorney." Belva was an attorney and she had been practicing for three years. With astonishment, the judges watched and listened as Belva was introduced to the Supreme Court for the third time. She presented her case.

They eventually responded with the pathetic excuse that there was no precedent. A woman could not be admitted unless there was a precedent that a woman had previously been admitted. But how could any woman ever be admitted if no woman was ever admitted? The decision was absolutely ludicrous, unjust, chauvinistic, and redundant. It was simply maddening. Queens had ruled in other countries for centuries and ruled admirably, including England, upon which many precedents in America's law had been established. Queen Elizabeth of England ruled for forty-five years, and the chief administrator and ruler in England during Belva's lifetime was Queen Victoria, who ruled for over sixty-three years. Why was the bias against women so prevalent in America?

Belva's response to her rebuff from the Supreme Court was, "I shall ask again to be admitted to the bar of the Supreme Court; I shall draft a bill and ask its introduction into both houses of Congress."[15]

On to Congress!

There were men sympathetic to women's issues and, in particular, to Belva's situation. She received recognition from the press and certain congressmen. Belva petitioned Congress with a legal brief, "Declaratory Act, or Joint Resolution to the effect . . . no woman otherwise qualified, shall be debarred from practice before any United States Court on account of sex."

In 1876 Congressman Benjamin F. Butler assisted Belva in drafting a bill that would specify that female lawyers could appear in front of the United States Supreme Court. It circulated through Congress and was defeated. Belva would not retreat. In 1877 yet another bill was drafted by Belva. Her comrade this time was Congressman William G. Lawrence. It did not succeed. In Belva's words, it "died almost before it was born."[16] Yet again, a third bill was introduced in the latter half of 1877, reiterating that women should have the right to appear in front of the Supreme Court. This particular bill was drafted by Belva and her new supporter, Congressman John M. Glover. Mr. Glover introduced this third bill—H.R. 1077—to Congress. Belva was summoned to speak before the House Judiciary Committee to argue its value and importance. The committee was convinced by Belva's supreme oratory skills, and the bill was recommended to the House for a vote. It was passed by a two-thirds majority. Success in one-half of the Congress!

Senator Aaron A. Sargent was the senator who believed in Belva and the bill. He presented it to the Senate Judiciary Committee. The committee denied the recommendation of the bill. They argued that the Supreme Court had no statement claiming that they would not technically allow women to appear in front of the Supreme Court; thus, why should they recommend a bill that states specifically that a woman be allowed to appear in front of the Supreme Court? In April 1878 they denied the bill's passage. In other words, the Supreme Court rules claimed that an "attorney" who had argued for three years at the highest court could be admitted. Belva and her allies knew, however, that they would always use the "no precedent" ruling until they were specifically forced not to do so.

Wasting no time, Senator Sargent resubmitted the bill to the committee. Again they refused it. With a determination matching Belva's, Senator Sargent was adamantly determined and decided to circumvent the committee and take it directly to the Senate floor. Hope! Then suddenly, the momentum of the bill was halted. Senator Sargent became ill and had to return home. The efforts on behalf of the bill and Belva stopped. Unbelievable.

Belva, who must have been absolutely deflated, still did not succumb to defeat. It took her yet another year, but she finally persuaded Senators Joseph E. McDonald and George F. Hoar to reissue the bill. It was presented to the Senate floor on February 1879, and Senator Sargent, who had recently recovered, appeared to help muster support. On the floor he passionately defended the bill, claiming it was "merely a measure of justice." He followed with the statement, "In this land, man has ceased to dominate over his fellow. Let him cease to dominate over his sister."[17] Senator Hoar chimed in with the scenario that if a man hired a female lawyer, he would not be allowed to have his attorney represent him in the higher court. This had happened with one of Belva's clients. Senator Hoar thus summarized that the bill would be positive for both women and men.

Belva roamed the halls of Congress in her black-velvet gowns accentuated with flowers adorning her hair. She visited with senator after senator, stating her cause with her infinite powers of persuasion. She recalled, "Nothing was too daring for me to attempt. I addressed senators as though they were old familiar friends, and with an earnestness that carried with it conviction."[18] On February 7, 1879, the bill was passed by the Senate with thirty-nine yeas and twenty nays and seventeen absent. It was done!

It took Belva over *five* years, beginning with her fight to be admitted to the District Supreme Court, but it was finally accomplished. Could any other woman have had the mental, emotional, and spiritual fortitude to pursue the endless, erroneous prejudices? Belva was motivated by her insatiable desire for justice and fairness. Her bill was signed promptly by President Rutherford B. Hayes. Belva's immediate path led her directly to the United States Supreme Court. Imagine the faces of the judges as Belva swept into the room and made her place in the history books as the first woman to be admitted to the bar of the United States Supreme Court. She had given them their precedent. She was the first woman; now other women could follow.

Belva and Lura celebrated. Sweet was the victory. Ezekiel was not present with them as they celebrated, because two years earlier, on April 23, 1877, Ezekiel had passed away. When he had become ill, Belva had sat endlessly at his bedside. Ezekiel had been her kind lover and generous friend. She was deeply saddened when he died. They had been married for nine years. By the age of forty-six, Belva had lost two husbands, her eighteen-month-old baby, a sister, and her father, who died two months after Ezekiel. These emotional challenges surely etched scars of sorrow upon her heart.

Belva and Lura remained inseparable, consoling and supporting one another. Belva's sorrows were lessened by Lura and her grandchildren, as they ran joyfully around her house. Belva had also alleviated her sorrows by resuming her passions, which included women's suffrage. In 1877 she was chosen to be the primary speaker for the National Woman Suffrage Association's convention. She spoke arduously to the crowd, which included the Association's founders, Susan B. Anthony and Elizabeth Cody Stanton. (She had recently been rebuffed by the Supreme Court.) Elizabeth Cody Stanton described Belva's commanding presence with the following words:

Tall, well proportioned, with dark hair and eyes, regular features, in velvet dress and train, with becoming indignation at such injustice, marched up and down the platform, and rounded out her glowing periods, she might have fairly represented the Italian Portia at the bar of Venice. No more effective speech was ever made on our platform.[19]

Belva's rousing speech motivated the crowd:

I have been told that there is no precedent for admitting a woman to practice in the Supreme Court of the United States. The glory of each generation is to make its own precedents. As there were none for Eve in the Garden of Eden, so there need be none for her daughters on entering colleges, the church, or the courts.[20]

Belva also joined the Universal Peace Union. It was organized in Philadelphia by a Quaker named Alfred Love. Belva always held her head high. When in the depths of sorrow or victimized by society, she would reach out to help others who were suffering similar fates. All of Belva's quests benefited her fellow human beings. She yearned to bring dignity to the suppressed and peace to her country.

In 1879 after her success with the Supreme Court, Belva bought a twenty-room house on F Street, and Lura, DeForest, and their children all moved under one roof with her. Her law offices were also in the house where she partnered with other female lawyers. She became well known for her unique mode of transportation, which was a giant tricycle. With her skirts billowing in the wind and flowers falling from her hair, she would pedal to her destinations.

Most of Belva's clients were soldiers who needed assistance in obtaining back pay. She also sponsored Samuel R. Lowry for admission to the Supreme Court bar. He was the fourth black man and the first black man from the South to be admitted shortly after the Civil War. Even though she had a thriving legal practice, she still found time to lecture on equal rights for women. She would command the stage, walking back and forth, passionately arousing audiences with fiery speeches including sentiments such as, "We shall never have rights until we take them. Nor respect until we command it."[21]

The women's movement chose Belva to represent women for the Republican Party at the national convention in Chicago. They wanted the party to embrace the idea that women had a right to vote. The men disregarded Belva's efforts. So the women tried again in 1884, receiving the same response.

Running for President

The Equal Rights Party was a new party that organized in San Francisco. The party's platform was equal rights for everybody with a strong emphasis on humanity. They proposed a unified education across the country, pensions for disabled soldiers, an increase in work wages for both men and women, and the right for Indians to govern themselves. Who did they think would best represent their party? Belva Lockwood!

In 1884 Belva, fifty-three years old and a single woman, was nominated for the office of president of the United States on the Equal Rights Party ticket. She was stunned. Flattered. She and Lura collaborated about what was the best course of action. Surprisingly, Susan B. Anthony and Elizabeth Stanton Cody did not embrace the idea.

They thought it would be a distraction from the women's movement. Belva thought quite the opposite; she thought it would bring national attention to their cause. She would be traveling and lecturing across the country. What an opportunity! Belva also believed that the messages of the party were sincere and noble. As the country's first female candidate for president, the first to actually make the ballot, she would garner much attention, and their causes would gain much consideration. Belva and Lura decided Belva should accept this great honor. It would require much dedication and devotion from both of them, but these were traits deeply ingrained in both their souls.

Belva, Lura, and her granddaughter, Hannah, three generations of women, traveled to Maryland to accept the nomination. Her campaign platform included women's suffrage, property rights for women, and "equal and exact justice to every class of . . . citizens, without distinction of color, sex, or nationality."[22] Many reporters attended the event. Ironically, a woman had been nominated for president before women even had the right to vote. Belva recalls her inaugural evening, "It grew dark before I rose to speak. I have vivid recollection when my turn came of seeing nine reporters on railroad ties, trying to take down my words by the light of one flickering candle."[23] Just as exists in modern-day politics, Belva became the victim of much ridiculous gossip. They wrote things such as she dyed her hair black, she tried to bribe a judge with chocolate caramels, and she wore scarlet underwear while riding her tricycle. Outrageous! Would these words have been written about a male presidential nominee? Would anyone dare to question the color of his underwear? Belva endured the arduous task of touring the country, shaking hands, and making her renowned motivational speeches. One of her campaign speeches addressed an absurdity:

> There are 10,500,000 male voters in the country to 12,500,000 adult women taxpayers. Yet this country is supposed to be governed by the will of the majority . . . Women can no longer be relegated to the cradle and the kitchen. The full-fledged American woman stands ready for the workshop, the pulpit or

the forum, and she demands equal protection from the Constitution and equal justice from the law.[24]

She, of course, did not win and never expected to do so. She won the electoral votes from the state of Indiana, which were overturned. She received the following votes:

New Hampshire 379
New York 1336
Michigan 374
Illinois 1008
Maryland 318
California 734 [25]

Votes were counted entirely by hand, and some of Belva's votes were simply discarded. The state of Pennsylvania disrespectfully dumped her votes into the trash can. Belva had received 4,149 votes. And of course these votes were from men, the only gender allowed to vote. Belva's candidacy for president of the United States was a landmark event, not to be rivaled until Hillary Clinton over one hundred and twenty years later. Belva felt confident and proud that she had "awakened the women of the country."[26]

Belva had a burning desire for worldwide peace. She wrote a revolutionary bill and submitted it to Congress. The bill presented her idea that an international court should be created to preserve the peace throughout the world. Her idea was the precursor to the League of Nations and the United Nations. Her bill was not acknowledged by the Congress. However, in 1886 the United States State Department asked her to represent America by attending the Congress of Charities and Corrections in Geneva, Switzerland. It was the world's first international peace conference. Belva used this platform to read her proposal in front of the entire international community. Many countries were intrigued by her idea and asked for copies of her bill. In 1887 she was asked to represent America again at the Second International Peace Conference. It was held in Budapest, Hungary. Belva once again undertook the transatlantic ocean voyage. Always seeking opportunities to advance women's suffrage, she stopped in London to attend the International Women's Congress.

Belva was asked by the Equal Rights Party to run for president again during the 1888 election. She was nominated for president, and the party's creator, Alfred H. Love, ran for vice president. Belva, absolutely tireless, toured the country for the second time. She wore a banner that was inscribed with the word "Peace" on one side and "Women's Rights" on the other. She created quite a stir and drew huge crowds. The newspapers described her as both an "intellectual treat" and "brains are what Belva is troubled with."[27] Describing her awesome tenacity, she commented, "I am very simple minded. When I wish to do a thing, I only know one way—to keep at it till I get it."[28] Once again they didn't win, but Belva created intrigue and a vast awareness for women's suffrage throughout the country.

Belva was a delegate to four more international peace conferences. She traveled by boat to Paris in 1889, to London in 1890, to Rome in 1891, and at the age of sixty-two, to Switzerland in 1892. Belva's physical stamina matched her intellectual stimulation. Lura was holding down the fort in Washington, D.C. She managed Belva's law firm, and in 1890 she gave birth to her third child, a boy named DeForest. Belva was thrilled to have a grandson.

THE TRAIL OF TEARS

In 1891 Jim Taylor, a Cherokee Indian from North Carolina who was a friend of Belva's and a former client, approached her to represent a major case for the Cherokee Indians. In 1835 the Treaty of New Echota was signed by seventy-nine Cherokee Indians. This treaty affected the sixteen thousand Cherokees living in North Carolina, Tennessee, Alabama, and Georgia. It was signed without the approval of the masses. This treaty agreed that they would move to Oklahoma. The majority of the Cherokees didn't agree and did not want to move. Subsequently, they were rounded up and inhumanely forced to travel by foot to Oklahoma. This journey was called the Trail of Tears. Fourteen thousand Indians were relocated. In the process, four thousand died. They were supposed to be paid for their lands, yet they never received the money. They hired Belva to help them retrieve their money. Belva didn't want to simply get the million dollars they had been denied. She wanted interest on the million dollars to be paid for the fifty-six years the government didn't pay. This project took years to prepare, as Belva was representing fourteen thousand people, and it required extensive travel.

In 1894 tragedy befell Belva. Lura, her beloved daughter, died suddenly after a brief illness at the age of forty-five. Belva was immobilized with despair. Lura had been her joy, her gift, her companion, her cherished daughter. Belva and Lura had been inseparable for forty-five years. They had experienced many chapters of life together, and through the fifteen years she had raised Lura as a single mother, they developed a bond that was inseverable, until now. Belva's remorse felt like an endless purgatory.

Lura's children were grown, except for DeForest, who was still a young boy. DeForest's father decided that it would be mutually beneficial for DeForest and Belva to live together. Belva cherished the opportunity, and at age sixty-four she became a single grandmother. DeForest was her saving grace, and she took a considerable amount of comfort in his presence. She took him with her everywhere. He would ride with Belva on her tricycle as she worked on her law cases. He witnessed her spunk and tenacity as she was fighting for justice for those who couldn't do it for themselves. He stood by her side as she orated fervently onstage. He would travel with her as she diligently fought for retribution for the Cherokee Indians. DeForest was receiving images of life that broadened his horizons and etched a sense of responsibility into his character.

When DeForest was ten years old, his father died, and thus, Belva was truly his sole guardian. Belva never doubted or despaired over her ability to mesh the two worlds of motherhood and occupation. She had always had to work. There had been no one else to provide for Lura and herself. She, unlike the angst many working mothers feel today, felt no guilt about working. It was a necessity. It was a passion. It was simply accepted. God gave her gifts and she knew it. She did not deny her God, her child, or her grandchild. She felt confident that she was serving them well.

Coming into Their Own

Belva's case with the Cherokee Indians would take fifteen years to resolve. In the meantime Belva, as a single grandmother, would put her talents, her heart, and her soul into a bill that would be the most far-reaching, monumentally important bill to benefit women and their children. This bill was, perhaps, comparable only to the Nineteenth Amendment, guaranteeing women the right to vote.

This important bill dealt with many issues that were gravely overdue. It was the Married Woman's Property Act. This act would provide a fair inheritance law for married women. It would also give them the right to sue. They would finally have the right to buy and sell property, enter into contracts, and conduct business. The most valuable aspect of this bill, however, was that women would have the right to guardianship of their children. A man could no longer automatically keep the children. A woman would not have to endure an abusive marriage out of the fear of losing her children. And children would no longer have to be victims of violent households. In regard to divorce, the man would no longer have the right to the children unless he could prove that the mother was negligent and unfit.

This bill was centuries overdue. How different Rachel Lavein Fawcett's life would have been if this law had existed during her lifetime. Belva helped shape the bill with the contributions of her brilliant mind and her compassionate heart. She also helped lobby the bill, and it was passed and signed into law by President McKinley on June 1, 1896.

This new law was a huge victory for women. It repealed the bondage that had unjustly controlled the fate of married women's lives for centuries and now blessed these women with fairness, dignity, safety, and opportunity. Future generations of women would reap the rewards granted by the tenacious efforts of Belva and the other contributors who fought on their behalf for the Married Woman's Property Act.

Victory at Last

In 1905, fourteen years after Belva had begun her work on the Cherokee Indians' case, the *Eastern and Emigrant Claims v. United States* finally came to fruition. It was initially heard in the United States Court of Claims. Ironically, the presiding judge was Charles C. Nott. He had fought against Belva's admittance to the court in 1874 with the scornful words, "A woman is without legal capacity to take office of attorney."[29] Now, thirty-one years later, he admitted that the Cherokee Indians were admirably represented by Mrs. Belva Lockwood.

Judge Nott announced his decision on March 20, 1905. He stipulated that the United States had "broken and evaded the letter of the spirit"[30] of the treaty of Echota. Yet he refused to allow the interest on the million dollars to be claimed. This was partial victory, but Belva was not going to settle for a partial victory. She appealed to the United States Supreme Court. Belva considered the million dollars that was owed to the Cherokee Indians an interest-bearing fund.

One year later, on April 30, 1906, Chief Justice Fuller delivered the Supreme Court's decision: "We agree that the United States are liable. The monies should be paid directly to the equitable owners."[31] Victory! Belva Lockwood, a seventy-seven-year-old single grandmother, had won the largest case in United States history. Her diligence, superior intellect, and blood, sweat, and tears of fifteen years of her life had won the Cherokee Indians five million dollars, four million more than if she had accepted Judge Nott's decision from the District Court. Belva's fee was approximately fifty thousand dollars.

Always a fierce protector, Belva, after winning the case, traveled to Oklahoma to personally make sure that all of the eligible recipients of the money received their monies due. This included approximately six thousand Cherokees. This extra effort of Belva's was not accomplished until she was approximately eighty years old.

At the age of seventy-nine she received an honorary degree of Doctor of Laws from Syracuse University. She continued to attend every peace conference until 1911, spanning the twenty-five years from 1886 to 1911. At the age of eighty-three, in 1912, she could still be seen in three different courts in one day. Perhaps her vigorous health could have been attributed to her ten-mile-a-day tricycle excursions.

Unfortunately Belva was swindled by bad investment advice, and she lost all of her savings. This must have been catastrophic for her at her age. She had always been frugal and had accomplished so much in her life with so little money.

To add to her financial woes, after her friend Jim Taylor died, his Native American heirs sued Belva for money. Belva, who had given over fifteen years of her life to their cause and had accomplished a victorious Supreme Court ruling, was now a recipient of bitter discourse. Jim had most likely dismissed whatever business dealing that was pending, a mutual contract regarding commission. He had not sought it. His heirs, however, did. It was fought in court and Belva lost. They demanded money from her that she had unfortunately lost to the unscrupulous investor. Belva appealed to the Cherokee people, but they refused to help her. At the age of eighty-three she had to move out of her home. Belva had been born poor, so she could certainly die poor. But her spirit was rich. Her life was full of rewards.

Belva once again faced the seas and made her last crossing for peace at the age of eighty-three. She argued her final case at eighty-four. She actively campaigned for Woodrow Wilson, and her support was considered a political advantage; thus, the Wilson campaign circulated her endorsement. Belva still had a dream of an international peace committee represented by her earlier bill and by her numerous efforts abroad. She ardently hoped that Woodrow Wilson would establish a League of Nations. In regard to her lifelong effort toward women's suffrage, many states were now granting women the right to vote, such as Wyoming, Utah Territory, Colorado, and Idaho. By 1915 women could vote in twelve states and in the Alaskan Territory. The women's suffrage amendment had been routinely introduced and denied in Congress for *thirty-seven* years. Yet, witnessing the movement of the many states that were granting women the right to vote, Belva felt hopeful. She commented on October 30, 1815, her eighty-fifth birthday, "Suffrage is no longer an issue, it is an accomplished fact. Those states which have denied it to women will come around."[32]

In April of 1917 Belva didn't feel well. She was taken to the George Washington Hospital, where she died in her sleep on May 20, 1917, at the age of eighty-six. She didn't live to see the Nineteenth Amendment pass, but she had heralded, by sheer will, many great accomplishments that benefited and continue to benefit women today.

Three years after her death, in 1920, the Nineteenth Amendment was passed, giving women the right to vote in America. In the 1984 presidential election, when Ronald Reagan was reelected, seven million more women voted than men. As Belva had proclaimed, only with the power to vote will women's voices be heard.

BELATED RECOGNITION

It is, to me, unfathomable that Belva Lockwood is not more widely known. But recognition has slowly begun to emerge. In 1983 Belva was inducted into the National Women's Hall of Fame in Seneca Falls, New York. She was deservedly the thirtieth subject of the United States Postal Service's series of Great Americans. Belva's hometown Girl Scouts remember Belva with a badge they instituted in 1975. They have been known to call themselves the "Belva Dears." In 1888 the *Morning Journal* in Washington tagged Belva with the nickname Belva Dear, initiated by this poem,

> *We'll not vote for Ben or Grove*
> *Belva, dear; Belva, dear;*
> *For our choice is you and "Love"*
> *Belva, dear; Belva, dear;*
> *We endorse your views in full*
> *For we know you're sound as "wool"*
> *With a husband's hair to pull,*
> *Belva, dear; Belva, dear;*
> *With a husband's hair to pull,*
> *Belva, dear; Belva, dear.*[33]

There is no doubt that Belva's influence, her countless speeches, her inexhaustible travels, her burning path through the halls of Congress, her undeniable and unyielding determination all contributed greatly to the surge of awareness and ultimate, unswerving stand that women should be heard. The *Suffragist* wrote a tribute to her after her death, including these words regarding her efforts on behalf of women's rights: "the candidacy of such a woman served brilliantly to bring the federal amendment for suffrage before the country as it had never been brought before."[34]

These same passions permeated all the causes for which she endeavored, whether they were for retrieving pensions for helpless widows or instigating the peace movement, women's suffrage or the Married Women's Property Act, fighting for admission to the Supreme Court or running for the office of president of the United States, getting an African American nominated for the Supreme Court or insisting that Native Americans get full retribution, insisting soldiers receive their due pay or young schoolgirls have classes in public speaking. Whatever projects she pursued, she represented them with sacrifice and honor.

Belva's ultimate passion, however, was for her daughter, Lura. She was a stoic, brave, devoted, and exemplary single mother. Belva surely knew fear, most assuredly felt the depths of sadness, and routinely was subjected to ridicule and scorn for her beliefs. Great people are never without circumstances beyond their control or desires, they simply stand bravely to face them. Belva didn't just stand, she walked through the flames of fire again and again. She aptly commented about her endeavors:

I have not raised the dead but I have awakened the living; and if I have not been able to walk on water, the progressive spirit of this age may soon accomplish this feat. The general effect of attempting things beyond us, even though we fail, is to enlarge and liberalize the mind. With work and school, I soon abandoned the miracles, but few undertakings were so great that I did not aspire to them.[35]

HOLDING HER HEAD HIGH

In the process, Belva exhibited for her daughter the coping skills required for life, granting her the freedom to dream. Belva wanted a better life for herself, for her daughter, for all women. She wasn't afraid to be who she was, to manifest her God-given talents, and to be a mother at the same time. She validated the perspective that as mothers bring their talents to fruition, they are giving their children a gift—the confidence to know that they, too, are capable of facing the world's challenges. By gallantly defending the victims of humanity with compassion and empathy, Belva provided her child with a perspective beyond her own limited view of life. Lura's childhood was full of adventure, color, stimulation, and comforts. She received from her mother love, sensitivity, strength, and an educated mind. Later her grandson, DeForest, was the recipient of these same devotions. He commented, "All the progressive and advanced women of the day visited our house."[36] Surely his life with his grandmother was intriguing.

Belva took all the injustices she had experienced, all her wounds, and rolled them into a huge, loud, incessant cannonball that burst through the walls of chauvinism, discrimination, bigotry, and intolerance. She was personally a victim of these narrow-minded prejudices, but she held her head high and turned her woes into countless victories for people experiencing similar fates. It was only because she had felt a similar despair that she could render a response, a hope, a solution. She lifted victims from inequality with the grasp of an eagle's talons. She fought her battles with unceasing determination. Her most impressive accomplishment was as a single mother. Belva is the icon of the single working mother—radiant, reliable, resourceful, resilient, renegade.

LIFE LESSON: SOAR ON EAGLE'S WINGS

I have had a lot of guilt about working as a single mother, feeling absolutely torn in two by my responsibilities toward my work and my all-consuming dedication to my daughter. I had fallen into a belief that, in order to be a good mother, I must diminish my pursuits. I do believe that our children are only babies for a short amount of time; then they are grown and on their own. I do believe that our most important and relevant job is developing our children's character and religious foundation, nurturing them with boundless love. Other than God, my love for my daughter has no equal.

Yet, Belva Lockwood has opened my eyes to the adventures of life. By her example I now believe I'm capable of blending my daughter's blessings with my gifts. Perhaps now my guilt as a single working mother will alleviate. Our children learn by our examples. What good are our talents if we don't utilize them for God's purpose? By limiting our scopes, we limit our children's fields of vision as well.

I realize now that I should soar on eagle's wings and accept God's plan for our lives. Wherever God leads me, He has already carved a place for my daughter. As single mothers we must work. The courts certainly do not afford us the luxury to be stay-at-home single moms. But we have power over our perspectives. Without fear and without guilt we can become all we are meant to be. God gave us wings to fly.

God will raise you and your children on eagle's wings. Fly with the eagle! Rest on God's mighty wings. Soar free from guilt. God's not going to drop you. He is only going to lift you and your children to higher stratospheres of success. Soar! When we are inspired, we inspire our children. God places no limitations on your divine path, nor must you.

America and the world are better places because Belva Lockwood allowed herself to soar as a single mother. Don't limit what you have to offer. Let go. Believe. Hold your head high and soar on eagles' wings.

Has God given one-half of his creatures talents and gifts that are not a mockery—wings but not to fly? Reasoning ability, but not to think, the power of poetry, but not to write? The power to sway the multitude with her eloquence but not to voice the thoughts? We tell you nay![37]

—Belva Lockwood

Virtual Conversations

So when the great word "Mother" rang out once more,
I saw at last its meaning and its place,
Not the blind passion of the brooding past,
But Mother—the World's Mother—come at last,
To love as she had never loved before—
To feed and guard and teach the human race.[1]

—CHARLOTTE PERKINS GILMAN

After months of delving into the realms of these rare, wonderful women, I felt as if I had actually ventured into their eras, their lives. During this process, Juliette and I visited the National Portrait Gallery in Washington, D.C., to see Belva Lockwood's portrait. There she was in her long, black gown with white ruffles, her intelligent eyes peering out at me.

I started jumping up and down like a child shouting, "Belva! Belva! Hi! It's me!" I felt like an idiot, but I couldn't control my thrill. Afterward I pondered, *What if each of these women were to walk into my home today? What if we could have a virtual conversation? Wouldn't that be fun?* So I lit my imagination. Come on in!

Helena Augusta. I would welcome her into our house and ask her if she would like a cool glass of water. We would sit by the pool, because I know how they loved their "baths" back then. I would have her describe the days of the Roman Empire in detail. What did the cities look like, and how did the men treat the women? I would ask Helena how she felt when the father of her child left her. She must have loved him very much. I would share with her that I, too, was separated from the man I loved and that it was immeasurably distressing. I was pregnant at the time, and thus, the intensity of the pain was magnified. And even though I gave birth alone, my sorrows were immediately lightened the moment I laid eyes on my baby girl. Her every breath awakened my senses of devotion. My life was forever, irreversibly, gorgeously altered.

I would ask Helena about how she listened for God's higher calling and her consequent transformation as a Christian. What a moment that would have been! I would share with her one of my many defining moments as a Christian: I remember one hot summer day, standing in the aisles of my church. I was pregnant. I was with my mother. I had always been a Christian, but now that I was pregnant and alone, I felt the call of Christ assuring me that He was going to be my husband and my daughter's father. I knew He would not forsake us. I joined my new church that day, and I remember, as I walked to the front of the church and said my affirmations, how I felt the love and acceptance of my fellow Christians. That is the way all churches should be, for that is how Jesus was. That day I felt the grace of Christ and I have felt it ever since.

I would most certainly ask Helena about her son Constantine and the Council of Nicea. I would tell her that I had just recited the Nicene Creed in church today and how cool it is to think of her. How amazing that her son was the one responsible for its creation.

I would ask her about Jerusalem and about her discovery of the three crosses. She would be amazed to know the magnificent influence crosses are in our religion and across the world today. I bet she would be pleased. I would show her the cross around my neck and the crosses in my house and in my car. I would introduce her to my daughter and ask her to tell me about her son. If she could stay for dinner, I wonder what she would like to eat? Domino's pizza?

If **Blanche of Castille** dropped by for a chat, I would ask her to join me in my living room. I bet she would like to hear Juliette play the piano. As she sipped on apple cider (I don't drink, so there is no wine in our house), I would ask her about what made her dry her tears in that drafty old castle when she was twelve years old. What made her choose God's greatness? I would discuss with her how I have felt powerless over situations in my life many times and I am usually weeping too. I would share with her how, during these times, I imagine a little flame burning within my chest and how I will not allow anyone to blow it out. With this determination, I always fall to my knees and pray to God. It is God's flame, a gift to me of His peace and destiny. No one has the right to touch it.

I, like Blanche, choose God's greatness. I would discuss with her how God always reveals Himself; it just may not be how, when, or where I was expecting it. I would ask her how she felt when she saw her son, the future king, feeding bread to the peasants in disguise. I would share with her that I have read the Bible with my daughter religiously since she was born. I would show her our hip, new, informational study Bible. I bet she would get a kick out of that.

If **Christine De Pizan** stopped by, I would promptly show her this book! I would discuss with her the challenges and joys of writing. I would ask her about her days of enduring malicious gossip after she became a widow. I would share with her how I have had to withstand my share of gossip as a single mother too. I would relish telling her how I tell Juliette exactly what she told her children in regard to gossip. God, Juliette, and I know the truth, and that is all that matters. I would ask her about Paris and the Louvre.

I would take Christine to my ranch and show her a longhorn cow. I bet she would be shocked. I would ask her how it felt to write away her woes. I would share with her how I often purge my emotions by writing a letter that I never mail. I may simply rip it up, but it feels so good to get all of those feelings out and on paper. The paper carries the pain away. I would tell her that I have taught Juliette how to write these emotional eliminating letters, and that she really wanted me to title her chapter "Write Away Your Woes." I would explain to her that

I chose "Turn Tribulations into Triumphs" because she, Christine, so eloquently turned all of her trials and tribulations into a victorious message for women and mankind and her children.

I think I would really like Christine. Maybe she would like to spend the night. I wonder if she would like to watch Fox News, the theatrical journalists of the day?

Rachel Lavein Fawcett. I would love to see her. I'd have her sit in the kitchen, and I'd make her a cup of hot Starbucks coffee. I would tell her that I felt so badly about her wretched death to yellow fever, but I would cheer her with the invigorating accomplishments of her son Alexander Hamilton. She probably already knows about this, however.

I would ask her about how it felt to be in that dismal jail cell and how horrible it must have been to leave her firstborn son. How tragic it must have been to leave her firstborn son. I would tell her about Belva's bill eliminating the father's automatic rights to the children. She would, no doubt, be relieved to hear about that.

I'd tell Rachel how I am a single mother and that at times I, too, have had to hold my head high. I would share with her how, at those junctures, I hold on to the unassailable truths of the situation and walk with God. I imagine God literally there beside me, holding my hand. I would also tell her that no one has the right to judge. Only God is the Judge.

I would ask her how it felt when the father of her children walked away from her and her boys. I would express to her that I admired and appreciated how she started her own business and succeeded. I would discuss with her how it felt to be the sole provider for her boys. I have worked, providing for Juliette, and at times it's perplexing to have to be both the sole provider and the nurturer. I would share with her how I imagine Alexander relishing the opportunity to work beside his mother and that I always recognize a spark of inspiration from my daughter when she observes me at work. She has watched me write and type so much lately that she has announced that she wants to be a writer. I would apologize to Rachel that we are not conveniently located to an ocean in North Texas, but I would ask her if she would like to go to the local Water World. (They have an ocean wave.)

If **Eliza Pinckney** dropped by, I would ask her to appraise my pecan tree and ask her why it is peaked. She would likely be able to give me some advice. I would question her about life on a plantation and commend her for sharing her discovery of indigo and for daring to dream. I would confide with her about how I started my career at the age of fifteen too. How I loved moving to New York City and, though it was stressful, I thrived on having many responsibilities.

I would tell her that I could appreciate how her early successes helped define her children, and I would share with her how my early successes have given me the opportunity to provide for my daughter and a platform upon which to reinvent myself so that I may continue to provide for her. I would tell her that I worry about this sometimes and that I know that times were tough for her on the plantation too. I would commend her for somehow making it all work and for managing to pay for her sons' extensive college educations.

I would tell her how I love my country and that I thank her for being such a brave patriot during the Revolutionary War and for raising such dedicated patriots. I would share with her how her sacrifices were worth it and what a magnificent country America has grown to be. I would share with her how my father graduated from West Point Military Academy and flew jets for the U.S. Air Force. I would explain how my daughter has been able to sing the National Anthem since she could talk, that we read educational books about the United States and the past presidents over dinner. I would include how we pray for our country, our president, and our troops. I would express my fervent passion for my country. Juliette and I would then take her for a walk around the ranch. I bet she would be amazed by a four-wheeler.

If **Isabella Graham** came for a visit, I would take her to my Methodist church. I would pray with her and let her hear the fabulous orchestra, choir, and Dr. John McKellar preach his inspired sermon with intelligence and humor. I would ask her if preachers were amusing in the 1700s.

I would commend her for her bravery on that sinking ship with her infant son and baby daughters. I would tell her that I am impressed with how she always put God first and how I try to do that as well. I would tell her that I appreciated how she prayed for her children's souls and yearned that they would have a bond with God. I would reveal to her that I read the Bible front to back in 2002 and that my daughter and I are now reading the New Testament together. It's wonderful to hear it read orally, and my daughter and I make it very theatrical, especially with Paul, who was so dramatic.

I would tell Isabella how she is a role model for me. I keenly believe in volunteerism, and I try to be of service frequently. I take my daughter with me because I believe one is never too young to witness the hardships of others and feel the quintessence of charity. I would take Isabella to visit some charitable organizations of our day, like the American Red Cross and Boys and Girls Clubs. Juliette and I hosted some children from the Boys and Girls Clubs at our ranch last year. As we are driving I would turn on the radio and let her hear Michael W. Smith cranking out a Christian tune.

If **Elizabeth Timothy** arrived at my house, I would promptly show her our computer and high-speed Internet. I would show her Google and how it pulls up information around the world. I bet it would boggle her mind.

I would discuss with her how I agree with her philosophy to go the extra mile. I would convey to her how many times I have had to go the extra mile, or two, or three in my career. I would relay how I always tell my daughter, "If at first you don't succeed, try, try again."

I would ask her how she dealt with the laboriousness of the printing press in those days and how she found the energy to print the newspaper twice a week with so many children running around the house. I would share with her how, when I am overwhelmed with the task of running a business and nurturing my daughter, I don't relent to negative voices.

When I was breast-feeding Juliette as a newborn and infant, it required getting up numerous times during the night. There was no father to do the midnight or three a.m. feedings. There was only me.

I was so tired sometimes the crib would spin, but I would say, "I can do this. I can do this. It is my greatest joy to do this." It worked. I breast-fed for a year, even as I was filming two movies (much to the producer's chagrin). I would ask Elizabeth if she wanted to see the newspaper online or Word Perfect and Digital Photoshop. She might stay for days.

Abigail Adams. Oh, my, if Abigail Adams rang my doorbell, I think I would faint. I would invite her into the kitchen and ask her if she would like some tea; well, perhaps not tea, because of her memories of the Boston Tea Party. I would offer her some hot chocolate and sugar cookies. She would be impressed with my refrigerator and Horizons milk cartons.

I would thank Abigail for being such a glorious compatriot and lavish her with embarrassing compliments about her splendid letters. I would tell her that, yes, we do appreciate the hardships and sufferings she endured, and how it took over a hundred years after her death for women to receive the right to vote. After she recovers from the shock, I would share with her the good news about how women have made tremendous strides. I would tell her that I am raising my daughter to believe that she is capable of accomplishing anything she desires, because the social limitations are now removed.

I would laud Abigail for the beautiful, inspirational letters to her son that motivated commitment to God and country. I would thank her for inspiring the phrase "champion your children." I would share with her how, before my daughter goes to bed, we say our prayers and then I praise her with affirmations such as, "You are a good person, a talented person, you are sweet and loving and kind." The world is cold and cruel, and in my home Juliette needs verifications of her virtues. Why let others dictate my child's sense of self-worth?

I would thank Abigail for her sacrifices for our great country and acknowledge how she spent so many years alone. I would ask her how she did it during an era of scarcities, sickness, and war. I would confide in her how some of my most frightening times as a single mother have been when my daughter was sick. Sometimes she would awaken in the middle of the night with stridor, which is a type of croup that gets stuck in the throat, making it almost impossible to breathe. I would rush her to the shower and call 911. Nothing is more terrifying than riding in an ambulance with your ailing baby, especially when you are all alone. It was times like these that I thanked God for my mother, who always arrived at the hospital shortly after we did.

I would thank Abigail for aiding the genesis of our country, and I would offer her another sugar cookie and tell her stories about how America is one of the most compassionate, thriving, brilliant countries on earth. I would tell her to relay this happy news to John.

Harriet Jacobs. If Harriet Jacobs knocked on my door, I would run to answer it and give her a big hug. I would invite her in and offer her a glass of iced tea. I would ask her how her life progressed after she completed writing her book and what happened to her children. I would praise God for her freedom and her children's freedom. I would pay tribute to her foresight, valor, and immensity of self-sacrifice. I would agree with her insistence that half-measures avail nothing, and I'd share with her how I, too, am like a mama bear when it comes to the welfare of my child.

I would ask Harriet how she managed to live in that attic for seven years. I would do it too if it were in the best interest of my daughter. I would also tell her that I would never want to leave the attic either if I could still hear my daughter's sweet voice, validating that she was okay. I would relay to Harriet that I appreciate her grandmother's mother-wit, because my mother is just as devoted. It's my mother I call in the middle of the night, who I call during good times and bad, whose advice I seek, and who has always been there for me.

I would tell Harriet that I'm so happy she eventually gained her God-given right to freedom and that I admire her for breaking the cycle. I have broken dysfunctional cycles in my life, too, and I can relate to the enormity of the effort. I would tell her that I appreciated how she didn't give up before the miracle, and I would thank her for holding her head high. Then I would have her autograph my copy of her book.

Oh, if **Elinore Pruitt Stewart** rapped on my door, I would whoop with happiness. We would promptly saddle up the horses and go for a gallop. As we slowed to a trot, I would tell her how I loved reading about her adventures on the plains with her two-year-old daughter, Jerrine. I would tell her what pleasure I reaped from visualizing her marvelous sense of adventure. I would share with Elinore how my baby, Juliette, received her first horse at the age of two and how horseback riding is one of our favorite things to do together.

I would convey my appreciation of her ability to see the best in every person she met and how she made every situation seem easy, even when it wasn't. I would commend her fabulous sense of humor and her ability to communicate it through her written stories. I would ask her how she learned to write so admirably since her schoolteacher met an early demise. I would relay that, as she did, I try to look at every person I meet and greet them with friendliness and humor. My daughter is watching how I treat everyone we encounter and I want her to be a compassionate human being. I would praise Elinore because, even when times were tough, she would heal with humor. I would then ask her if she would like to fry some fish. We could catch it in my pond, and I know she would be able to whip up a campfire and skin the catch. What fun!

Aunt Clara Brown. It would be a glorious moment if she graced our doorstep. I would dash to the door and welcome her with open arms. I would ask her to sit in the dining room and have a slice of apple pie. Then I would proceed to pour accolades on her. I would tell her that I was so sorry that she lost her whole family to the auction block, due to the vile and hideous blight upon our country, slavery. I would extend my awe in regard to how she learned to persevere with praise. There are so many days that I have to ride the wave of faith and know that God will show me the way. Perseverance. I pray verbally with my daughter about our worries and surround them with affirmations of His grace. I also try to praise God even when I feel too overwhelmed to do so. God *is* great.

I would applaud Aunt Clara for her witness for Christ, always feeling free to raise her arms to her Lord in adoration and drop to her knees in prayer. I always pray on my knees, because it just feels more reverent. Children are our mirrors, so now Juliette prays on her knees too. In order to not overwhelm Aunt Clara, I would heap one, last praise upon her. I would commend her for holding her head high and for her amazing faith as she waited for forty-six years to be reunited with her daughter, Eliza Jane. Then I would let her eat her pie.

Belva Lockwood. It would be divine to have Belva tap quietly on our door with her white-ruffled hand. She would enter our house in her black flowing gown with flowers adorning her hair. I would escort her to the den and offer her a cup of hot tea.

I would besiege Belva with compliments about her innumerable contributions to women's suffrage, humanity, and our country. I would start with the Married Woman's Property Act that she helped compose, finally giving mothers the rights to their children. I would tell her that I stand with her on all of her issues: women's rights, temperance, abolition, peace.

I would tell Belva that, due to her influence, I am now feeling inspired to soar on eagles' wings myself. In fact, my daughter and I took a daring step and moved to New York City while this book was being completed, thanks to her. We've stepped out of our Texas comfort zone in order to pursue new opportunities and learning experiences together. The bond that Belva and her daughter, Lura, enjoyed through all their exciting exploits reinforces my sense of adventure and willingness to listen to God's plan. I have learned that when I am entrenched in *my* will, God is not able to work, but as soon as I turn it all over to *Him*, God leads in exciting ways.

I would thank Belva for being a tireless, relentless activist. I have often had to be relentless in my pursuits, because if I didn't, no one else would. Success is never given; it is pursued. I would tell her that finally another woman is running for president, that it has taken another 120 years for this to happen. I would tell her that, if she were to run for president today, she most certainly would have my vote!

HOLD YOUR HEAD HIGH

It's fun to improvise, and wouldn't it be amazing if we really could sit and visit with our historical heroes? But there is one reality, one definitive. No matter what troubles you may incur, know that you, like these women, have what it takes to overcome them. Look at what these ordinary women did in extraordinary circumstances. They turned their tribulations into triumphs, championed their children, and changed history. With you lie the seeds of stamina, breadth of talents, and abilities beyond your wildest imagination. These seeds can flower into a menagerie of moments you will cherish as a woman.

As a mother you shape the lives of your children, those precious God-given souls. You share their secrets and their joys. You know the source of their tears. You hold the power to design their dreams and regulate their fantasies. You are the keeper of future generations.

Within you is the magic that molds our nation. You are a mother. You have a gift. Find it, keep it in your heart, share it with your children. Teach them, with the faithfulness of God, how to better themselves and their nation. Illuminate their paths. You are their hope.

And even if you are a single mother, like me, you're not alone. History provides the warmth and comfort of women who have done it successfully before you. They say, "Come on, it's okay. I did it. Now, you can do it too." You are the daughter of the King of the universe; so look Life in the eye, square your shoulders, step out boldly, and hold your head high.

Stand up and hold up your head,
because your redemption is drawing near!

—LUKE 21:28 PARAPHRASED

NOTES

Introduction: How Did a Baptist Girl from Texas End Up as a Single Mom?
1. Sam Roberts, "51% of Women Are Now Living Without Spouse," *The New York Times,* 16 January 2007.

Chapter One: The Roman Empire—Setting the Stage
All quotations within this chapter are taken from James Carroll, *Constantine's Sword* (New York: Houghton Mifflin, 2002).

Chapter Two: Listen for God's Higher Calling—Helena Augusta
1. James Carroll, *Constantine's Sword* (New York: Houghton Mifflin, 2002).
2. Ibid.
3. Jan Willem Drijvers, *Helena Augusta: The Mother of Constantine the Great and the Legend of Her Finding of the True Cross* (New York: EJ Brill, 1992), 64.
4. Eusebius Pamphilus. "The Life of the Blessed Emperor Constantine." In *Nicene and Post-NiceneFathers,* 2d ser. Vol. 1, *Eusebius: Church History, Life of Constantine the Great, and Oration in Praise of Constantine,* edited by Philip Schaff and Henry Wace. Peabody, MA: Hendrickson, 1994.
5. Ibid.
6. Carroll, *Constantine's Sword.*
7. Ibid., 183.
8. Drijvers, *Helena Augusta.*
9. Pamphilus. "The Life of the Blessed Emperor Constantine."
10. Drijvers, *Helena Augusta,* 64.
11. Sozomen, *Historia Ecclesiastica,* J. Bidez & G.C. Hansen, ed. (London: G. Bell and Sons, Ltd., 1960).
12. Pamphilus. "The Life of the Blessed Emperor Constantine."

Chapter Three: The Middle Ages—Setting the Stage
1. Richard Eugene Sullivan, Bede K. Lackner, Kenneth R. Philp, Essays on *Medieval Civilization* (Austin: University of Texas Press, 1978), 118.
2. Benedict of Nursia, *Regula Monachorum 63* (CSEL 75.160).
3. Vincent of Beauvais, *Biblioteca Mundi.*

Chapter Four: Choose God's Greatness—Blanche of Castile
1. Petit-Dutaillis, Ch., *Etude sur la vie et le regne de Louis VIII* (1187–1226). Parrs 1894.
2. Regine Pernoud, *Blanche of Castile,* Translated by Henry Noel (New York: Coward, McCann & Geoghegan, Inc., 1975), 97.
3. Matthew Paris, *Chronica Majora,* ed. H.R. Luard, 1872–84. 7 vols. Rolls Series No. 57, 211.
4. Pernoud, *Blanche of Castille,* 113.
5. Kahil Gabran, *The Prophet* (New York: Knopf, 1923), 11.
6. Pernoud, *Blanche of Castille,* 114.
7. Ibid.

8. Ibid.
9. Etienne de Bourbon: *Anecdotes,* published by Lecoy de la Marche, No. 513, 443.
10. Pernoud, *Blanche of Castille,* 151.
11. Ibid, 13.
12. *Guillaume de Saint-Pathus,* Queen Margaret's confessor, *Vie de Saint Louis.* Pub. H.F. Delaborde, Paris, 1899.
13. Jean de Joinville (c. 1224 – December 24, 1317) was one of the great chroniclers of medieval France.
14. Etienne de Bourbon: *Anecdotes,* No. 58, 63.
15. *Chronique de Jean Eleemosyna.* Cf. my works: *Les Croises,* 243.
16. Tales of the Minstrel of Rheims, circa 1260.
17. Agnes of Harcourt is an important though little known thirteenth-century author. In the 1280s Agnes wrote a substantial biography of Isabelle of France, as well as a brief letter detailing Louis IX's involvement with the abbey. These texts were based on Agne's first-hand observations and contained many lively stories about their royal subjects.
18. Pernoud, *Blanche of Castille.*
19. Ibid.
20. Matthew Paris, *Chronica Majora,* ed. H.R. Luard, 1872–84. 7 vols. Rolls Series No. 57.
21. Pernoud, *Blanche of Castille,* 246.

Chapter Five: Turn Tribulations into Triumphs—Christine De Pizan
1. Charity Cannon Willard, *The Writings of Christine de Pizan* (New York: Persea Books, 1994), 22.
2. Ibid, 7.
3. Ibid, 9.
4. Ibid.
5. Ibid.
6. Ibid.
7. Christine wrote this poem after the death of her husband in 1389.
8. Willard, *The Writings of Christine de Pizan,* 10.
9. Christine de Pizan, *The Treasure of the City of Ladies.* Trans. by Sarah Lawton (New York: Penguin, 1985), xxiii.
10. Willard, *The Writings of Christine de Pizan,* 10.
11. Ibid, 11.
12. Ibid, 13.
13. Ibid.
14. Ibid.
15. Ibid.
16. *The Tale of the Rose* was written in 1402.
17. Willard, *The Writings of Christine de Pizan,* 22.
18. This ballad was also included by Christine in the collection of "Autres Balades," of which it is the sixth in the Roy edition. See *Oeuvres poetiques de Christine de Pisan,* I, pp. 213–214.
19. Willard, *The Writings of Christine de Pizan,* 22.
20. Ibid.

21. Ibid, 23.
22. Ibid, 16.
23. Ibid.
24. Ibid, 15.
25. Ibid.
26. Ibid, 23.
27. Written in 1400.
28. Willard, *The Writings of Christine de Pizan*, 190.
29. Ibid.
30. Ibid, 24.
31. This poem was possibly written in 1398 when Christine's son left Paris for England.
32. Willard, *The Writings of Christine de Pizan*, 19.
33. Ibid.
34. Christine de Pizan, *A Medieval Woman's Mirror of Honor: The Treasure of the City of Ladies*. Trans. by Charity Cannon Willard (New York: Bard Hall Press, 1989), 197.
35. Ibid.
36. Christine de Pizan, *The Treasure of the City of Ladies,* trans. Sarah Lawson (New York: Penguin, 2003), xxv.
37. Christine de Pizan, *The Book of the City of Ladies*, III.4. Trans. Rosalind Brown-Grant (New York: Penguin, 1999), 220.
38. *The Book of the City of Ladies,* III.18, 236.
39. *The Treasure of the City of Ladies*, III. 4.
40. Ibid.
41. *The Book of Peace* (1414) addressed to Dauphin, Louis de Guyenne, urged him to prudence.
42. Translated from *Le Ditie de Jebanne d'Arc*, eds. Angus J. Kennedy and Kenneth Varty (London: Oxford, 1977).
43. Madeleine Pelner Cosman, "Christine de Pizan's Well-Tempered Feminisim," in Christine de Pizan, *Mirror of Honor*, 14–15.
44. Christine de Pizan, *The Writings of Christine de Pizan*. Sel. and ed. Charity Cannon Willard. New York: Persea Books, 1994.

Chapter Seven: Define Your Own Destiny—Rachel Lavein Fawcett

1. James Thomas Flexner, *The Young Hamilton* (New York: Fordham University Press, 1997), 21.
2. Ibid, 11.
3. Forrest McDonald, *Alexander Hamilton* (New York: W.W. Norton, 1979), 6.
4. Ibid.
5. Broadus Mitchell, *Alexander Hamilton: A Concise Biography* (New York: Barnes & Noble, 1999), 6.
6. Flexner, *The Young Hamilton*, 13.
7. Willard Sterne Randall, *Alexander Hamilton* (New York: Harper Collins, 2003), 14.
8. Ibid.
9. Flexner, *The Young Hamilton*, 14.

10. Ron Chernow, *Alexander Hamilton* (New York: Penguin, 2004), 16.
11. Harold C. Syrett ed., *The Papers of Alexander Hamilton*, Vol. 2 (New York: Columbia University Press, 1961), 539.
12. Randall, *Alexander Hamilton*, 18.
13. Mitchell, *Alexander Hamilton*, 6.
14. Ibid.
15. Chernow, *Alexander Hamilton*, 29.
16. John C. Hamilton, *Life of Alexander Hamilton*, Vol. 1 (Boston: Houghton, Osgood, 1879), 42.
17. Allan McLane Hamilton, *The Intimate Life of Alexander Hamilton* (New York: Charles Scribner, 1911), 13.

Chapter Eight: Dare to Dream—Eliza Pinckney
1. Frances Leigh Williams, *Plantation Patriot* (New York: Harcourt, 1967).
2. Susan and John Lee, *Eliza Pinckney* (Chicago: Childrens Press, 1977), 9.
3. Frances Leigh Williams, *Plantation Patriot*.
4. Susan and John Lee, *Eliza Pinckney*, 13.
5. Ibid, 22.
6. Frances Leigh Williams, *Plantation Patriot*, 128.
7. Ibid.
8. Ibid.
9. Carole Chandler Waldrup, *Colonial Women* (Jefferson, NC: MacFarland & Co., 1999, 129.
10. Frances Leigh Williams, *Plantation Patriot*, 130–131.
11. Susan and John Lee, *Eliza Pinckney*, 16.
12. Frances Leigh Williams, *Plantation Patriot*.
13. Susan and John Lee, *Eliza Pinckney*, 18.
14. Frances Leigh Williams, *Plantation Patriot*, 123.
15. Ibid.
16. Carole Chandler Waldrup, *Colonial Women*, 137.
17. Susan and John Lee, *Eliza Pinckney*.
18. Harriott Horry Ravenel, *Eliza Pinckney* (New York, 1896), 113-114.
19. Susan and John Lee, *Eliza Pinckney*, 31.
20. Ibid.
21. Ibid, 39.
22. Ibid, 44.
23. Ibid, 45.
24. Carole Chandler Waldrup, *Colonial Women*, 135.

Chapter Nine: Put God First—Isabella Marshall Graham
All quotations within this chapter are taken from *The Power of Faith: The Life and Writings of Isabella Graham* by Joanna Bethune. Copyright by American Tract Society, 1843. Joanna Bethune was the daughter of Isabella Graham.

Chapter Ten: Go the Extra Mile—Elizabeth Timothy
1. Benjamin Franklin, *The Private Life of Benjamin Franklin*, London © 1791.

2. Brown, Richard Maxwell, *Notable American Women*, Vol. 4, Cambridge, MA: Harvard University Press, 1971.
3. Franklin, *The Private Life of Benjamin Franklin*.

Chapter Eleven: Champion Your Children—Abigail Adams
All quotations within this chapter were taken originally from *The Adams Papers*, a collection of letters, diaries, and family papers housed in the Massachusetts Historical Society in Boston.

Chapter Twelve: Single Mothers of Slavery—Setting the Stage
1. Alonzo Johnson and Paul Jersild, *Ain't Gonna Lay My 'Ligion Down* (Columbia: University of South Carolina Press, 1996), 72.
2. Ibid, 82.
3. Frederick Douglass, *My Bondage and My Freedom* (New York: Miller, Orion, and Mulligan, 1855).
4. Ibid, 35.
5. Johnson, 84.
6. Douglass, *My Bondage and My Freedom*, 56.
7. Johnson, *Ain't Gonna Lay My 'Ligion Down*, 78.

Chapter Thirteen: Don't Give Up Before the Miracle—Harriet Jacobs
All quotations within this chapter are taken from *Incidents in the Life of a Slave Girl* by Harriet Jacobs (Boston: Dover Press, 2001). Originally published in 1861 in Boston. A new introductory note was added by General Editor, Paul Negri, concerning the names of certain people being changed by Harriett "to protect the identities of those dear to her."

Chapter Fourteen: Pioneer Single Mothers—Setting the Stage
1. Emerson Hough, *The Passing of the Frontier* (New Haven, CT: Yale University Press, 1918).
2. Ruth Barnes Moynihan, "Children and Young People on the Overland Trail," *Western Historical Quarterly* 6, no. 3 (July 1975): 292.
3. Ibid.
4. Linda Peavy & Ursula Smith, *Pioneer Women: The Lives of Women on the Frontier* (Norman: University of Oklahoma Press, 1996), 43.
5. Emmy Werner, *Pioneer Children on the Journey West* (San Francisco: Westview Press, 1995), 12.
6. Peavy, *Pioneer Women*, 42.
7. Ibid.
8. Marilyn Irvin Holt, *Orphan Trains* (Winnipeg: Bison Books, 1994), 54.
9. Werner, *Pioneer Children on the Journey West*, 2.

Chapter Fifteen: Heal with Humor—Elinore Pruitt Stewart
Excerpts within this chapter, unless otherwise noted, are taken from *Letters of a Woman Homesteader* by Elinore Pruitt Stewart (Boston: Houghton Mifflin, 1988). Used by permission.

1. Susanne K. George, *The Adventures of The Woman Homesteader* (Lincoln: The University of Nebraska, 1992), 11.
2. Ellery Sedgwick, *The Happy Profession* (New York: Little, Brown & Co., 1946), 198.

Chapter Sixteen: Persevere with Praise—Aunt Clara Brown

1. William Byers, "A Women in a Thousand," *Rocky Mountain News* ,quoted in Linda Lowery, *One More Valley, One More Hill: The Story of Aunt Clara Brown* (New York: Random, 2002), 169.
2. Told to a reporter by Clara Brown quoted in Linda Lowery, *One More Valley*, 10.
3. Linda Lowery, *One More Valley, One More Hill: The Story of Aunt Clara Brown* (New York: Random, 2002), 14.
4. Ibid, 48.
5. Ibid, 86.
6. Horace Greeley, *The New York Tribune* ©1860, quoted in Linda Lowery, *One More Valley, One More Hill: The Story of Aunt Clara Brown* (New York: Random, 2002), 109.
7. Written in the *City Miners Register,* date unknown, quoted in Linda Lowery, *One More Valley, One More Hill,* 142.
8. Linda Lowery, *One More Valley, One More Hill,* 167.
9. William Byers, "A Women in a Thousand," *Rocky Mountain News* ,quoted in Linda Lowery, *One More Valley, One More Hill,* 169.
10. Newspaper articled quoted in Linda Lowery, *One More Valley, One More Hill,* 182.
11. *Central City Register-Call* ©1879, quoted in Linda Lowery, *One More Valley, One More Hill,* 183–84.
12. *Denver Republican* quoted in Linda Lowery, *One More Valley, One More Hill,* 190.
13. "Story of Two Lives," *Denver Republican* 18 February 1882, quoted in Linda Lowery, *One More Valley, One More Hill,* 192.
14. Quoted in Linda Lowery, *One More Valley, One More Hill,* 201.
15. Ibid, 204.
16. Ibid.

Chapter Seventeen: Soar on Eagle's Wings—Belva Lockwood

1. Belva A. Lockwood, "My Efforts to Become a Lawyer," *Lippincott's Monthly Magazine,* February, 1888: 225. Found on http://janetkagan.com/MyEfforts.html.
2. Ibid, 215.
3. Drollene P. Brown, *Belva Lockwood Wins Her Case* (Niles, IL: Albert Whitman, 1987), 9.
4. Quoting Belva's March 21, 1895 statement as an alumna of Syracuse University as found on http://www.stanford.edu/group/WLHP/papers/lockwood.htm.
5. Drollene P. Brown, *Belva Lockwood Wins Her Case,* 19.
6. Ibid, 20.
7. Ibid.
8. Mary Virginia Fox, *Lady for the Defense: A Biography of Belva Lockwood* (New York: Harcourt, 1975), 119.
9. Quoted in Terry Dunnahoo, *Before the Supreme Court: The Story of Belva Ann Lockwood* (Boston: Houghton Mifflin, 1984), 66.

10. Quoted in Drollene P. Brown, *Belva Lockwood Wins Her Case,* 29.
11. Barbara Babcock. *Belva Ann Lockwood: For Peace, Justice, and President,* ©1997. www.stanford.edu/group/WLHP/papers/lockwood.htm.
12. Quoted in Drollene P. Brown, *Belva Lockwood Wins Her Case,* 30.
13. Quoted in Mary Virginia Fox, *Lady for the Defense,* 107.
14. Terry Dunnahoo, *Before the Supreme Court,* 117.
15. Belva A. Lockwood, *Lippincott's Monthly Magazine,* 227.
16. Ibid.
17. Drollene P. Brown, *Belva Lockwood Wins Her Case,* 37.
18. Belva Lockwood, *Lippincott's Monthly Magazine.*
19. Elizabeth Cady Stanton, "Letter from Mrs. Stanton," *Ballot Box,* February 1877.
20. Drollene P. Brown, *Belva Lockwood Wins Her Case,* 35.
21. "Changing Worlds, Moving Mountains, A Long Way To Go, A Full Life, Amendment Xix," found on http://law.jrank.org/pages/12250/Lockwood-Belva-Ann.html.
22. Belva Ann Lockwood, "How I Ran for the Presidency," *National Magazine* ©1903: 728.
23. Drollene P. Brown, *Belva Lockwood Wins Her Case,* 46.
24. "Belva Lockwood on the Hustings," *New York Tribune,* Oct. 20, 1884.
25. Mary Virginia Fox, *Lady for the Defense,* 139.
26. Drollene P. Brown, *Belva Lockwood Wins Her Case,* 50.
27. Article written in *Brooklyn Daily Eagle,* July 27, 1888.
28. Drollene P. Brown, *Belva Lockwood Wins Her Case,* 53.
29. Mary Virginia Fox, *Lady for the Defense,* 152.
30. Ibid, 153.
31. Ibid, 154.
32. "Attorneys Representing the Indian Nations," *The New York Times,* May 20, 1917. www.congresionalcemetery.org.
33. "Belva, dear," *Morning Journal* ©1888, quoted in Drollene P. Brown, *Belva Lockwood Wins Her Case,* 59.
34. "Belva A. Lockwood," *The Suffragist,* May 26, 1917.
35. Belva Lockwood, *Lippincott's Monthly Magazine,* 216.
36. Frances Willard Kerr, "Lady's Chapeau in Ring in 1880's," *Washington Post,* July 6, 1952.
37. Drollen P. Brown, *Belva Lockwood Wins Her Case,* 4.

Conclusion: Virtual Conversations
1. Charlotte Perkins Gilman, *The Home, Its work and Influence* (New York: Charlton, 1910), p.xi, but written earlier, probably in 1904.

Inwood House

Inwood House is an internationally recognized leader in teen pregnancy and HIV/AIDS prevention, youth development, and teen family support programming. Since 1830, Inwood House has been dedicated to helping young people take charge of their lives and become healthy and self-reliant adults. Inwood House programs address all aspects of teenage pregnancy. For information about Inwood House programs and research, go to www.inwoodhouse.com.

We Help Teens Take Charge Of Their Lives

Boys & Girls Clubs of America

Boys & Girls Club of America comprises a national network of more than 4,000 neighborhood-based facilities, with 4.8 million youth served through Club membership and community outreach, in all 50 states and on U.S. military bases worldwide. Known as "The Positive Place for Kids," the Clubs provide guidance-oriented character development programs on a daily basis for children 6–18 years old, conducted by a full-time professional staff. Key Boys & Girls Club programs emphasize leadership development, education and career exploration, financial literacy, health and life skills, the arts, sports, fitness and recreation, and family outreach.

For more information or to find a Club nearest you,
please visit www.bgca.org or call 1-800-854-CLUB.

Single Parent Outreach

The Single Parent Family Ministry of the Richland Hills Church of Christ is dedicated to assisting and encouraging single-parent families to walk closer with the living God, strengthen the bond between parent and child, meet and fellowship with others like ourselves, and seek out answers to real-life issues. These goals are accomplished through Bible study, special single-parent family events, Christian counseling, and in many other ways. We are simply a ministry of love and understanding, operating in the name of Jesus Christ.

Single Parent Family Ministry
Richland Hills Church of Christ
6300 N. E. Loop 820
North Richland Hills, TX 76180
(817) 581-3301
www.RHChurch.org

If you are interested in volunteering and finding an opportunity near you
please visit www.volunteer.com. Bring good cheer, *volunteer*!